INSIDE MACINTOSH

Overview

Addison-Wesley Publishing Company

Reading, Massachusetts   Menlo Park, California   New York
Don Mills, Ontario   Wokingham, England   Amsterdam   Bonn
Sydney   Singapore   Tokyo   Madrid   San Juan
Paris   Seoul   Milan   Mexico City   Taipei

2 3 4 5 6–MU–96959493
Second printing, August 1993

Addison-Wesley books are available for bulk purchases by corporations, institutions, and other organizations. For more information please contact the Corporate, Government and Special Sales Department at (617) 944-3700 x 2915.

The paper used in this book meets the EPA standards for recycled fiber.

Contents

Chapter 7   Dialog Boxes   131

Chapter 8   Menus   149

Chapter 9   Processes   163

Afterword   Going Further   183

Figures, Tables, and Listings

About This Book

This book, *Inside Macintosh: Overview,* provides a general introduction to programming for Macintosh computers and to the *Inside Macintosh* library of reference books. Unless you are already an experienced developer of software for Macintosh computers, you should read this book for a general overview of the Macintosh system software and of the programming techniques that you should use when developing your application.

This book is written for both professional developers and "hobbyists." It assumes only that you understand fundamental programming concepts and that you have had experience using a high-level programming language such as Pascal or C. It is helpful, but not necessary, to have some experience programming for a graphic user interface (like the Macintosh desktop metaphor). At the very least, you should already have extensive experience *using* one or more applications on a Macintosh computer. Before you start programming, you need to understand what the basic elements of the Macintosh desktop metaphor are (windows, menus, scroll bars, and so forth) and how the user expects those elements to operate.

This book leads by example. From the very first page, the fundamental programming techniques are illustrated by source code that you can compile into actual, working routines and applications. Gradually, you will learn how to implement the major features of a Macintosh application, including

- responding to user actions and other events

- creating and managing windows and dialog boxes

- handling menu selections

- storing application data in resources

- managing your application's memory efficiently

- sharing processing time and available memory with other open applications

- checking available system software features

- handling errors or unexpected occurrences safely

This book also provides guidelines on how to maximize your application's compatibility with the entire family of Macintosh computers and minimize the amount of work required to localize your application (that is, to adapt it for use in other geographic locations). Compatibility and localizability are features that you should always plan in advance. In general, your best guide to writing software that follows these guidelines is to use the techniques illustrated throughout the *Inside Macintosh* series of books.

About *Inside Macintosh*

The *Inside Macintosh* library of books is a complete technical reference to the system software provided for Macintosh computers by Apple Computer, Inc. You'll need some or all of the *Inside Macintosh* books—in addition to the documentation for your specific software development environment—to write applications and other software components that run in the Macintosh Operating System.

Books in the *Inside Macintosh* series are designed primarily as reference books and not as step-by-step tutorials. (The main exception to that rule is this book, *Inside Macintosh: Overview*, which is a general introduction to programming on Macintosh computers and to the other *Inside Macintosh* books.) Nonetheless, there is sufficient "how-to" material in each book that you should be able to successfully implement the features of some particular part of the Macintosh system software by reading the appropriate chapters in *Inside Macintosh*. Moreover, some of these books contain special introductory chapters that explain general concepts and provide implementation details for specific parts of the system software. For example, the chapter "Introduction to File Management" in the book *Inside Macintosh: Files* provides a complete explanation of how to implement the typical File menu commands.

If you are new to programming for the Macintosh system software, you should begin by reading this book, *Inside Macintosh: Overview*. Once you understand the material presented here, you can then usefully turn to other *Inside Macintosh* books. In all likelihood, you'll next want to look at two books covering the Macintosh Toolbox:

- *Inside Macintosh: Macintosh Toolbox Essentials*
- *Inside Macintosh: More Macintosh Toolbox*

If your application is concerned with either text or graphics, you need to look at one or both of:

- *Inside Macintosh: Imaging*
- *Inside Macintosh: Text*

You'll also need to learn more about the main parts of the Macintosh Operating System. You can get most of the information you need from these three books:

- *Inside Macintosh: Memory*
- *Inside Macintosh: Files*
- *Inside Macintosh: Processes*

See the Afterword, beginning on page 183, for a more detailed description of the contents of these and other books in the *Inside Macintosh* series.

The New *Inside Macintosh*

The original *Inside Macintosh* library of books appeared in six volumes from 1985 to 1991. Those volumes each focused on a particular version of the system software, sometimes prompted by the release of new hardware configurations. Often, the later volumes of the original *Inside Macintosh* described only new system software components or changes to existing system software components.

The new *Inside Macintosh* books are intended to replace the original *Inside Macintosh* books and to provide a more complete and more useful reference to the Macintosh system software. The most obvious improvement in the new books is that they are organized principally by topic. For example, the book *Inside Macintosh: Files* contains virtually all the available information related to files, including complete descriptions of the File Manager, the Standard File Package, the Alias Manager, and the Disk Initialization Manager. Similarly, the book *Inside Macintosh: Text* contains all information about handling text. This topic-oriented organization of books makes it easier for you to find the information you need. It also makes it easier for Apple to add books to the *Inside Macintosh* suite as new technologies emerge in the years ahead.

At the same time that the entire suite of books was reorganized, the chapters in the new *Inside Macintosh* books were completely rewritten. Information that may have been previously scattered across multiple volumes of the original *Inside Macintosh* is now combined into easily accessible chapters. Information that is no longer relevant or useful has been removed. Most importantly, the new *Inside Macintosh* provides far more explanatory material and source code samples than the original. Where appropriate, material from the Macintosh Technical Notes has been incorporated into the new *Inside Macintosh*. Finally, each chapter has been extensively reviewed by Apple engineers, testing personnel, and Developer Technical Support staff.

Conventions Used in This Book

Inside Macintosh uses various conventions to present information. Words that require special treatment appear in specific fonts or font styles. Certain information, such as parameter blocks, appears in special formats so that you can scan it quickly.

Special Fonts

All code listings, reserved words, and the names of actual data structures, constants, fields, parameters, and routines are shown in Courier (`this is Courier`).

Words that appear in **boldface** are key terms or concepts and are defined in the Glossary.

Types of Notes

There are several types of notes used in *Inside Macintosh*.

Note

A note like this contains information that is interesting but possibly not essential to an understanding of the main text. (An example appears on page 8.) ◆

IMPORTANT

A note like this contains information that is essential for an understanding of the main text. (An example appears on page 5.) ▲

▲ **WARNING**

Warnings like this indicate potential problems that you should be aware of as you design your application. Failure to heed these warnings could result in system crashes or loss of data. (There are no warnings in this book.) ▲

Development Environment

The system software routines described in this book are available using Pascal, C, or assembly-language interfaces. How you access these routines depends on the development environment you are using. This book shows system software routines in their Pascal interface using the Macintosh Programmer's Workshop (MPW).

All code listings in this book are shown in Pascal. They show methods of using various routines and illustrate techniques for accomplishing particular tasks. All code listings have been compiled and, in most cases, tested. However, Apple Computer does not intend that you use these code samples in your application.

This book occasionally uses *GreetMe* and *Venn Diagrammer* as the names of sample applications for illustrative purposes; these are not actual products of Apple Computer, Inc.

For More Information

APDA is Apple's worldwide source for over three hundred development tools, technical resources, training products, and information for anyone interested in developing applications on Apple platforms. Customers receive the quarterly *APDA Tools Catalog* featuring all current versions of Apple development tools and the most popular third-party development tools. Ordering is easy; there are no membership fees, and application forms are not required for most of our products. APDA offers convenient payment and shipping options, including site licensing.

To order products or to request a complimentary copy of the *APDA Tools Catalog*, contact

APDA
Apple Computer, Inc.
P.O. Box 319
Buffalo, NY 14207-0319

Telephone	800-282-2732 (United States)
	800-637-0029 (Canada)
	716-871-6555 (International)
Fax	716-871-6511
AppleLink	APDA
America Online	APDA
CompuServe	76666,2405
Internet	APDA@applelink.apple.com

If you provide commercial products and services, call 408-974-4897 for information on the developer support programs available from Apple.

For information of registering signatures, file types, Apple events, and other technical information, contact

Macintosh Developer Technical Support
Apple Computer, Inc.
20525 Mariani Avenue, M/S 75-3T
Cupertino, CA 95014-6299

IMPORTANT

See the section "Using Developer Services" beginning on page 189 in the Afterword for more information about Apple developer programs and services. ▲

Introduction

Contents

Introduction

Welcome inside. This chapter begins the discussion of programming for Macintosh computers by describing the general organization of the **Macintosh system software,** a collection of routines that you'll use to simplify your development of Macintosh applications. The system software provides, among other things, routines that you can use to create and manage the essential parts of your application's user interface. This chapter illustrates the organization and content of the system software by dissecting a very simple sample application.

Getting Started

Let's begin by looking at the source code for a simple application. Consider Listing 1-1.

Listing 1-1   A simple Macintosh application

```pascal
PROGRAM GreetMe;
VAR
    gWindow:     WindowPtr;              {pointer to a window record}
    gString:     Str255;                {the string to display}
    gRect:       Rect;                  {the window's rectangle}
BEGIN
    InitGraf(@thePort);                 {initialize QuickDraw}
    InitFonts;                          {initialize Font Manager}
    InitWindows;                        {initialize Window Manager}
    InitCursor;                         {initialize the cursor to an arrow}

                                        {set the position of the window}
    SetRect(gRect, 100, 100, 400, 200);
    gString := 'Hello, world!';         {set the greeting to be displayed}

                                        {create a window}
    gWindow := NewWindow(NIL, gRect, '', TRUE, dBoxProc, WindowPtr(-1),
                        FALSE, 0);
    SetPort(gWindow);                   {set the current drawing port}
    WITH gWindow^.portRect DO           {set the position of the pen}
        MoveTo(((right - left) DIV 2) - (StringWidth(gString) DIV 2),
                (bottom - top) DIV 2);
    TextFont(systemFont);               {set the font}
    DrawString(gString);                {draw the string}

    REPEAT                              {loop until the mouse button is pressed}
    UNTIL Button;
END.
```

Introduction

Introduction

The application GreetMe defined by Listing 1-1 simply displays the window shown in Figure 1-1 and exits as soon as the user presses the mouse button.

Figure 1-1   The window created by the simple application

This application is remarkably simple, but also quite revealing about some important aspects of Macintosh programming. Consider the call that creates the window in which the greeting is drawn:

```
gWindow := NewWindow(NIL, gRect, '', TRUE, dBoxProc,
                     WindowPtr(-1), FALSE, 0);
```

This call to the NewWindow function creates a window at the specified location in front of any existing windows on the screen. The NewWindow function is a good example of the kind of routines provided by the system software. These routines greatly simplify the creation of the standard "look and feel" of Macintosh applications. By using these routines, you can ensure that your application conforms as closely as possible to the standard Macintosh user interface and hence that users find your application easy to learn and use.

Let's take a closer look at the call to NewWindow. The NewWindow function requires eight parameters, whose meanings are described in Table 1-1.

Table 1-1   Parameters passed to NewWindow in Listing 1-1

Parameter	Meaning
NIL	The address of a window record, a data structure that contains information about the new window. Specifying NIL as the address of this structure instructs the system software to allocate that required storage itself.
gRect	The window's bounding rectangle. This is the rectangle that encloses the new window. The values of the desired rectangle are specified by the previous call to SetRect, which defines the upper-left and lower-right corners of the rectangle.
' '	The window's title. The new window has no title bar, so this parameter is specified as the empty string.

Table 1-1   Parameters passed to `NewWindow` in Listing 1-1 (continued)

Parameter	Meaning
`TRUE`	An indication of whether the new window should initially be visible or not. This parameter is set to `TRUE` to indicate that the window is indeed to be made visible.
`dBoxProc`	The type of window you want to create. The Macintosh user interface includes a great variety of window types for different purposes. For present purposes, the standard modal dialog box is appropriate. The constant `dBoxProc` identifies that type of window.
`WindowPtr(-1)`	The new window's initial plane (or layer) relative to any other existing windows. This parameter is a window pointer to the window behind which you want the new window to appear. The system software recognizes two special values here. If you pass `NIL` in this parameter, the new window appears *behind* all other windows. If you pass –1, the new window appears *in front of* all other windows. Because the `NewWindow` function expects a window pointer in this parameter, you need to typecast the special value –1 as `WindowPtr(-1)`.
`FALSE`	An indication of whether the window has a close box or not. This parameter is set to `FALSE` to indicate that no close box is desired.
`0`	An application-specific reference number. This number is put into a particular field of the new window record, and can be useful to you if the window has specific data associated with it. Because there is no such data associated with this window, this parameter is set to 0.

The `NewWindow` function returns a window pointer, which is the address in memory of a window record. The window record contains important information about the window (such as its current location on the screen and the current font and size of text that is to be drawn in the window). When you call a system software routine to perform some operation on a window, you'll typically pass a window pointer as a parameter to that routine. For example, in Listing 1-1, the window pointer is passed to the `SetPort` procedure to set the new window as the current drawing window.

IMPORTANT

You need to call `SetPort` before you do anything at all that affects the contents of a window, such as drawing graphics or text in the window, or even just erasing the contents of the window. ▲

Another notable element of Listing 1-1 is the `DrawString` procedure, which draws the specified string in the current font at the current drawing location. By default, the current drawing location in a new window is the upper-left corner. In this case, remaining at that location would make the greeting unreadable, because `DrawString` uses the vertical coordinate of the current point as the baseline of the text to be printed. Instead, GreetMe calls the `MoveTo` procedure to move the current pen location to a point that centers the greeting in the window:

```
WITH gWindow^.portRect DO          {set the position of the pen}
    MoveTo(((right - left) DIV 2) - (StringWidth(gString) DIV 2),
           (bottom - top) DIV 2);
```

The `MoveTo` procedure requires 2 parameters, the horizontal and vertical coordinates within the window of the new drawing position. The origin—point (0,0)—of a window is at its upper left corner. Horizontal coordinates increase as you move from left to right, and vertical coordinates increase as you move from top to bottom. The coordinates passed to `MoveTo` are calculated from the left, top, bottom, and right coordinates of the window (obtained from the `portRect` field of the window record).

The Macintosh System Software

The richness of the Macintosh user interface is closely matched by the richness of the Macintosh system software routines. There are currently several thousand system software routines that, like `NewWindow`, are available to application developers for use in writing applications for the Macintosh operating system. Fortunately, you don't need to learn all of those routines before starting to develop applications for the Macintosh. The sample application defined in Listing 1-1 uses only a dozen or so system software routines. A typical application might directly call a few hundred of these routines.

The entire collection of system software routines is logically divided into functional groups—usually known as **managers**—that handle specific tasks or user interface elements. For example, the `NewWindow` routine belongs to the Window Manager, the part of the Macintosh system software that allows you to create, move, hide, resize, and otherwise manipulate windows. Similarly, the parts of the system software that allow you to create and manipulate menus belong to the Menu Manager.

Your application calls system software routines to create standard user interface elements and to coordinate its actions with other open applications. The main other application that your application needs to work with is the **Finder,** which is responsible for keeping track of files and managing the user's desktop. Usually, the user launches your application by double-clicking its icon (or one of its document's icons) in a Finder window. The Finder isn't really part of the Macintosh system software, but it is such an important piece of the Macintosh graphic user interface that it's sometimes difficult to tell where the Finder ends and the systems software begins. In fact, the system software provides a set of routines—known as the Finder Interface—that you can use to interact with the Finder.

As shown in Figure 1-2, most of the system software routines are part of either the Macintosh Operating System or the Macintosh Toolbox.

Figure 1-2 Overview of the system software

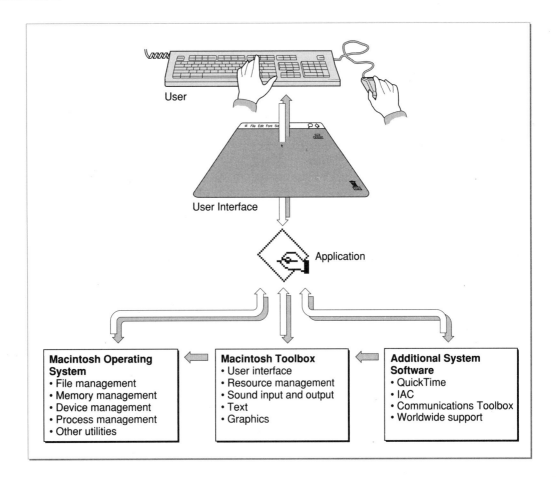

This section describes the division of the Macintosh system software into its logical parts. Understanding this division of system software into managers and other units is essential to understanding Macintosh programming, as well as the general organization of *Inside Macintosh*.

The Macintosh Toolbox

The system software routines used in Listing 1-1 allow you to manage elements of the Macintosh user interface. These parts of the system software belong to the **Macintosh Toolbox** (sometimes also called the **Macintosh User Interface Toolbox**). By offering a common set of routines that every application can call to implement the user interface, the Toolbox not only ensures familiarity and consistency for the user, but also helps reduce your application's code size and development time. At the same time, the Toolbox offers a great deal of flexibility; your application can, whenever appropriate, use its own code instead of Toolbox routines, and it can define its own types of windows, menus, and controls. In general, however, you should use the Toolbox routines to maximize compatibility with present and future versions of the system software.

Introduction

Figure 1-3 illustrates the main parts of the Macintosh Toolbox.

Figure 1-3   Parts of the Macintosh Toolbox

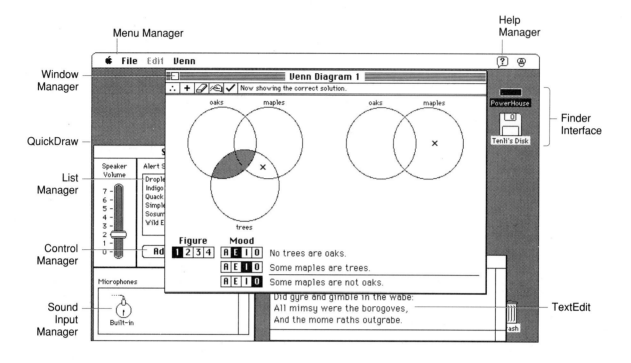

Note

For historical reasons, some collections of system software routines are
referred to as packages. One example is the Standard File Package
(which allows you to present the standard file opening and saving
dialog boxes). In general, the distinction between managers and
packages is unimportant. Accordingly, the new *Inside Macintosh* has,
whenever appropriate, adopted the practice of renaming packages as
managers. For instance, the Disk Initialization Manager (described in the
book *Inside Macintosh: Files*) was previously known as the Disk
Initialization Package. ◆

Consider the first few lines of Listing 1-1 on page 3:

```
InitGraf(@thePort);              {initialize QuickDraw}
InitFonts;                       {initialize Font Manager}
InitWindows;                     {initialize Window Manager}
InitCursor;                      {initialize cursor to arrow}
```

Introduction

These lines of code perform standard initialization of some essential Toolbox managers. You need to initialize these managers in order to set up the drawing environment for your application and to prepare parts of the Toolbox for further use. The `InitGraf` procedure initializes **QuickDraw,** the part of the Macintosh Toolbox that handles drawing and other graphics operations. Because the Macintosh user interface is largely a graphic user interface, QuickDraw routines are called by virtually all the other Toolbox managers. For example, the Window Manager calls QuickDraw to draw the window frame and any other required parts of a window (for instance, the title bar). For this reason, you need to initialize QuickDraw before you initialize the other main Toolbox Managers.

Note
QuickDraw gets its name from the fact that it's designed to perform basic graphics operations exceptionally fast. This is important for a user interface that relies so heavily on graphics. ◆

Your application will also call QuickDraw directly, usually to draw inside a window or to set up constructs (like rectangles) that you'll need when making other Toolbox calls. QuickDraw provides a rich array of routines that let you

- change, hide, and display the cursor

- manipulate the current drawing port

- set characteristics of the drawing pen

- draw text

- manage colors

- define rectangles, ovals, arcs, and other basic geometric shapes

- define arbitrarily shaped regions

- perform operations on shapes and regions

The essential thing to keep in mind is that if you can see something on the screen, then QuickDraw is lurking somewhere behind it, either directly (you drew it there) or indirectly (you called a Toolbox routine that called QuickDraw to draw it there).

The `InitFonts` procedure initializes the Font Manager, which supports the use of various character fonts when you draw text with QuickDraw. The `TextFont` routine sets the current font to that whose font number is passed as a parameter. GreetMe passes the special constant `systemFont`, which requests the font used by the system (for drawing menu titles and commands in menus, for example).

The `InitWindows` procedure initializes the Window Manager, and the `InitCursor` procedure (which belongs to QuickDraw) sets the cursor to the standard arrow cursor. Every application needs to call these routines before creating windows or handling any user actions.

Notice that Figure 1-3 depicts a number of other Toolbox managers that are not used by GreetMe. You'll encounter many of these as you progress through this book. For now, take a look at Table 1-2 for a brief description of the most commonly used Macintosh Toolbox managers.

Table 1-2   The Macintosh Toolbox

Manager	Description
QuickDraw	Performs all screen display operations, including all drawing of graphics and text.
Window Manager	Allows you to create and manage windows of various types.
Dialog Manager	Allows you to create and manage dialog boxes, which are special kinds of windows. Typically you'll use dialog boxes to alert the user to unusual situations or to solicit information from the user.
Control Manager	Allows you to create and manage controls, such as buttons, radio buttons, checkboxes, pop-up menus, scroll bars, and application-defined controls.
Menu Manager	Allows you to create and manage your application's menu bar and the menus it contains. Also handles the drawing of menus and user actions within a menu.
Event Manager	Reports to your application events describing user actions and changes in the processing status of your application. Also allows you to communicate with other applications.
TextEdit	Provides simple text-formatting and text-editing capabilities, such as text input, selection, cutting, and pasting. Applications that are not primarily concerned with text processing can use TextEdit to handle most text manipulation.
Resource Manager	Allows your application to read and write resources. Any static data (such as menus, cursors, and windows) used by your application can usefully be stored as a resource. The system software provides a number of standard resources, and your application can define its own custom resources.
Finder Interface	Allows your application to interact with the Finder, the application that helps keep track of files and manages the user's desktop display.
Scrap Manager	Allows your application to support cutting and pasting of information among applications.
Standard File Package	Provides the standard dialog boxes that allow the user to select a file to open or a location and name for a file to be saved.
Help Manager	Allows your application to provide Balloon Help on-line assistance, information that describes the actions, behaviors, and properties of elements of your application.

Table 1-2   The Macintosh Toolbox (continued)

Manager	Description
List Manager	Allows your application to create lists of items.
Sound Manager	Provides sound output capabilities.
Sound Input Manager	Provides sound input capabilities for Macintosh computers equipped with a sound input device such as a microphone.

The Macintosh Operating System

The Macintosh Operating System provides routines that allow you to perform basic low-level tasks such as file input and output, memory management, and process and device control. The Macintosh Toolbox is a level above the Operating System and, as you've seen, provides routines that help you implement the standard Macintosh user interface for your application. The Toolbox calls the Operating System to do low-level operations, and you'll also need to call the Operating System directly yourself.

The Macintosh Toolbox allows you to create and manage parts of your application's user interface, and in some sense mediates your application and the user. By contrast, the Macintosh Operating System essentially mediates your application and the Macintosh hardware. For example, you'll read and write files not by reading data directly from the medium on which they are stored, but rather by calling appropriate File Manager routines. The File Manager locates the desired data within the logical hierarchical structure of files and directories that it manages; then it calls another part of the Operating System, the Device Manager, to read or write the data on the actual physical device. The File Manager and the Device Manager thereby insulate your application from the low-level details of interacting with the available data-storage hardware.

Similarly, the Memory Manager helps you allocate and dispose of memory within your application's logical address space. The Memory Manager takes care of mapping that logical address space onto the physical address space provided by the available RAM. It also helps manage your application's memory by moving allocated blocks of memory when necessary to create space for new blocks you want to allocate. Table 1-3 briefly describes the main parts of the Macintosh Operating System.

Table 1-3   The Macintosh Operating System

Manager	Description
Process Manager	Handles the launching, scheduling, and termination of applications. Also provides information about open processes.
Memory Manager	Manages the dynamic allocation and releasing of memory in your application's memory partition.

continued

Table 1-3   The Macintosh Operating System (continued)

Manager	Description
Virtual Memory Manager	Provides virtual memory services (the ability to have a logical address space that is larger than the total amount of available RAM).
File Manager	Provides access to the file system; allows applications to create, open, read, write, and close files.
Alias Manager	Helps you locate specified files, directories, or volumes.
Disk Initialization Manager	Manages the process of initializing disks.
Device Manager	Provides input from and output to hardware devices attached to the computer.
SCSI Manager	Controls the exchange of information between a Macintosh computer and peripheral devices attached through the Small Computer Standard Interface (SCSI).
Time Manager	Allows you to execute a routine periodically or after a specified time delay.
Vertical Retrace Manager	Allows you to synchronize the execution of a routine with the redrawing of the screen.
Shutdown Manager	Allows you to execute a routine while the computer is shutting down or restarting.

Additional System Software Services

The Macintosh system software includes a number of other parts that don't historically belong to either the Macintosh Toolbox or the Macintosh Operating System. The system software provides an extremely powerful set of services you can use to handle text and to support the varying text-handling requirements of different languages and writing systems. Other system software components include the interapplication communications architecture, QuickTime, and the Communications Toolbox.

Text Handling

Text handling on the Macintosh has two basic aspects that make it so powerful. First, it is fundamentally graphic; text is drawn as a sequence of graphic elements; therefore the full power and flexibility of the Macintosh graphic interface is available for drawing text in sophisticated ways.

Second, text handling is designed to function properly across multiple languages and writing systems. As you develop applications for worldwide markets, you need to consider differences in scripts, languages, and regions. The Macintosh system software presents one of the most flexible architectures for developing applications that can support more than one script.

A **script**, such as Roman, Kanji, or Arabic, is a writing system for a human language such as English, Japanese, or Arabic. Scripts have different characteristics; for example, they can differ in the direction in which their characters and lines run and in the number of characters in their character sets. The way in which you need to input, display, render, and edit text may change depending on the script in use.

A Macintosh **script system** is a set of system resources that support text input, manipulation, and display for a given writing system. The **Macintosh script management system** consists of system software managers and the WorldScript extensions, which together give your application the power to create and work with text of any script system. These are the essential text-handling managers:

■ **QuickDraw** is the graphics manager of Macintosh system software. Your application makes QuickDraw calls to write text to the screen or to a printer. When QuickDraw draws text, it draws it according to the settings of the current window's graphics port record, which includes the location information and complete font information. QuickDraw can draw text of any script system. Figure 1-4 shows some of QuickDraw's text-drawing capabilities.

Figure 1-4   A multiscript line of text drawn by QuickDraw

■ The **Font Manager** supports QuickDraw by providing the fonts that QuickDraw needs, in the typefaces, sizes, and styles that QuickDraw requests. The Font Manager keeps track of all fonts available to an application, and supports fonts for all script systems.

■ The **Text Utilities** are an integrated collection of routines for performing a variety of operations on text, ranging from sorting strings to formatting dates and times to finding word breaks. The Text Utilities work in conjunction with the Macintosh script management system and can take into account the differences in text handling among script systems. If you use these routines, you can handle text operations in a manner that is transportable to different parts of the world.

■ The **Script Manager** is at the center of the Macintosh script management system. It initializes script systems, maintains important data structures, supports switching text input among different script systems, and provides several text-manipulation services.

■ The **Text Services Manager** supports *text service components* such as input methods. If your application uses the Text Services Manager, it can support the special kinds of text input needed for 2-byte script systems such as Japanese, Chinese, and Korean.

Introduction

Figure 1-5 shows how you can use the Text Services Manager to convert Japanese text.

Figure 1-5   Input and conversion of Japanese text using the Text Services Manager

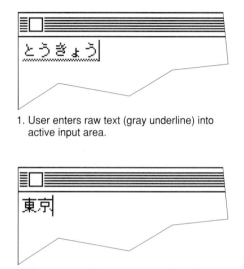

1. User enters raw text (gray underline) into active input area.

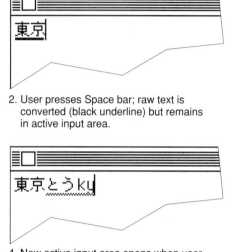

2. User presses Space bar; raw text is converted (black underline) but remains in active input area.

3. User presses Return; converted text is confirmed (no underline). Active input area closes.

4. New active input area opens when user enters more raw text.

You can use the script management system to achieve any level of text-handling sophistication, from simple display of static text in one language to highly sophisticated multilanguage word processing and page layout. The simplest way to achieve basic worldwide flexibility in text handling is to use **TextEdit,** which provides simple text-handling capabilities for text of any script system, including multiscript text. TextEdit automatically handles text with more than one script, style, and direction. For example, TextEdit supports mixing English text (a left-to-right directional script) with Arabic text (a right-to-left directional script) in the same line (as you saw in Figure 1-4).

Note

For complete information on text handling, including multiscript text handling, see *Inside Macintosh: Text*. For information on individual script systems and how to localize your software for markets around the world, see *Guide to Macintosh Software Localization*. ◆

Interapplication Communication

The **interapplication communications (IAC) architecture** provides a standard and extensible mechanism for communication among Macintosh applications. The IAC architecture includes these main parts:

- The **Edition Manager** allows applications to automate copy and paste operations between applications, so that data can be shared dynamically.

■ The **Apple Event Manager** allows applications to send and respond to Apple events.

■ The **Event Manager** allows applications to send and respond to high-level events other than Apple events.

■ The **Program-to-Program Communications (PPC) Toolbox** allows applications to exchange blocks of data with each other by reading and writing low-level message blocks. It also provides a standard user interface that allows a user working in one application to select another application with which to exchange data.

The parts of the IAC architecture depend upon each other in fairly straightforward ways. The Edition Manager uses the services of the Apple Event Manager to support dynamic data sharing. The Apple Event Manager, in turn, relies on the Event Manager to send Apple events as high-level events, and the Event Manager uses the services of the PPC Toolbox.

If you want your application to exchange data with another application, you'll probably use either the Edition Manager or the Apple Event Manager. The Edition Manager allows users to copy data from one application's document to another application's document, updating the information automatically when the data in the original document changes. Figure 1-6 shows how you can use the Edition Manager to create a poster whose elements (an illustration, a title, and some text) all originate in documents created by other applications. If, for example, the user changes the illustration in the original document, the copy of that illustration in the poster could be updated automatically.

Figure 1-6   Sharing dynamic data with other applications

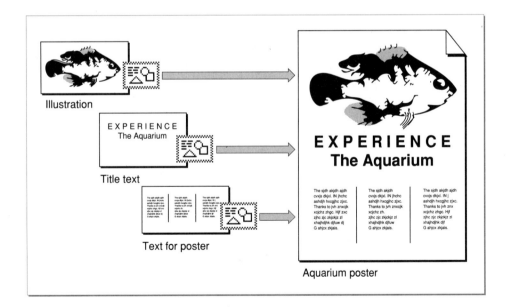

Introduction

The Apple Event Manager allows you to send and receive Apple events, which are high-level events that conform to the Apple Event Interprocess Messaging Protocol. The *Apple Event Registry: Standard Suites* describes a standard vocabulary of Apple events that you can use to communicate with other open applications. Typically you use Apple events to request services and information from other applications, or to provide services and information in response to such requests.

Communication between two applications that support Apple events is initiated by a client application, which sends an Apple event to request a service or information. For example, a client application might request services such as printing specific files, checking the spelling of a list of words, or performing a numerical calculation; or it might request information, such as one customer's address or a list of names and addresses of all customers living in Ohio. The application providing the service or the requested information is called a server application. The client and server applications can reside on the same local computer or on remote computers connected to a network.

Figure 1-7 shows the relationships among a client application, the Apple Event Manager, and a server application. The client application uses Apple Event Manager routines to create and send the Apple event, and the server application uses Apple Event Manager routines to interpret the Apple event and respond appropriately. If the client application so requests, the server application sends back a reply Apple event.

Figure 1-7   Sending and responding to Apple events

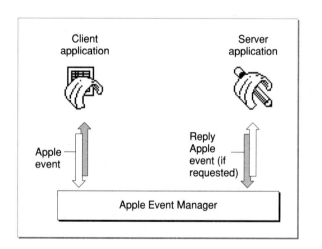

As you might imagine, there are many predefined kinds of Apple events, corresponding to the many services one application might request of another. Apple events are grouped into standard suites or groups of related events. Usually, you implement all the events in a given suite at the same time. The standard Apple event suites include the following:

- The *Required suite* consists of four basic Apple events that your application must support if it supports any Apple events at all. These events are Open Documents, Open Application, Print Documents, and Quit Application. The Finder uses these events for launching and terminating applications.

- The *Core suite* consists of the basic Apple events that nearly all applications use to communicate, including Get Data, Set Data, Move, Delete, and Save. You should support all the Apple events in the Core suite that make sense for your application.

- A *functional-area suite* consists of a group of Apple events that support a related functional area. One example of a functional area is the Text suite, which includes events related to text processing.

If an Apple event is one of these standard events, the client application can construct the event and the server application can interpret it according to the standard definition for that event. To ensure that your application can respond to Apple events sent by other applications, you should support the standard Apple events that are appropriate for your application.

Note

See the book *Inside Macintosh: Interapplication Communication* for complete details about the interapplication communications architecture. ◆

QuickTime

QuickTime is a collection of managers and other system software components that allow your application to control time-based data. QuickTime allows you to integrate time-based data (such as video clips, animation sequences, sound sequences, or time-indexed scientific data) into your application and to let users manipulate it in the same easy, intuitive way that they manipulate other elements of the Macintosh user interface. With QuickTime, your application can allow users to display, edit, copy, and paste time-based data much as they do text and graphics.

A movie is a collection of one or more streams of data, called tracks. Each track represents a stream of data of a particular type, such as video, sound, still images, or animation. Depending on the way the tracks are defined, one or more tracks can be active at certain times while the movie is playing.

QuickTime consists mainly of these pieces:

- the Movie Toolbox

- the Image Compression Manager

- a set of predefined components

Introduction

Many applications that incorporate QuickTime capabilities are interested only in playing movies. To do so, they call the Movie Toolbox, which provides routines that allow you to store, retrieve, and manipulate time-based data stored in QuickTime movies. Figure 1-8 illustrates the relationship between the various QuickTime managers and components.

Figure 1-8   Playing a QuickTime movie

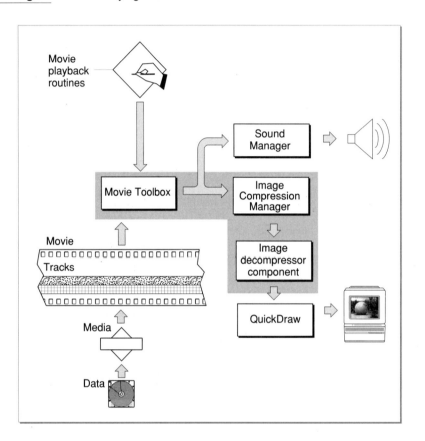

Note
See the books *Inside Macintosh: QuickTime* and *Inside Macintosh: QuickTime Components* for complete details about QuickTime. ◆

Communications Toolbox

The **Communications Toolbox** is a collection of system software managers that you can use to provide your application with basic networking and communications services. You're likely to use the Communications Toolbox only if your application is specifically concerned with communication between computers. Examples of such applications include telecommunications packages and electronic bulletin board applications. By using the Communications Toolbox, you can insulate your application from the details of the actual physical connection between your computer and the remote computer.

Introduction

The Communications Toolbox consists of four managers:

- The Connection Manager, which you can use to create and maintain a network connection.

- The Terminal Manager, which you can use to emulate a particular terminal during a network connection.

- The File Transfer Manager, which you can use to transfer files between your computer and the remote computer to which you are connected.

- The Communications Resource Manager, which you can use to register and keep track of communications resources.

Note

For complete information about the Communications Toolbox, see the book *Inside the Macintosh Communications Toolbox.* ◆

System Software Routines

By now, you might be wondering how these various system software routines are made available to your application. In traditional programming environments, you gain access to such special routines by linking a subroutine library—which contains the actual executable code of those routines—to your application. The code of the special routine is contained in your application, just like the code of any application-defined routine.

One main drawback of such an approach is that it tends to result in very large applications. As you might imagine, the code comprising the thousands of system software routines takes up quite a bit of space. It would be impractical to link all that code, or whatever subset of it an application actually used, to each application.

Another important drawback of the traditional approach is the difficulty of revising system software routines to provide new capabilities or to fix bugs. You would need to obtain a new subroutine library and then rebuild your application so that the new code is included in it.

The original Macintosh system software circumvented these problems by adopting a fairly novel approach. The software routines that make up the Macintosh Toolbox and the Macintosh Operating System reside mainly in **read-only memory (ROM),** provided by special chips contained in every Macintosh computer. When your application calls a Toolbox routine like `NewWindow`, the Operating System intercepts the call and executes the appropriate code contained in ROM.

This mechanism provides a simple way for the Operating System to substitute the code that is executed in response to a particular system software routine. Instead of executing the ROM-based code for some routine, the Operating System might choose to load some substitute code into the computer's **random-access memory (RAM);** then, when your application calls the routine in question, the Operating System intercepts the call and executes that RAM-based code.

Introduction

RAM-based code that substitutes for ROM-based code is called a **patch.** Patches are usually stored in the **System file,** located in the System Folder. The System file also contains collections of static data, known as resources, that applications can use to help present the standard Macintosh user interface.

The System file can also contain system software components that are not in a computer's ROM. To make one of these components available to your application, the Operating System simply loads it into RAM. This is like a patch, except that the new routines aren't replacing any existing ROM routines. Originally these sorts of RAM-based system software components were called **packages;** they were read into RAM only when some application called any one of the routines contained in them. However, because some of these packages have been included in later revisions of the ROM, the distinction between managers and packages has faded with time.

The current method for adding capabilities to the system software is to include the executable code of the new routines as a **system extension.** Extensions are stored in a special location (namely, in the Extensions folder in the System Folder) and are loaded into memory at system startup time. QuickTime, for example, is currently distributed as an extension.

When your application calls a system software routine, it doesn't matter, in general, whether the code that is executed in response resides in ROM, is a patch in RAM loaded from the System file, or is part of a RAM-based extension. It is, however, important that the appropriate code exist in at least one of these locations, because your application will crash if you attempt to call a routine that isn't defined anywhere. So, especially for code contained in extensions, you'll need to make sure that the code is present in the current operating environment before trying to call it. You can use the `Gestalt` function to determine whether a particular part of system software is available. For details on calling `Gestalt`, see the chapter "Gestalt Manager" in *Inside Macintosh: Operating System Utilities*.

There is one further twist in this picture that is worth mentioning. Some routines that are declared in your development system's header files are provided by the development system itself, not by the system software. These routines, known as **glue routines** (or just **glue**), are constructed by modifying available system software routines in some way. Consider the Memory Manager function `NewHandle`, which allocates a new relocatable block of memory. A call to `NewHandle` compiles into an executable instruction word. When that instruction is executed, the ROM code (or its RAM patch, if one exists) reads several of the bits in that word to determine exactly what to do. If, for instance, bit 9 of the instruction word is set, the ROM code allocates a block of the requested size and then clears all the bytes in that block to 0.

If you're programming in assembly language, you can set the bits of an instruction word directly. However, if you're programming in a high-level language like Pascal, you can't do that. Instead, you need to call a glue routine, in this case `NewHandleClear`, that takes care of calling `NewHandle` and setting the appropriate bits in the instruction word. Essentially, `NewHandleClear` is nothing but `NewHandle` together with some assembly-language code to set a bit in the instruction word. This translation is handled automatically by your development system at the time your application is compiled.

You'll encounter several other kinds of glue routines. Some glue routines translate high-level routines into low-level routines. Most of the high-level File Manager routines are of this variety. There is, for example, no code in ROM or the System file corresponding to the `FSpCreate` function. Instead, calling `FSpCreate` invokes some glue code that creates a parameter block, fills out some of the fields appropriately, and then passes that parameter block to the low-level function `PBHCreate`.

Some other glue routines are pure assembly-language instructions which don't call any system software routines. You might use glue like this to move a function result or other data from a register onto the stack.

You don't usually need to know whether a particular routine is implemented as glue code, except when you're doing low-level assembly-language debugging. For the time being, you can consider all the routines defined in *Inside Macintosh* as part of the Macintosh system software.

The Sample Application

The remainder of this book illustrates how to write a Macintosh application by gradually dissecting the source code of a very simple sample application, called Venn Diagrammer. This application allows the user to use Venn diagrams as a method of determining whether a given syllogism is valid (that is, whether the conclusion must be true if both premises are true). This section briefly describes the operation of the Venn Diagrammer application.

IMPORTANT

The account of syllogisms and Venn diagrams given here is inadequate for a full understanding of these topics. Most programmers, however, have encountered Venn diagrams at some point in their lives. For a more complete account, consult a good textbook on introductory logic. ▲

Introduction

When the user launches the Venn Diagrammer application, it opens a Venn diagram window, shown in Figure 1-9.

Figure 1-9   A typical Venn diagram window

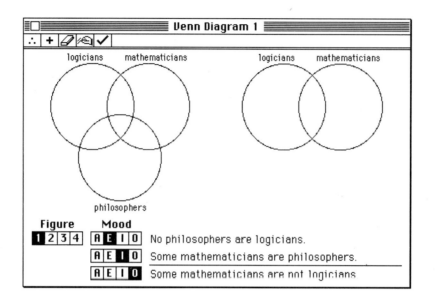

This window contains a number of distinct parts, shown in Figure 1-10.

Figure 1-10   The parts of a Venn diagram window

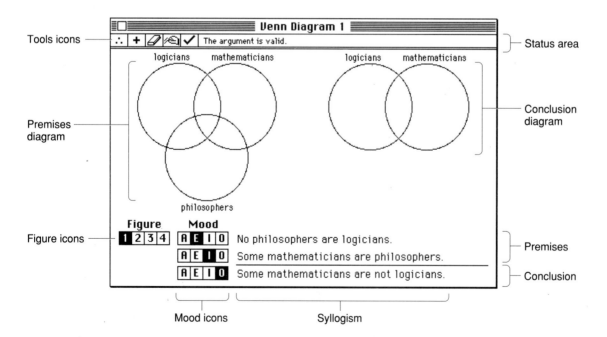

Introduction

This window is designed to let the user select a syllogism and then assess the validity of the syllogism by appropriately modifying the Venn diagram (the five overlapping circles). The user graphs the information contained in the two premises in the three circles on the left and the information in the conclusion in the two circles on the right.

As you can see, a syllogism is an argument containing two premises and one conclusion. These three statements must each be of one of four specific forms, known as the statement's mood. The four moods are often designated by the letters A, E, I, and O, as follows:

A   All philosophers are logicians.

E   No philosophers are logicians.

I   Some philosophers are logicians.

O   Some philosophers are not logicians.

Syllogisms are further classified by figure, which determines the order of the terms in the two premises. A syllogism is completely determined by the three terms involved, the moods of the three statements, and the figure.

The user can graph the information in a syllogism by clicking in the overlapping regions in the circles. If a region is white, nothing is known about the region. If the region is shaded, it's known that there is nothing in that region (that is, the region is empty). Finally, if an X appears in the region, it's known that there is something in that region. A correctly graphed syllogism is shown in Figure 1-11.

Figure 1-11   A correctly constructed Venn diagram

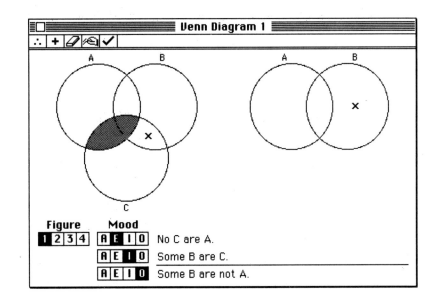

Introduction

At the top of the window, just below the title bar, are a set of tool icons and an empty status area. The tool icons allow the user to perform various operations on the diagram without having to move out of the window. For instance, clicking the tool in the middle (the eraser) clears the Venn diagram. These same operations can also be invoked using the Venn menu, as shown in Figure 1-12.

Figure 1-12　　The Venn menu

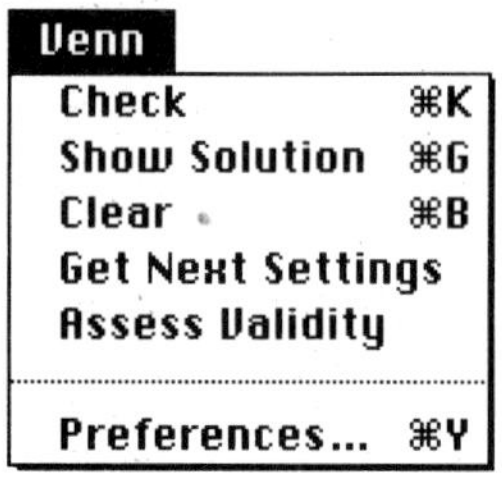

```
┌─────────────────────────┐
│ Venn                    │
├─────────────────────────┤
│ Check            ⌘K     │
│ Show Solution    ⌘G     │
│ Clear            ⌘B     │
│ Get Next Settings       │
│ Assess Validity         │
│·························│
│ Preferences...   ⌘Y     │
└─────────────────────────┘
```

The Venn Diagrammer application displays information in the window's status area. For example, if the user clicks the leftmost tool icon (or chooses the Assess Validity menu command), the application determines whether the currently displayed syllogism is valid or invalid. If it's valid, the application displays the message "The argument is valid." in the status area; otherwise, it displays the message "The argument is invalid."

Conventions for Sample Code

The sample code presented throughout this book follows a number of conventions to help you understand the code and to distinguish application-defined routines from system software routines. For the most part, the sample code listings presented throughout the *Inside Macintosh* suite of books follow these conventions as well.

■ Constants defined by the Venn Diagrammer application begin with the letter k. For example, the number of tools in a Venn diagram window is specified by the constant kNumTools. There are, however, several exceptions to this rule:

   □ Constants specifying resource IDs begin with the letter r. For example, the resource ID of the menu bar is specified by the constant rMenuBar.

   □ Constants specifying menu resource IDs begin with the letter m. For example, the resource ID of the File menu is specified by the constant mFile.

   □ Constants specifying menu commands begin with the letter i. For example, the number of the Quit command in the File menu is specified by the constant iQuit.

   □ Constants specifying messages displayed to the user in a window's status area begin with the letter e. For example, the message "The argument is valid." is specified by the constant eArgIsValid.

Introduction

- Application global variables have names beginning with the letter g. For example, the global variable that indicates whether the user wants to quit the application is called gDone. There are no exceptions to this rule.

- Application-defined routines have names beginning with either the prefix Do or the prefix My. For example, the routine that handles window updating is called DoUpdate. Similarly, the routine that returns a random number is called MyRandom. There is one exception to this rule:

  □ Application-defined routines that return Boolean values have names beginning with the prefix Is. For example, the routine that determines whether a window is a dialog box is called IsDialogWindow. Several system software routines have similar-sounding names. (For instance, the Dialog Manager provides the IsDialogEvent routine.)

- Application-defined data structures and types have names beginning with the prefix My. For example, the structure that holds information about a document window is called MyDocRec. A pointer to a record of type MyDocRec is of type MyDocRecPtr.

- Routine parameters and local variables have names beginning with the prefix my. For example, many of the routines in the Venn Diagrammer application require a window pointer as one of the parameters; this parameter is usually called myWindow. This convention has, however, many exceptions.

IMPORTANT

These naming conventions are adopted in this book (and elsewhere in *Inside Macintosh*) solely for reasons of consistency and clarity. They might not be suitable for your purposes. ▲

It's worth mentioning in advance that Venn Diagrammer takes a minimalist approach to error-handling: it tries to detect any errors that might adversely affect its further processing and to work around those errors in such a way as to avoid those adverse effects. In fact, this strategy is far too simple for most applications. Your application should provide far more extensive error detection and reporting to the user. See "Handling Errors" beginning on page 176 for some further discussion of error-handling techniques.

Memory

Contents

Memory

This chapter provides a brief introduction to memory management on Macintosh computers. It describes the organization of the partition of memory assigned to your application when it is launched and explains the basic data types used by the Macintosh Toolbox and Operating System. This chapter also describes how you can allocate portions of that memory partition for specific purposes and how the Memory Manager helps to maintain an orderly partition.

This chapter provides only the minimum information about memory that you'll need to understand the rest of this book and to begin reading other *Inside Macintosh* books. For a more detailed description of basic memory management strategies, see the chapter "Introduction to Memory Management" in the book *Inside Macintosh: Memory*.

About Memory

In the cooperative multitasking environment provided by the Macintosh Operating System, your application can use only part of the total amount of RAM available on a computer. Some of the available RAM is reserved for use by the Operating System itself, and the remainder of the available memory is shared among all open applications.

When the Operating System starts up, it divides the available RAM into two broad sections. It reserves for itself a zone or **partition** of memory known as the **system partition.** The system partition always begins at the lowest addressable byte of memory (memory address 0) and extends upward. The system partition consists of two main parts:

- a system heap
- a set of global variables

In general, the memory in the system partition is for use by the Operating System alone. Your application probably won't need to read or write that memory.

All memory outside the system partition is available for allocation to applications or other software components. In the cooperative multitasking environment, the user can have multiple applications open at once. When an application is launched, the Operating System assigns it a section of memory known as its application partition. In general, an application uses only the memory contained in its own application partition.

Figure 2-1 illustrates the organization of memory when several applications are open at the same time. The system partition occupies the lowest position in memory. Application partitions occupy some or all of the remaining space. Note that application partitions are loaded into the top part of memory first. An application partition consists of three main parts:

- an application heap
- a stack
- an A5 world, which includes the application's global variables

Figure 2-1   Memory organization in the cooperative multitasking environment

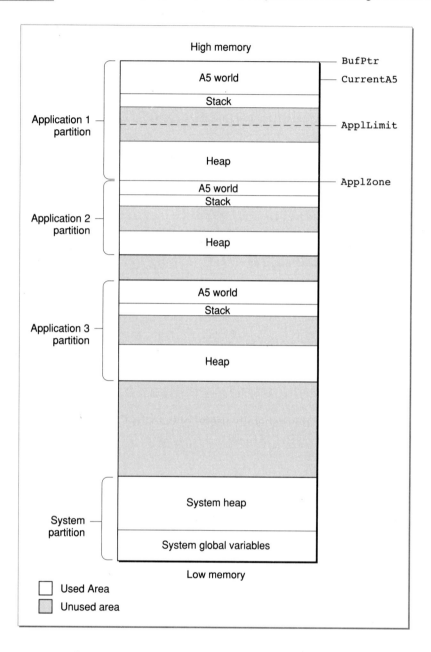

The System Heap

The main part of the system partition is an area of memory known as the **system heap.** In general, the system heap is reserved for exclusive use by the Operating System and other system software components, which load into it various items such as system resources, system code segments, and system data structures. All system buffers and queues, for example, are allocated in the system heap.

The system heap is also used for code and other resources that do not belong to specific applications, such as code resources that add features to the Operating System or that provide control of special-purpose peripheral equipment. System patches and system extensions (stored as code resources of type 'INIT') are loaded into the system heap during the system startup process. Hardware device drivers (stored as code resources of type 'DRVR') are loaded into the system heap when the driver is opened.

The System Global Variables

The lowest part of memory is occupied by a collection of global variables called **system global variables** (or **low-memory system global variables**). The Operating System uses these variables to maintain different kinds of information about the operating environment. For example, the `Ticks` global variable contains the number of ticks (sixtieths of a second) that have elapsed since the system was most recently started up. Similar variables contain, for example, the height of the menu bar (`MBarHeight`) and pointers to the heads of various operating-system queues (`DTQueue`, `FSQHdr`, `VBLQueue`, and so forth). Most low-memory global variables are of this variety: they contain information that is generally useful only to the Operating System or other system software components.

Other low-memory global variables contain information about the current application. For example, the `ApplZone` global variable contains the address of the first byte of the active application's partition. The `ApplLimit` global variable contains the address of the last byte the active application's heap can expand to include. The `CurrentA5` global variable contains the address of the boundary between the active application's global variables and its application parameters. Because these global variables contain information about the active application, the Operating System changes the values of these variables whenever a context switch occurs (that is, whenever an application takes control of the CPU from another application).

In general, it is best to avoid reading or writing low-memory system global variables. Most of these variables are undocumented, and the results of changing their values can be unpredictable. Usually, when the value of a low-memory global variable is likely to be useful to applications, the system software provides a routine that you can use to read or write that value. For example, you can get the current value of the `Ticks` global variable by calling the `TickCount` function.

Application Partitions

When your application is launched, the Operating System allocates for it a partition of memory called its **application partition.** That partition contains required segments of the application's code as well as other data associated with the application. Figure 2-2 illustrates the general organization of an application partition.

Figure 2-2   Organization of an application partition

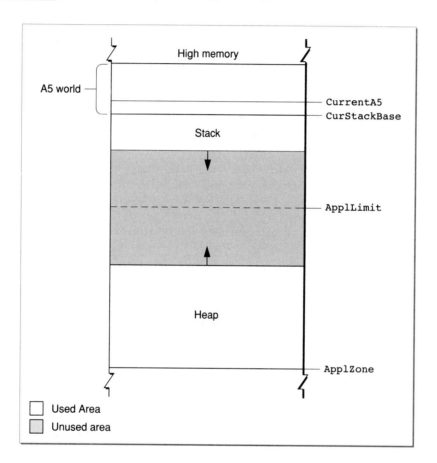

Your application partition is divided into three major parts:

- the application stack
- the application heap
- the application global variables and A5 world

The heap is located at the low-memory end of your application partition and always expands (when necessary) toward high memory. The A5 world is located at the high-memory end of your application partition and is of fixed size. The stack begins at the high-memory end of the A5 world and expands downward, toward the top of the heap.

As you can see in Figure 2-2, there is usually an unused area of memory between the stack and the heap. This unused area provides space for the stack to grow without encroaching upon the space assigned to the application heap. In some cases, however, the stack might grow into space reserved for the application heap. If this happens, it is very likely that data in the heap will become corrupted.

The ApplLimit global variable marks the upper limit to which your heap can grow. If you call the MaxApplZone procedure at the beginning of your program, the heap immediately extends all the way up to this limit. If you were to use all of the heap's free space, the Memory Manager would not allow you to allocate additional blocks above ApplLimit. If you do not call MaxApplZone, the heap grows toward ApplLimit whenever the Memory Manager finds that there is not enough memory in the heap to fill a request. However, once the heap grows up to ApplLimit, it can grow no further. Thus, whether you maximize your application heap or not, you can use only the space between the bottom of the heap and ApplLimit.

Unlike the heap, the stack is not bounded by ApplLimit. If your application uses heavily nested procedures with many local variables or uses extensive recursion, the stack could grow downward beyond ApplLimit. Because you do not use Memory Manager routines to allocate memory on the stack, the Memory Manager cannot stop your stack from growing beyond ApplLimit and possibly encroaching upon space reserved for the heap. However, an Operating System task checks approximately 60 times each second to see if the stack has moved into the heap. If it has, the task, known as the "stack sniffer," generates a system error.

The Application Stack

The **stack** is an area of memory in your application partition that can grow or shrink at one end while the other end remains fixed. This means that space on the stack is always allocated and released in LIFO (last-in, first-out) order. The last item allocated is always the first to be released. It also means that the allocated area of the stack is always contiguous. Space is released only at the top of the stack, never in the middle, so there can never be any unallocated "holes" in the stack.

By convention, the stack grows from high-memory addresses toward low-memory addresses. The end of the stack that grows or shrinks is usually referred to as the "top" of the stack, even though it's actually at the lower end of memory occupied by the stack.

Because of its LIFO nature, the stack is especially useful for memory allocation connected with the execution of functions or procedures. When your application calls a routine, space is automatically allocated on the stack for a stack frame. A **stack frame** contains the routine's parameters, local variables, and return address. Figure 2-3 illustrates how the stack expands and shrinks during a function call. The leftmost diagram shows the stack just before the function is called. The middle diagram shows the stack expanded to hold the stack frame. Once the function is executed, the local

Memory

variables and function parameters are popped off the stack. If the function is a Pascal function, all that remains is the previous stack with the function result on top.

Figure 2-3   The application stack

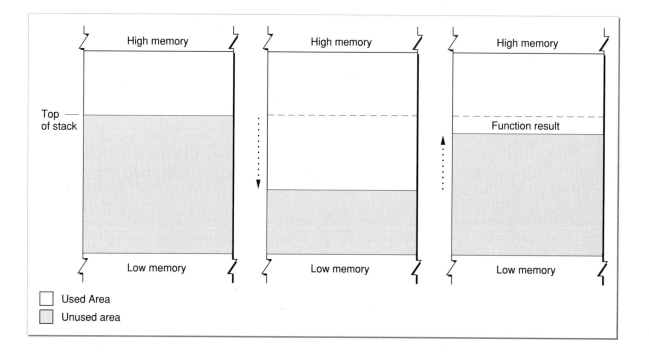

Note
Dynamic memory allocation on the stack is usually handled automatically if you are using a high-level development language such as Pascal. The compiler generates the code that creates and deletes stack frames for each function or procedure call. ◆

The Application Heap

An **application heap** is the area of memory in your application partition in which space is dynamically allocated and released on demand. The heap begins at the low-memory end of your application partition and extends upward in memory. The heap contains virtually all items that are not allocated on the stack. For instance, your application heap contains the application's code segments and resources that are currently loaded into memory. The heap also contains other dynamically allocated items such as window records, dialog records, document data, and so forth.

You allocate space within your application's heap by making calls to the Memory Manager, either directly (for instance, using the `NewHandle` function) or indirectly (for instance, using a routine such as the Window Manager's `NewWindow`, which in turn calls Memory Manager routines). Space in the heap is allocated in **blocks,** which can be of any size needed for a particular object.

The Memory Manager does all the necessary housekeeping to keep track of blocks in the heap as they are allocated and released. Because these operations can occur in any order, the heap doesn't usually grow and shrink in an orderly way, as the stack does. Instead, after your application has been running for a while, the heap can tend to become fragmented into a patchwork of allocated and free blocks, as shown in Figure 2-4. This fragmentation is known as **heap fragmentation.**

Figure 2-4   A fragmented heap

One result of heap fragmentation is that the Memory Manager might not be able to satisfy your application's request to allocate a block of a particular size. Even though there is enough free space available, the space is broken up into blocks smaller than the requested size. When this happens, the Memory Manager tries to create the needed space by moving allocated blocks together, thus collecting the free space in a single larger block. This operation is known as **heap compaction.** Figure 2-5 shows the results of compacting the fragmented heap shown in Figure 2-4.

Figure 2-5   A compacted heap

Heap fragmentation is generally not a problem as long as the blocks of memory you allocate are free to move during heap compaction. There are, however, two situations in which a block is not free to move: when it is a nonrelocatable block, and when it is a relocatable block that is temporarily locked in place. To minimize heap fragmentation, you should use nonrelocatable blocks sparingly, and you should lock relocatable blocks only when absolutely necessary. See "Memory Blocks" starting on page 38 for a description of relocatable and nonrelocatable blocks.

Memory

The Application Global Variables and A5 World

Your application's global variables are stored in an area of memory near the top of your application partition known as the application **A5 world.** The A5 world contains four kinds of data:

- application global variables
- application QuickDraw global variables
- application parameters
- the application's jump table

Each of these items is of fixed size, although the sizes of the global variables and of the jump table vary from application to application. Figure 2-6 shows the standard organization of the A5 world.

Figure 2-6   Organization of an application's A5 world

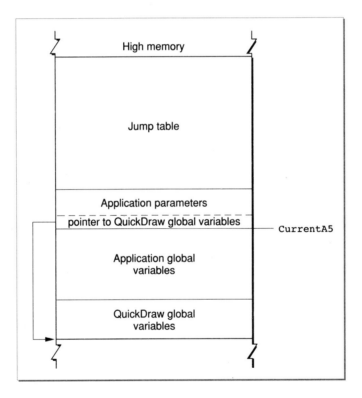

Note

An application's global variables may appear either above or below the QuickDraw global variables. The relative locations of these two items are determined by your development system's linker. In addition, part of the jump table might appear below the boundary pointed to by `CurrentA5`. ◆

The system global variable `CurrentA5` points to the boundary between the current application's global variables and its application parameters. For this reason, the **application's global variables** are found as negative offsets from the value of `CurrentA5`. This boundary is important because the Operating System uses it to access the following information from your application: its global variables, its QuickDraw global variables, the application parameters, and the jump table. This information is known collectively as the A5 world because the Operating System uses the microprocessor's A5 register to point to that boundary.

Your application's **QuickDraw global variables** contain information about its drawing environment. For example, among these variables is a pointer to the current graphics port.

Your application's **jump table** contains an entry for each of your application's routines that is called by code in another segment. The Segment Manager uses the jump table to determine the address of any externally referenced routines called by a code segment. For more information on jump tables, see the chapter "Segment Manager" in *Inside Macintosh: Processes*.

The **application parameters** are 32 bytes of memory located above the application global variables; they're reserved for use by the Operating System. The first long word of those parameters is a pointer to your application's QuickDraw global variables.

Memory Blocks

You can use the Memory Manager to allocate two different types of blocks in your heap: nonrelocatable blocks and relocatable blocks. A **nonrelocatable block** is a block of memory whose location in the heap is fixed. In contrast, a **relocatable block** is a block of memory that can be moved within the heap (perhaps during heap compaction). The Memory Manager sometimes moves relocatable blocks during memory operations so that it can use the space in the heap optimally.

The Memory Manager provides data types that reference both relocatable and nonrelocatable blocks. It also provides routines that allow you to allocate and release blocks of both types.

Nonrelocatable Blocks

To reference a nonrelocatable block, you can use a **pointer** variable, defined by the `Ptr` data type.

```
TYPE
    SignedByte     = −128..127;
    Ptr            = ^SignedByte;
```

A pointer is simply the address of an arbitrary byte in memory, and a pointer to a nonrelocatable block of memory is simply the address of the first byte in the block, as illustrated in Figure 2-7. After you allocate a nonrelocatable block, you can make copies of the pointer variable. Because a pointer is the address of a block of memory that cannot be moved, all copies of the pointer correctly reference the block as long as you don't dispose of it.

Figure 2-7   A pointer to a nonrelocatable block

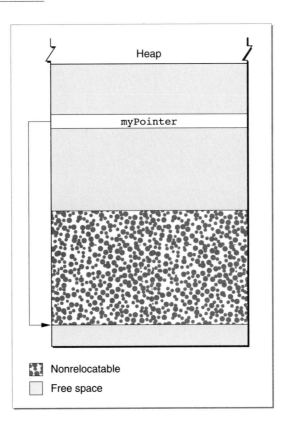

You can allocate a nonrelocatable block of memory by calling the Memory Manager function `NewPtr`. The Venn Diagrammer application uses the following line of code to allocate a new window record each time the user creates a new document window:

```
myPointer := NewPtr(sizeof(WindowRecord));
```

Here, `myPointer` is of type `Ptr`. (To see this line of code in context, look at Listing 6-6 on page 117.)

Relocatable Blocks

To reference relocatable blocks, the Memory Manager uses a scheme known as **double indirection.** The Memory Manager keeps track of a relocatable block internally with a **master pointer,** which itself is part of a nonrelocatable **master pointer block** in your application heap.

Note

The Memory Manager allocates one master pointer block (containing 64 master pointers) for your application at launch time, and you can call the `MoreMasters` procedure to request that additional master pointer blocks be allocated. ◆

When the Memory Manager moves a relocatable block, it updates the master pointer so that it always contains the address of the relocatable block. You reference the block with a **handle,** defined by the `Handle` data type.

```
TYPE
    Handle        = ^Ptr;
```

A handle contains the address of a master pointer. The left side of Figure 2-8 shows a handle to a relocatable block of memory located in the middle of the application heap. If necessary (perhaps to make room for another block of memory), the Memory Manager can move that block down in the heap, as shown in the right side of Figure 2-8.

Figure 2-8   A handle to a relocatable block

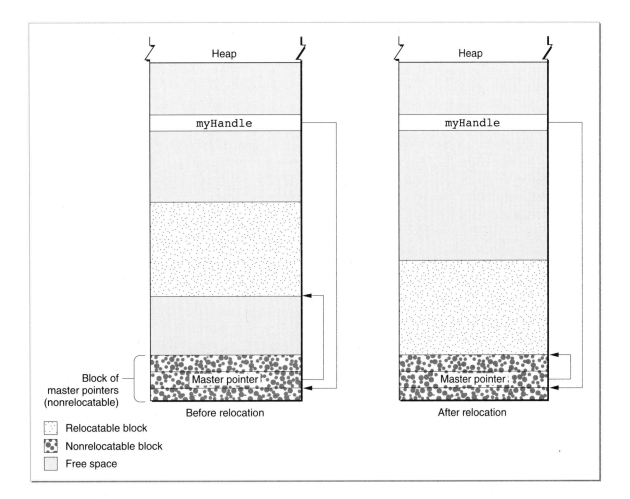

Master pointers for relocatable objects in your heap are always allocated in your application heap. Because the blocks of master pointers are nonrelocatable, it is best to allocate them as low in your heap as possible. You can do this by calling the `MoreMasters` procedure when your application starts up.

You can allocate a relocatable block of memory by calling the Memory Manager function `NewHandle`. The Venn Diagrammer application uses the following line of code to allocate a new document record each time the user creates a new document window:

```
myHandle := MyDocRecHnd(NewHandleClear(sizeof(MyDocRec)));
```

Here, `myHandle` is of type `MyDocRecHnd`. The `NewHandleClear` function is a variant of `NewHandle` that clears all bytes in the new block to 0. (To see this line of code in context, look at Listing 6-6 on page 117.)

Whenever possible, you should allocate memory in relocatable blocks. This gives the Memory Manager the greatest freedom when rearranging the blocks in your application heap to create a new block of free memory. In some cases, however, you may be forced to allocate a nonrelocatable block of memory. When you call the Window Manager function `NewWindow`, for example, the Window Manager internally calls the `NewPtr` function to allocate a new nonrelocatable block in your application partition. You need to exercise care when calling Toolbox routines that allocate such blocks, lest your application heap become overly fragmented.

Using relocatable blocks makes the Memory Manager more efficient at managing available space, but it does carry some overhead. As you have seen, the Memory Manager must allocate extra memory to hold master pointers for relocatable blocks. It groups these master pointers into nonrelocatable blocks. For large relocatable blocks, this extra space is negligible, but if you allocate many very small relocatable blocks, the cost can be considerable. For this reason, you should avoid allocating a very large number of handles to small blocks; instead, allocate a single large block and use it as an array to hold the data you need.

As you have seen, a heap block can be either relocatable or nonrelocatable. The designation of a block as relocatable or nonrelocatable is a permanent property of that block. If relocatable, a block can be either locked or unlocked; if it's unlocked, a block can be either purgeable or unpurgeable. These attributes of relocatable blocks can be set and changed as necessary. The following sections explain how to lock and unlock blocks, and how to mark them as purgeable or unpurgeable.

Locking and Unlocking Relocatable Blocks

Occasionally, you might need a relocatable block of memory to stay in one place. To prevent a block from moving, you can **lock** it, using the `HLock` procedure. Once you have locked a block, it won't move. Later, you can **unlock** it, using the `HUnlock` procedure, allowing it to move again.

In general, you need to lock a relocatable block only if there is some danger that it might be moved during the time that you read or write the data in that block. This might happen, for instance, if you dereference a handle to obtain a pointer to the data and (for increased speed) use the pointer within a loop that calls routines that might cause memory to be moved. If, within the loop, the block whose data you are accessing is in fact moved, then the pointer no longer points to that data; this pointer is said to **dangle.**

Using locked relocatable blocks can, however, hinder the Memory Manager as much as using nonrelocatable blocks. The Memory Manager can't move locked blocks. In addition, except when you allocate memory and resize relocatable blocks, it can't move relocatable blocks around locked relocatable blocks (just as it can't move them around nonrelocatable blocks). Thus, locking a block in the middle of the heap for long periods can increase heap fragmentation.

Locking and unlocking blocks every time you want to prevent a block from moving can become troublesome. Fortunately, the Memory Manager moves unlocked, relocatable blocks only at well-defined, predictable times. In general, each routine description in *Inside Macintosh* indicates whether the routine could move or purge memory. If you do not call any of those routines in a section of code, you can rely on all blocks to remain stationary while that code executes.

Purging and Reallocating Relocatable Blocks

One advantage of relocatable blocks is that you can use them to store information that you would like to keep in memory to make your application more efficient, but that you don't really need if available memory space becomes low. For example, your application might, at the beginning of its execution, load user preferences from a preferences file into a relocatable block. As long as the block remains in memory, your application can access information from the preferences file without actually reopening the file. However, reopening the file probably wouldn't take enough time to justify keeping the block in memory if memory space were scarce.

By making a relocatable block **purgeable,** you allow the Memory Manager to free the space it occupies if necessary. If you later want to prohibit the Memory Manager from freeing the space occupied by a relocatable block, you can make the block **unpurgeable.** You can use the `HPurge` and `HNoPurge` procedures to change back and forth between these two states.

IMPORTANT

A block you create by calling `NewHandle` is initially unlocked and unpurgeable. As a result, you don't have to worry about the block being purged unless you make the block purgeable. ▲

Once you make a relocatable block purgeable, you should subsequently check handles to that block before using them if you call any of the routines that could move or purge memory. If a handle's master pointer is set to `NIL`, then the Operating System has purged its block. To use the information formerly in the block, you must reallocate space for it (perhaps by calling the `ReallocateHandle` procedure) and then reconstruct its contents (for example, by rereading the preferences file). Figure 2-9 illustrates the purging and reallocating of a relocatable block. When the block is purged, its master pointer is set to `NIL`. When it is reallocated, the handle correctly references a new block, but that block's contents are initially undefined.

Figure 2-9   Purging and reallocating a relocatable block

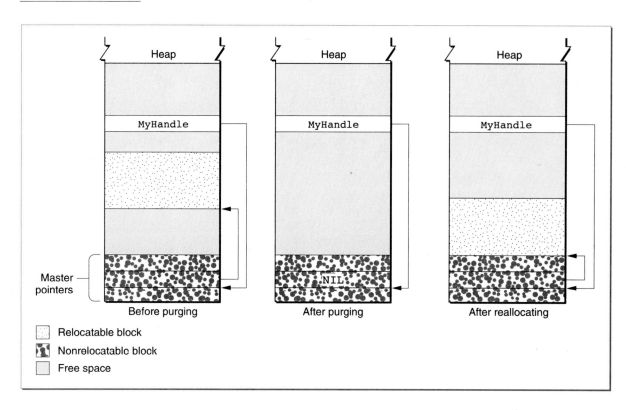

Data Types

This section describes some of the general-purpose data types that the Memory Manager defines. These data types are used throughout the Macintosh Toolbox and Operating System.

Pointers and Handles

As you've seen, the Memory Manager uses pointers and handles to reference nonrelocatable and relocatable blocks, respectively. The data types `Ptr` and `Handle` define pointers and handles as follows:

```
TYPE
    SignedByte   = —128..127;        {any byte in memory}
    Byte         = 0..255;           {an unsigned byte}
    Ptr          = ^SignedByte;      {address of a signed byte}
    Handle       = ^Ptr;             {address of a master pointer}
```

The `SignedByte` data type stands for an arbitrary byte in memory, just to give `Ptr` and `Handle` something to point to. The `Byte` data type is an alternative definition that treats byte-length data as an unsigned rather than a signed quantity.

The Pascal language defines the special symbol `NIL`, which can be the value of any pointer type. You can assign `NIL` to any pointer (and hence to any handle) to indicate that the pointer has a defined value but does not point anywhere useful. Some system software routines return `NIL` as the value of a pointer or handle if the routine fails to perform the requested action. For example, the `NewHandle` routine returns `NIL` if the requested amount of memory is not available in the application heap.

For C, the type declarations look like this:

```
typedef char SignedByte;        /*any byte in memory*/
typedef unsigned char Byte;     /*an unsigned byte*/
typedef char *Ptr;              /*address of a signed byte*/
typedef Ptr *Handle;            /*address of a master pointer*/
```

Unlike Pascal, the C language does not contain a reserved symbol for a nil pointer. Most development systems, however, include definitions of both `nil` and `NULL`:

```
#define NULL 0
#define nil 0
```

Because of C's loose type conventions, you can assign the values `nil` and `NULL` to data types other than pointers and handles. In Pascal, the compiler generates an error if you try to assign the value `NIL` to an object whose data type is not defined as a pointer to some data type.

Strings

The Macintosh system software uses strings in arrays of up to 255 characters, with the first byte of the array storing the length of the string. Some Toolbox routines allow you to pass such a string directly; others require that you pass a pointer or a handle to a string. The Memory Manager provides the following type definitions that define character strings in terms of the Pascal `String` data type:

```
TYPE
    Str15        = String[15];
    Str27        = String[27];
    Str31        = String[31];
    Str63        = String[63];
    Str255       = String[255];
    StringPtr    = ^Str255;
    StringHandle = ^StringPtr;
```

The C language treats strings differently than Pascal does. In C, strings are of variable length, with the end of the string marked by a special delimiter, usually the null character (ASCII 0). If you are using C, you must make certain to pass Pascal-style strings to Toolbox routines or to use special versions of the Toolbox routines that accept C strings. Check the documentation for your development environment for complete details.

Procedure Pointers

For treating procedures and functions as data objects, the Memory Manager defines the `ProcPtr` data type:

```
TYPE
    ProcPtr        = Ptr;            {pointer to a procedure}
```

For example, after the declarations

```
VAR
    myProcPtr:     ProcPtr;


PROCEDURE MyProc;
BEGIN
    ...
END;
```

you can make `myProcPtr` reference the `MyProc` procedure by using Pascal's @ operator, as follows:

```
myProcPtr := @MyProc;
```

With the @ operator, you can assign procedures and functions to variables of type `ProcPtr`, embed them in data structures, and pass them as arguments to other routines. Notice, however, that the data type `ProcPtr` technically points to an arbitrary byte, not an actual routine. As a result, there's no way in Pascal to access the underlying routine via this pointer in order to call it. Only routines written in assembly language can actually call routines designated by pointers of type `ProcPtr`.

Note

You can't use the @ operator to reference procedures or functions whose declarations are nested within other routines. ◆

Type Coercion

Because of Pascal's strong typing rules, you can't directly assign a pointer value to a variable of some other pointer type, or pass a pointer variable to a routine requesting some other pointer type. Instead, you have to coerce the pointer from one type to another.

For example, you can call the HLock procedure to lock a relocatable block of memory. The HLock procedure requires a parameter of type Handle. If the block you want to lock isn't referenced by a variable of type Handle, you must coerce the variable to the required type. Here's an example:

```
HLock(Handle(myData));
```

Similarly, the GetDialogItem procedure returns in a VAR parameter a handle to an item in a dialog box. If you were to use the procedure to obtain the handle to a button in the variable itemHand of type Handle, you might need to access the button as a control. For example, you could access the button's enclosing rectangle with the code:

```
ControlHandle(itemHand)^^.contrlRect;
```

You can use this same syntax to equate any two variables of the same length. For example:

```
VAR
    myChar:     Char;
    myByte:     Byte;


myByte := Byte(myChar);
```

You can also use the functions ORD, ORD4, and POINTER to coerce variables of different length from one type to another. For example:

```
VAR
    myInteger:  Integer;
    myLongInt:  LongInt;
    myPointer:  Ptr;


myInteger := ORD(myLongInt);      {two low-order bytes only}
myInteger := ORD(myPointer);      {two low-order bytes only}
myLongInt := ORD(myInteger);      {packed into high-order bytes}
myLongInt := ORD4(myInteger);     {packed into low-order bytes}
myLongInt := ORD(myPointer);
myPointer := POINTER(myInteger);
myPointer := POINTER(myLongInt);
```

Note
Assembly-language and C language programmers don't need to bother with type coercion. ◆

Resources

Contents

Resources

This chapter describes how your application can use the Resource Manager to create and manage resources, collections of data stored in a file's resource fork that have a defined structure or type. The Macintosh Operating System and the Macintosh Toolbox define a large number of resource types. You'll need to include resources of some of these types in your application's resource file to meet various requirements of the system software. In addition, the system software provides a number of resources (such as fonts, patterns, and icons) that you can use to help create the standard Macintosh user interface for your application.

This chapter begins with a general description of resources. Then it shows how to

- use predefined system resources
- create resources of a standard type
- define your own custom resources and resource types

For a complete description of the capabilities of the Resource Manager and for code samples illustrating more advanced resource-handling techniques, see the chapter "Resource Manager" in *Inside Macintosh: More Macintosh Toolbox*.

About Resources

An experienced Macintosh programmer might cringe at several features of the GreetMe source code shown in Listing 1-1 on page 3. One of the main sins it commits is this line:

```
gString := 'Hello, world!';
```

The problem with this line is that it includes, as part of the source code of the application, the message string that is to be displayed in the output window. While such an intermixing of code and data might be standard in some programming environments, it's definitely nonstandard in the Macintosh environment. To change the message, or to produce a version of the message in a different language, you'd need to change the source code and recompile the application. It would be better to isolate the changing data (the message string) from the application's code.

When you're programming on the Macintosh, you can do this by creating a resource that contains the message string. A **resource** is any collection of data having a defined structure that is stored in a file designed to hold resources, known as a **resource file.** Then you can read the message string from the resource file using a call like this:

```
GetIndString(gString, kMessages, kGreetingString);
```

The GetIndString procedure reads the resource of type 'STR#' that has the resource ID kMessages in an open resource fork. This type of resource contains a string list, which is a sequential list of Pascal strings. Then GetIndString selects the string having the index kGreetingString. If there are at least that many strings in the string list, it puts the appropriate string into the first parameter (in this case, gString).

Note

The GetIndString procedure is not part of the Resource Manager, but it does call the Resource Manager. Many Toolbox and Operating System routines internally call the Resource Manager to retrieve information from resources. ◆

The resources used by an application can be created and changed separately from the application's code. This separation is the main advantage to having resource files. A change in a simple greeting or in the title of a menu, for example, won't require any recompilation of code, nor will translation to another language.

IMPORTANT

Properly written Macintosh applications should store *all* language- or location-sensitive data as resources, so that localization is largely a matter of editing the application's resources. ▲

Resource Paths

At any given time during your application's execution, there are usually two or more open resource files from which you can read information. The system resource file is opened by the Operating System at startup time. It contains standard resources, called **system resources,** shared by all applications. Among these are icons, fonts, sounds, and other collections of data. The system resource file also contains a number of code resources that you call indirectly to help create the standard Macintosh user interface. For example, the standard appearance and behavior of pull-down menus is governed by a menu-definition procedure, stored as a resource of type 'MDEF' in the system resource file. The system resource file also contains code resources that help you create standard windows and controls.

Your application's resource file is opened when your application is launched. You can call the CurResFile function early in your application's execution to get the reference number of your application's resource file.

```
gAppsResourceFile := CurResFile;
```

You need to keep track of your application's resource file because the Resource Manager always looks for resources in the current resource file, which can change. Each time you open a resource file, it becomes the current resource file. You're likely to open a number of different resource files at various points in your application's execution. For instance, many applications store the user's general preferences in a resource file in the **Preferences folder** in the System Folder. In addition, if your application supports document files, you'll probably store some of the document's settings in the document's resource file. Table 3-1 summarizes the typical locations of resources used by an application.

Table 3-1   Typical locations of resources

Resource file	Resources contained in file
System resource file	Standard elements of the Macintosh user interface (such as fonts, sounds, and icons) shared by all applications, and code resources that manage user interface elements (such as menus, controls, and windows)
Application resource file	Resources containing static data (such as menu titles, menu items, and text strings) used by the application
Application preferences file	Resources encoding the user's global preferences for the application
Document resource file	Resources used only in this document, or resources that govern the appearance of the document's window (such as its location on the screen)

When searching resource files, the Resource Manager generally begins with the most recently opened one. When you ask it to open a resource of a particular type and ID, it first looks in the current resource file. If the Resource Manager doesn't find the specified resource there, it then looks in the resource file opened just before the current resource file. As long as the resource remains unfound, the Resource Manager continues until it reaches the last resource file in the chain, which is probably the system resource file. If the specified resource isn't there either, the Resource Manager gives up and notifies your application that the resource can't be found.

Figure 3-1 illustrates a typical search path followed by the Resource Manager as it looks for a particular font.

Figure 3-1   Searching for a resource

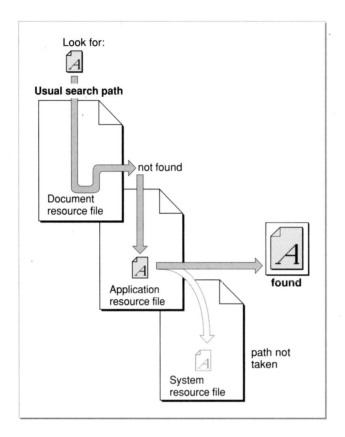

Note

Unlike the system resource file and your application's resource file, a document's resource file is not automatically opened when you open the document's data fork. If you want to include a document's resource fork in the chain of open resource files, you need to open it explicitly (for instance, using the `HOpenResFile` routine). ◆

In general it's best not to rely too much on the Resource Manager's ability to search through open resource files; instead, you should explicitly set the appropriate resource file as the current resource file (by calling `SetResFile`) before you read or write any resource data. In addition, you can restrict the Resource Manager's search for a resource to the current resource file by using special Resource Manager routines. For example, instead of calling `GetResource`, you can call `Get1Resource`. This instructs the Resource Manager to look only in the first resource file in the chain of open resource files.

Resource Types

As indicated above, resources are grouped logically by function into **resource types.** You refer to a resource by passing the Resource Manager a **resource specification,** which consists of the resource type and an ID number or a name. Any resource type is valid, whether one of those recognized by the Toolbox as referring to a standard Macintosh resource (such as a pattern), or a custom type created for use by your application.

Note

The Resource Manager knows nothing about the formats of the individual types of resources. Only the routines in the other parts of the Toolbox and Operating System that call the Resource Manager have this knowledge. ◆

A resource type can be any sequence of four alphanumeric characters, including the space character. You can create resource types for your application, provided that they consist of all uppercase letters and do not conflict with the standard resource types already created. A resource type is defined by the `ResType` data type:

```
TYPE ResType = PACKED ARRAY[1..4] OF CHAR;
```

IMPORTANT

Uppercase letters are distinguished from their lowercase counterparts in resource types. In addition, Apple reserves for its own use all resource types that include any lowercase letters. If you create custom resource types for use by your application, make sure that the type includes all uppercase letters. ▲

Table 3-2 lists the names and uses of some of the standard resource types used by the Macintosh system software. Uppercase resources are listed first.

Table 3-2   Some standard resource types

Resource type	Meaning
'ALRT'	Alert box template
'CODE'	Application code segment
'CURS'	Cursor
'DITL'	Item list in a dialog or alert box
'DLOG'	Dialog box template
'FONT'	Bitmapped font
'ICON'	Icon
'MBAR'	Menu bar
'MENU'	Menu
'PAT '	Pattern (The space in the resource type is required.)

continued

Table 3-2   Some standard resource types (continued)

Resource type	Meaning
'PICT'	QuickDraw picture
'SIZE'	Size of an application's partition and other information
'STR '	String (The space in the resource type is required.)
'STR#'	String list
'WIND'	Window template
'hdlg'	Help for dialog box or alert box items
'sfnt'	Outline font
'snd '	Sound (The space in the resource type is required.)

You pick out a particular resource by specifying its type together with a **resource name** or a **resource ID** number. In general, it's best to use resource IDs because they're guaranteed to be unique within any given resource file. By contrast, it's possible to have two different resources of the same type with the same name.

Resource Structure

A resource file consists of a number of individual resources together with a **resource map,** an indication of where in the resource file the data for a given resource is to be found. You usually don't need to know about the structure—or even the existence—of the resource map. The Resource Manager uses it to keep track of a resource file's resources. If you lengthen or shorten a resource, or remove one from the resource file entirely, the Resource Manager takes care of modifying the resource map accordingly.

Often, you don't even need to know about the structure of the individual resources you access in a resource fork. Sometimes you just need to open a resource and pass the handle you receive from the Resource Manager to some Toolbox routine. Here's an example:

```
FOR count := 1 TO 4 DO
    gEmptyPats[count] := GetPattern(kEmptyID + (count - 1));


FillRgn(myRegion, gEmptyPats[gEmptyIndex]^^);
```

At application startup time, the Venn Diagrammer application reads the four available emptiness patterns from the application's resource file. Later, when it is drawing the current contents of the Venn diagram, it might fill a specified region with the current pattern. The application itself knows nothing about the actual structure of a pattern.

Sometimes, however, you do need to know about the structure of the individual resources you want to use in your application. This is certainly true for any resources your application defines itself. Occasionally, you also need to know how the data in a system resource is structured. *Inside Macintosh* uses two general methods for displaying the structure of a resource's data: resource descriptions and resource diagrams.

The first method used in *Inside Macintosh* to describe the structure of a resource involves specifying a description in the Rez resource description language. Listing 3-1 shows the Rez input for a sample dialog box.

Listing 3-1   Rez input for the Preferences dialog box

```
resource 'DLOG' (rVennDPrefsDial, purgeable) {          /*dialog resource*/
    {84, 82, 264, 362},         /*rectangle for dialog box*/
    noGrowDocProc,              /*window definition ID for modeless dialog*/
    visible,                    /*display this dialog box immediately*/
    goAway,                     /*draw a close box*/
    0x0,                        /*initial refCon value of zero*/
    rVennDPrefsDial,            /*use item list with res ID rVennDPrefsDial*/
    "Venn Diagram Preferences",/*window title*/
    noAutoCenter                /*don't automatically center the window*/
};
```

Rez is a resource compiler: it takes a resource description like the one shown in Listing 3-1 and produces a compiled resource. As you can see, the Rez description includes information about the desired dialog box, including the box's rectangle, window definition ID, and initial window title.

Rez is provided as part of the Macintosh Programmer's Workshop (MPW) and as part of some third-party development environments. If you prefer, you can create and edit resources using tools like ResEdit, a graphic resource editor provided by Apple Computer, Inc. Using ResEdit, you'll create and modify resources in a slightly more friendly atmosphere, by manipulating windows like the one shown in Figure 3-2.

Figure 3-2   The ResEdit version of the Preferences dialog box

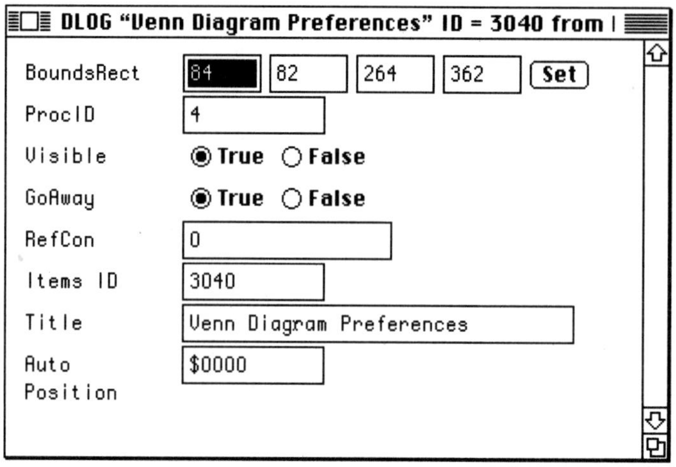

ResEdit uses an internal resource compiler to turn this graphic representation of a resource into a compiled resource.

Note

For most purposes, and especially for programmers new to the Macintosh environment, ResEdit is a perfectly adequate tool for creating and editing resources. For information about using ResEdit to create resources, see *ResEdit Reference*. For complete information about using Rez to compile resource descriptions into resources, see *Macintosh Programmer's Workshop Reference.* ◆

Whether you use Rez or ResEdit's internal resource compiler to create resources, the compiled resource will have the same structure. This structure is sometimes depicted in *Inside Macintosh* using a resource diagram, as illustrated in Figure 3-3.

Figure 3-3   A resource diagram

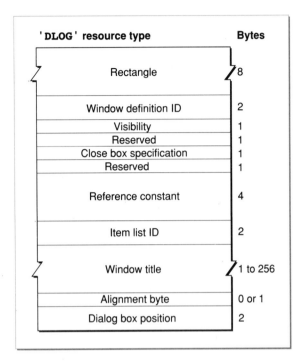

Using Standard Resources

In general, you'll need to create resources describing the standard user interface elements used by your application, including

■ dialog boxes

■ dialog box item lists

■ menus

■ windows

■ controls

For standard user interface elements, the Macintosh Toolbox provides special routines you can use to open the appropriate resources. For instance, you can call the Dialog Manager function GetNewDialog to read a dialog box resource (of type 'DLOG') and the corresponding item list (of type 'DITL') from your application's resource fork.

```
myDialog := GetNewDialog(myKind, myPointer, WindowPtr(-1));
```

Similarly, you can call the Window Manager routine GetNewWindow to open a window description resource (of type 'WIND'). Internally, these routines call Resource Manager routines such as GetResource to read the resource data from the resource file.

Some Toolbox routines are simply loosely disguised Resource Manager calls. For example, the code shown on page 56 which uses GetPattern to open four available emptiness patterns could be replaced by this functionally equivalent code:

```
FOR count := 1 TO 4 DO
    gEmptyPats[count] := GetResource('PAT ', kEmptyID + (count - 1));
```

Most Resource Manager routines that open resources return a handle to the specified resource data. You can pass that handle to other Resource Manager routines, or doubly dereference it to get at the resource data.

Using Custom Resources

In addition to using system resources to help create the standard Macintosh user interface for your application and standard resource types to help isolate its localizable data, you'll probably also want to create custom resources. This section illustrates how to define a custom resource type and how to create and manage resources of that type. The source code provided here shows how to handle a preferences file. This file stores the user's global preferences, and your application can retrieve them each time it is launched. When it starts up, the Venn Diagrammer application tries to open a preferences file, which contains a single resource with the following type and ID:

```
CONST
    kPrefResType     = 'PRFN';   {type of preferences resource}
    kPrefResID       = 259;      {ID of preferences resource}
```

As you've seen earlier in this book, the preferences file needs to contain information about the user's Venn diagram preferences, as displayed in the Preferences dialog box shown in Figure 3-4.

Resources

Figure 3-4   The Preferences dialog box

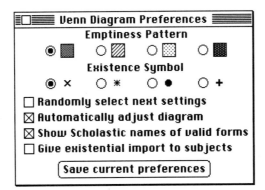

Here, there are six pieces of information that need to be tracked. To maintain this information, the Venn Diagrammer application defines a data structure of type `MyPrefsRec` (defined in Listing 3-2).

Listing 3-2   The structure of a resource containing Venn diagram preferences

```
TYPE
    MyPrefsRec = RECORD
        autoDiag:   Boolean;    {do we automatically fix the diagram?}
        showName:   Boolean;    {do we show names of valid arguments?}
        isImport:   Boolean;    {do subjects have existential import?}
        isRandom:   Boolean;    {do we select next setting randomly?}
        emptyInd:   Integer;    {index of the desired emptiness pattern}
        existInd:   Integer;    {index of the desired existence symbol}
    END;
    MyPrefsPtr = ^MyPrefsRec;
    MyPrefsHnd = ^MyPrefsPtr;
```

When it is first launched, the Venn Diagrammer application calls the application-defined routine `DoReadPrefs` (defined in Listing 3-3) to read the user's existing preferences settings. First, `DoReadPrefs` determines the name of the preferences file by reading a resource in the application's resource file that contains that name. By convention, the name of the preferences file consists of the name of the application followed by the string " Preferences", for instance, Venn Diagrammer Preferences.

Listing 3-3   Reading a user's preferences

```pascal
PROCEDURE DoReadPrefs;
   VAR
      myVRefNum:  Integer;
      myDirID:    LongInt;
      myName:     Str255;      {name of this application}
      myPrefs:    Handle;      {handle to actual preferences data}
      myResNum:   Integer;     {reference number of opened resource file}
      myResult:   OSErr;
   CONST
      kNameID = 4000;          {resource ID of 'STR#' with filename}
BEGIN
   {Determine the name of the preferences file.}
   GetIndString(myName, kNameID, 1);

   {Figure out where the preferences file is.}
   IF IsFindFolder THEN
      myResult := FindFolder(kOnSystemDisk, kPreferencesFolderType,
                             kDontCreateFolder, myVRefNum, myDirID)
   ELSE
      myResult := -1;

   IF myResult <> noErr THEN
      BEGIN
         myVRefNum := 0;       {use default volume}
         myDirID := 0;         {use default directory}
      END;

   {Open the preferences resource file.}
   myResNum := HOpenResFile(myVRefNum, myDirID, myName, fsCurPerm);

   {If no preferences file successfully opened, create one }
   { by copying default preferences in app's resource file.}
   IF myResNum = -1 THEN
      myResNum := DoCreatePrefsFile(myVRefNum, myDirID, myName);

   IF myResNum <> -1 THEN         {if we successfully opened the file...}
      BEGIN
         UseResFile(myResNum);   {make the new resource file current one}
         myPrefs := Get1Resource(kPrefResType, kPrefResID);
         IF myPrefs = NIL THEN
            exit(DoReadPrefs);
         WITH MyPrefsHnd(myPrefs)^^ DO
```

```
   BEGIN                         {read the preferences settings}
      gAutoAdjust := autoDiag;
      gShowNames  := showName;
      gGiveImport := isImport;
      gStepRandom := isRandom;
      gEmptyIndex := emptyInd;
      gExistIndex := existInd;
   END;


{Make sure some preferences globals make sense.}
IF NOT (gExistIndex IN [1..4]) THEN
   gExistIndex := 1;
IF NOT (gEmptyIndex IN [1..4]) THEN
   gEmptyIndex := 1;


{Reinstate the application's resource file.}
UseResFile(gAppsResourceFile);
   END;


gPreferencesFile := myResNum;            {remember its resource ID}
END;
```

After determining the name of the preferences file, DoReadPrefs calls the
application-defined utility IsFindFolder to see whether the operating environment
supports the FindFolder function. (See Listing 9-6 on page 179 for a definition of
IsFindFolder.) If it does, DoReadPrefs calls FindFolder to find the location of the
Preferences folder. The FindFolder function returns the volume reference number and
the directory ID of that folder, if it can be found. If FindFolder isn't available or if it
cannot find the Preferences folder, DoReadPrefs looks in the default directory on the
default volume.

IMPORTANT

Just looking in the default directory when you cannot find the
Preferences folder isn't really the best thing to do. Your application
would probably want to look in the System Folder to see if your
preferences file is there. ▲

Once the target folder is successfully located, DoReadPrefs calls the HOpenResFile
function to try to open a file having the required name in that folder. If no such file can
be opened (as indicated by a returned reference number of –1), DoReadPrefs calls the
application-defined function DoCreatePrefsFile to attempt to create a new
preferences file. (See Listing 3-4 for a definition of DoCreatePrefsFile.)

If the existing or newly created preferences file is successfully opened, then
DoReadPrefs calls UseResFile to make that file the current resource file. Then it
reads the resource of type kPrefResType and ID kPrefResID from that file. If all goes

Resources

well, `DoReadPrefs` reads the current settings from that resource and assigns them to the appropriate global variables:

```
WITH MyPrefsHnd(myPrefs)^^ DO
    BEGIN                    {read the preferences settings}
        gAutoAdjust := autoDiag;
        gShowNames := showName;
        gGiveImport := isImport;
        gStepRandom := isRandom;
        gEmptyIndex := emptyInd;
        gExistIndex := existInd;
    END;
```

Finally, `DoReadPrefs` ensures that the values of the two index variables are within acceptable limits and then restores the application's resource file as the current resource file by calling `UseResFile` once again. Notice that the preferences resource file is left open; this way, the Venn Diagrammer application need not reopen the file if the user wants to change the stored preferences settings.

The `DoCreatePrefsFile` function that is called by `DoReadPrefs` is defined in Listing 3-4. Essentially, `DoCreatePrefsFile` creates a resource file in the appropriate location and with the appropriate name; then it copies into that new resource file an existing set of preferences (stored in the application's resource fork).

Listing 3-4 Creating a preferences file

```
FUNCTION DoCreatePrefsFile (myVRefNum: Integer; myDirID: LongInt;
                            myName: Str255): Integer;
    VAR
        myResNum:    Integer;
        myResult:    OSErr;
        myID:        Integer;     {resource ID of resource in app's res fork}
        myHandle:    Handle;      {handle to resource in app's res fork}
        myType:      ResType;     {ignored; used for GetResInfo}
BEGIN
    myResult := noErr;
    HCreateResFile(myVRefNum, myDirID, myName);
    IF ResError = noErr THEN
        BEGIN
            myResNum := HOpenResFile(myVRefNum, myDirID, myName, fsCurPerm);
            IF myResNum <> -1 THEN
                BEGIN
                    UseResFile(gAppsResourceFile);
                    myHandle := Get1Resource(kPrefResType, kPrefResID);
                    IF ResError = noErr THEN
```

Resources

```
              BEGIN
                 GetResInfo(myHandle, myID, myType, myName);
                 myResult := DoCopyResource(kPrefResType, myID,
                                      gAppsResourceFile, myResNum);
              END
           ELSE
              BEGIN
                 CloseResFile(myResNum);
                 myResult := HDelete(myVRefNum, myDirID, myName);
                 myResNum := -1;
              END;
        END;

     DoCreatePrefsFile := myResNum;
   END;
END;
```

To copy the existing resource from the application's resource file to the new preferences resource file, `DoCreatePrefsFile` calls the application-defined routine `DoCopyResource`. A version of `DoCopyResource` is shown in Listing 3-5.

Listing 3-5   Copying a resource from one resource file to another

```
FUNCTION DoCopyResource (rType: ResType; rID: Integer; source: Integer;
                     dest: Integer): OSErr;
   VAR
      myHandle:   Handle;               {handle to resource to copy}
      myName:     Str255;               {name of resource to copy}
      myAttr:     Integer;              {resource attributes}
      myType:     ResType;              {ignored; used for GetResInfo}
      myID:       Integer;              {ignored; used for GetResInfo}
      myResult:   OSErr;
      myCurrent:  Integer;                {current resource file on entry}
BEGIN
   myCurrent := CurResFile;                {remember current resource file}
   UseResFile(source);                     {set the source resource file}
   myHandle := Get1Resource(rType, rID);  {open the source resource}
   IF myHandle <> NIL THEN
      BEGIN
         GetResInfo(myHandle, myID, myType, myName);  {get res name}
         myAttr := GetResAttrs(myHandle);              {get res attributes}
         DetachResource(myHandle);         {so we can copy the resource}
         UseResFile(dest);                 {set destination resource file}
```

```
    IF ResError = noErr THEN
        AddResource(myHandle, rType, rID, myName);
    IF ResError = noErr THEN
        SetResAttrs(myHandle, myAttr);{set res attributes of copy}
    IF ResError = noErr THEN
        ChangedResource(myHandle);      {mark resource as changed}
    IF ResError = noErr THEN
        WriteResource(myHandle);        {write resource data}
    END;


    DoCopyResource := ResError;              {return result code}
    ReleaseResource(myHandle);               {get rid of resource data}
    UseResFile(myCurrent);                   {restore original resource file}
END;
```

As you can see, DoCopyResource opens the resource to be copied. It copies that resource into the destination resource file by making the destination file the current resource file and then calling the Resource Manager routine AddResource. However, before calling AddResource, you need to disassociate the source resource from its resource file. Because AddResource requires a handle to some data in memory that is not a handle to an existing resource, you need to call the DetachResource procedure to cut the link between the resource data and its original resource file.

You can determine whether a Resource Manager call succeeded by calling the function ResError, which returns the result code from the most recently executed Resource Manager routine. The DoCopyResource function calls ResError repeatedly to make sure that the resource data was successfully added, that the resource attributes were successfully copied, that the destination resource was successfully marked as changed, and that the data was successfully written out to disk.

It's easy to see how to save a set of preferences to the user's preferences file. In essence, you simply need to reverse the strategy employed in reading the preferences. Listing 3-6 defines the DoSavePrefs procedure, which the Venn Diagrammer application calls whenever the user wants to save the current preferences settings. The DoSavePrefs procedure assumes that the application's preferences file is already open.

Listing 3-6   Saving current preferences settings

```
PROCEDURE DoSavePrefs;
    VAR
        myPrefData: Handle;     {handle to new resource data}
        myHandle:   Handle;     {handle to resource to replace}
        myName:     Str255;     {name of resource to copy}
        myAttr:     Integer;    {resource attributes}
        myType:     ResType;    {ignored; used for GetResInfo}
        myID:       Integer;    {ignored; used for GetResInfo}
```

```
BEGIN
   {Make sure we have an open preferences file.}
   IF gPreferencesFile = -1 THEN
      exit(DoSavePrefs);

   myPrefData := NewHandleClear(sizeof(MyPrefsRec));
   HLock(myPrefData);
   WITH MyPrefsHnd(myPrefData)^^ DO
      BEGIN
         autoDiag := gAutoAdjust;
         showName := gShowNames;
         isImport := gGiveImport;
         isRandom := gStepRandom;
         emptyInd := gEmptyIndex;
         existInd := gExistIndex;
      END;

   UseResFile(gPreferencesFile);                      {use preferences file}
   myHandle := Get1Resource(kPrefResType, kPrefResID);
   IF myHandle <> NIL THEN
      BEGIN
         GetResInfo(myHandle, myID, myType, myName);  {get res name}
         myAttr := GetResAttrs(myHandle);             {get res attributes}
         RmveResource(myHandle);
         IF ResError = noErr THEN
            AddResource(myPrefData, kPrefResType, kPrefResID, myName);
         IF ResError = noErr THEN
            WriteResource(myPrefData);
      END;

   HUnlock(myPrefData);
   ReleaseResource(myPrefData);
   UseResFile(gAppsResourceFile);                     {restore app's resource file}
END;
```

The DoSavePrefs procedure creates a new preferences record and fills in the fields as appropriate. Then it removes the existing preferences resource from the preferences file and adds a new resource. To make sure that the new resource data is written out to disk, DoSavePrefs calls the WriteResource procedure. Finally, DoSavePrefs restores the application's resource file as the current resource file.

Events

Contents

/

4

This chapter describes how you can use the Event Manager to receive information about user actions and to receive notice of changes in the processing status of your application. One of the key elements of a well-written Macintosh application is its "user-centered" design. This means, among other things, that instead of carrying out a sequence of steps in a predetermined order, the application is driven primarily by user actions (such as moving the mouse, pressing the mouse button, and typing characters) whose order cannot in general be predicted. This chapter describes how the Macintosh system software reports user actions to your application and shows how to structure your application to facilitate the implementation of user-centered design.

This chapter begins by describing some of the features of a good user-centered design and some general ways to implement them. Then it shows how to

- initialize the basic Toolbox managers

- receive information from the Event Manager about user actions

- respond to user actions

For a complete description of the capabilities of the Event Manager, see the chapter "Event Manager" in *Inside Macintosh: Macintosh Toolbox Essentials*. For the complete story on the features of a good user interface, see *Macintosh Human Interface Guidelines*.

About Events

Probably the most distinctive aspect of a well-written Macintosh application is that it puts users in control of the application, not the other way around. To be in control, the user should be able to perform, at any particular time, any of a wide array of actions. These actions might include pulling down one of your application's menus, choosing a menu command, typing some characters, moving a window, and so forth. A key concept here is that users should feel that your application is always ready to do something for them.

Even when your application is busy performing some lengthy operation (for instance, saving a document to disk) and you need to prevent the user from doing other things, you should provide some safe way for the user to cancel the operation and regain control. Typically you accomplish this by displaying a dialog box indicating that a lengthy operation is underway; the dialog box should indicate some safe way for the user to stop the operation.

The essence of this user-centered design is the use of an **event-driven programming model**. In other words, the system software breaks up the user's actions into their component **events,** which are passed one by one to your application for handling. For example, when the user presses a key on the keyboard, the system software sends your application information about that event. This information includes which key was pressed, when the key was pressed, whether any modifier keys (for instance, the Command key) were being held down at the time of the keypress, and so forth. Your application responds to the event by performing whatever actions are appropriate.

Events

Your application can receive many types of events. Events are usually divided into three categories:

- low-level events
- operating-system events
- high-level events

The Event Manager returns **low-level events** to your application for occurrences such as the user pressing the mouse button, releasing the mouse button, pressing a key on the keyboard, or inserting a disk. The Event Manager also returns low-level events to your application if your application needs to activate a window (that is, make changes to a window based on whether it is in front or not) or update a window (that is, redraw the window's contents). When your application requests an event and there are no other events to report, the Event Manager returns a **null event.**

The Event Manager returns **operating-system events** to your application when the processing status of your application is about to change or has changed. For example, if a user brings your application to the foreground, the Process Manager sends an event through the Event Manager to your application. Some of the work of reactivating your application is done automatically, both by the Process Manager and by the Window Manager; your application must take care of any further processing needed as a result of your application being reactivated.

The Event Manager returns **high-level events** to your application as a result of communication directed to your application from another application or process.

Note
Low-level events, except for update events and null events, are always directed to the foreground process. Operating-system events are also always directed to the foreground process. High-level events, update events, and null events can be directed to the foreground process or background processes. ◆

Figure 4-1 illustrates the various sources of events that can be passed to your application. As you can see, events originate from a number of different sources: the Operating System Event Manager, Window Manager, Process Manager, and PPC Toolbox.

Figure 4-1   Sources of events sent to your application

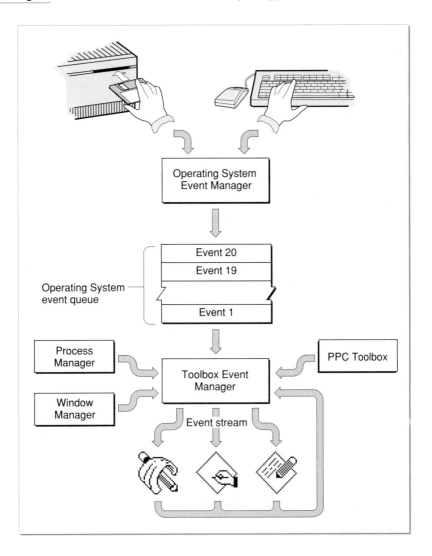

The Event Manager maintains, for each open application, an event stream containing those events that are available to that application. Your general strategy is to retrieve an event, process it, retrieve the next event, process it, and so on indefinitely. You stop this process only when the user elects to quit your application.

Initializing an Application

When your application first starts up, and even before you begin to receive and process events describing the user's actions, you need to do some initial setting up. As you've already seen (page 3), you need to initialize some of the Macintosh Toolbox managers. You also need to set up your menu bar and menus, and perform some other standard initialization. Listing 4-1 shows the code executed by the Venn Diagrammer application when it first starts up.

Listing 4-1   Initializing your application

```
DoInitManagers;                        {initialize Toolbox managers}
DoSetupMenus;                          {initialize menus}

gDone := FALSE;                        {initialize global variables}
gNumDocWindows := 0;                   {initialize count of open doc windows}
gPrefsDialog := NIL;                   {initialize ptr to Preferences dialog}

gAppsResourceFile := CurResFile;  {get refnum of the app's resource file}
gPreferencesFile := -1;                {initialize res ID of preferences file}

DoReadPrefs;                           {read the user's preference settings}

DoVennInit;
DoMainEventLoop;                       {and then loop forever...}
```

The first thing the Venn Diagrammer application does is call the application-defined routine `DoInitManagers` to set up its application partition and initialize several Toolbox managers. Then it calls `DoSetupMenus` to create its menu bar and menus. (See Listing 8-1 on page 155 for the definition of `DoSetupMenus`.)

After its menu bar has been created, Venn Diagrammer initializes several global variables and reads the user's current preferences from a preferences file. Then the application calls another routine, `DoVennInit`, to handle any other initialization. This includes defining the rectangles and regions in a Venn diagram window and displaying a window.

Note

The `DoVennInit` procedure is not defined in this book. ◆

Once the application has initialized itself, it starts executing its main event loop by calling the `DoMainEventLoop` procedure. In the main event loop, the application calls the Event Manager to get an event, responds to the event, then loops back to repeat the process. See Listing 4-4 on page 77 for a sample event loop.

Listing 4-2 defines the `DoInitManagers` routine. It begins by calling two Memory Manager routines to expand the heap zone to its limit and to create an additional block of master pointers.

Listing 4-2   Initializing the main Toolbox Managers

```
PROCEDURE DoInitManagers;
BEGIN
    MaxApplZone;                    {extend heap zone to limit}
    MoreMasters;                    {get 64 more master pointers}

    InitGraf(@thePort);             {initialize QuickDraw}
    InitFonts;                      {initialize Font Manager}
    InitWindows;                    {initialize Window Manager}
    InitMenus;                      {initialize Menu Manager}
    TEInit;                         {initialize TextEdit}
    InitDialogs(NIL);               {initialize Dialog Manager}

    FlushEvents(everyEvent, 0);     {clear event queue}
    InitCursor;                     {initialize cursor to arrow}
END;
```

Then `DoInitManagers` calls the standard Toolbox initialization routines. Finally, it clears the event queue and calls the QuickDraw routine `InitCursor` to make sure that the cursor is the standard arrow cursor.

Receiving Events

You receive events by calling an Event Manager routine, usually `WaitNextEvent`. When you ask for an event, the Event Manager returns the next available event according to its **event priority.** The Event Manager returns events in this order of priority:

1. activate events

2. mouse-down, mouse-up, key-down, key-up, and disk-inserted events in FIFO (first-in, first-out) order

3. auto-key events

4. update events (in front-to-back order of windows)

5. operating-system events (suspend, resume, mouse-moved)

6. high-level events

7. null events

To retrieve an event, you pass the `WaitNextEvent` function an **event record,** defined by
the `EventRecord` data type:

```
TYPE EventRecord =
    RECORD
        what:        Integer;        {event code}
        message:     LongInt;        {event message}
        when:        LongInt;        {ticks since startup}
        where:       Point;          {mouse location}
        modifiers:   Integer;        {modifier flags}
    END;
```

On return from `WaitNextEvent`, the what field of the event record contains an integer
that specifies the type of event received. The Event Manager uses this set of predefined
constants to indicate the event type:

```
CONST
    nullEvent        = 0;            {no other pending events}
    mouseDown        = 1;            {mouse button pressed}
    mouseUp          = 2;            {mouse button released}
    keyDown          = 3;            {key pressed}
    keyUp            = 4;            {key released}
    autoKey          = 5;            {key held down}
    updateEvt        = 6;            {a window needs updating}
    diskEvt          = 7;            {disk inserted}
    activateEvt      = 8;            {activate/deactivate window}
    osEvt            = 15;           {operating-system event}
    kHighLevelEvent  = 23;          {high-level event}
```

The `message` field of the event record contains additional information about the event.
The interpretation of this field depends on the type of event you've received. For some
events (such as null events, mouse-up, and mouse-down events), the value in the
`message` field is undefined. For keyboard events, the `message` field indicates which key
was pressed. For activate and update events, the `message` field contains a window
pointer to the affected window. For disk-inserted events, the `message` field contains the
drive number in the low-order word and the result code of the File Manager's attempt to
mount that disk in that drive. Listing 4-3 illustrates how an application reads parts of the
`message` field while handling disk-inserted events.

Listing 4-3   Handling disk-inserted events

```
PROCEDURE DoDiskEvent (myEvent: EventRecord);
    VAR
        myResult:    Integer;
        myPoint:     Point;
BEGIN
    IF HiWord(myEvent.message) <> noErr THEN
        BEGIN
            SetPt(myPoint, 100, 100);
            myResult := DIBadMount(myPoint, myEvent.message);
        END;
END;
```

If the disk was not successfully mounted (that is, if the high-order word of the `message` field does not contain `noErr`), then `DoDiskEvent` calls the system software routine `DIBadMount` to inform the user and allow the disk to be ejected or reformatted. (See the chapter "Disk Initialization Manager" in *Inside Macintosh: Files* for more information about handling disk-inserted events.)

The `where` field of the event record contains, for low-level events, the location of the cursor at the time the event was posted. You can use this information to determine where on the screen a mouse-down event occurred, for instance.

The `modifiers` field contains information about the state of the modifier keys and the mouse button at the time the event was posted. For activate events, this field also indicates whether the window should be activated or deactivated. (In System 7, it also indicates whether a mouse-down event caused your application to switch to the foreground.)

To handle an event, you simply take whatever action is appropriate for the kind of event it is. Listing 4-4 shows one way to structure an event-handling routine.

Listing 4-4   An event loop

```
PROCEDURE DoMainEventLoop;
    VAR
        myEvent:     EventRecord;
        gotEvent:    Boolean;                    {is returned event for me?}
BEGIN
    REPEAT
        gotEvent := WaitNextEvent(everyEvent, myEvent, 15, NIL);
        IF NOT DoHandleDialogEvent(myEvent) THEN
            IF gotEvent THEN
                BEGIN
                    CASE myEvent.what OF
```

```
            mouseDown:
                DoMouseDown(myEvent);                    {see page 120}
            keyDown, autoKey:
                DoKeyDown(myEvent);                      {see page 160}
            updateEvt:
                DoUpdate(WindowPtr(myEvent.message));  {see page 124}
            diskEvt:
                DoDiskEvent(myEvent);                    {see page 77}
            activateEvt:
                DoActivate(WindowPtr(myEvent.message),
                            myEvent.modifiers);          {see page 126}
            osEvt:
                DoOSEvent(myEvent);                      {see page 171}
            keyUp, mouseUp:
                ;
            nullEvent:
                DoIdle(myEvent);                         {see page 173}
            OTHERWISE
                ;
          END; {CASE}
        END
      ELSE
        DoIdle(myEvent);
    UNTIL gDone;                          {loop until user quits}
END;
```

The event loop defined in Listing 4-4 repeatedly calls the WaitNextEvent function to retrieve the next available event. This function returns a value of FALSE if there are no events of the desired type (other than null events) pending for your application. Otherwise, WaitNextEvent returns TRUE.

After the next available event is retrieved, the DoMainEventLoop procedure calls the application-defined function DoHandleDialogEvent (defined in Listing 7-5 on page 141) to determine whether the event applies to a dialog box. The DoHandleDialogEvent function returns TRUE if it handled the event and FALSE otherwise.

Note
Dialog boxes receive special treatment because the system software automatically handles many user actions in dialog boxes. For example, the Dialog Manager handles update events for dialog boxes, and it calls the Control Manager to handle user actions affecting any controls in the dialog box. ◆

If the event retrieved does not apply to a dialog box, and if it isn't a null event, then `DoMainEventLoop` branches into a Pascal `CASE` statement in which the labels are simply the predefined constants for each event type. As you can see, the event loop calls an application-defined routine to handle each particular kind of event. These routines are defined throughout this book.

Handling Events Outside the Main Event Loop

You'll notice that some types of events—for example, `keyUp` and `mouseUp`—are simply ignored by the main event loop defined in Listing 4-4. Key-up events are ignored because most applications don't need to know that a key was released, only that it was pressed. Similarly, you usually don't need to know when the mouse button was released, because you're more interested in knowing whether (and where) the mouse button was pressed. In certain cases, however, you will be interested in a mouse-up event. For example, if the user presses the mouse button while the cursor is in a window's close box but then moves the cursor outside the close box before releasing the mouse button, you don't want to handle the mouse-down event. (This is another good example of user-centered design: allowing users to change their minds.)

It might appear that a problem is lurking, because the main event loop defined in Listing 4-4 ignores mouse-up events. How, then, can your application determine that the user released the mouse button when the cursor was outside of the close box? The answer is simple: the system software provides a routine, `TrackGoAway`, that you call in response to a user click in the close box. The `TrackGoAway` function tracks user actions involving the close box; it returns the Boolean value `TRUE` if the cursor is still inside the close box when the button is released and `FALSE` otherwise. Listing 4-5 illustrates how to call `TrackGoAway`.

Listing 4-5   Tracking mouse events in the close box

```
PROCEDURE DoGoAwayBox (myWindow: WindowPtr; mouseloc: Point);
BEGIN
   IF TrackGoAway(myWindow, mouseloc) THEN
      DoCloseWindow(myWindow);
END;
```

The `TrackGoAway` function exits only when the mouse button is released. Because it determines internally when that happens, your application doesn't need to.

The system software provides routines to handle the three main cases in which you need to track the mouse and determine if the cursor is in a particular location when the button is released. Here are the main routines you'll use:

Mouse-tracking routine	Action
TrackBox	Track the cursor in a window's zoom box
TrackControl	Track the cursor within a control
TrackGoAway	Track the cursor in a window's close box

For various purposes, you might need to perform similar tracking on an arbitrary rectangle in a window. The function DoTrackRect defined in Listing 4-6 shows one way to define such a function.

Note
Venn Diagrammer calls DoTrackRect to handle mouse-down events in the tool icons. See Listing 6-9 beginning on page 121. ◆

Listing 4-6   Tracking the cursor in an arbitrary rectangle

```
FUNCTION DoTrackRect (myWindow: WindowPtr; myRect: Rect): Boolean;
   VAR
      myIgnore:    LongInt;
      myPoint:     Point;
BEGIN
   InvertRect(myRect);               {invert the rectangle}
   REPEAT
      Delay(kVisualDelay, myIgnore)
   UNTIL NOT StillDown;              {until mouse is released}
   InvertRect(myRect);

   GetMouse(myPoint);               {get mouse location}
   DoTrackRect := PtInRect(myPoint, myRect);
END;
```

The DoTrackRect function inverts the specified rectangle and keeps it inverted until the user releases the mouse button. The Event Manager function StillDown looks in your application's event queue for a mouse-up event; if none is found, StillDown returns TRUE; otherwise, StillDown returns FALSE. Note that DoTrackRect loops until StillDown returns FALSE, indicating that the corresponding mouse-up event has been found. The call to the Delay procedure within the loop is to ensure that the rectangle is inverted for some minimum, user-perceptible amount of time.

```
CONST
   kVisualDelay        = 6;       {wait 6 ticks (one-tenth second)}
```

The DoTrackRect function loops until StillDown detects the appropriate mouse-up event and then returns the specified rectangle to its original state by inverting it again. Next, DoTrackRect calls the Event Manager function GetMouse to determine the current position of the cursor. If, when the mouse button is released, the cursor is still inside the specified rectangle (as determined by the QuickDraw routine PtInRect), then DoTrackRect returns TRUE.

As you can see, you sometimes want to call Event Manager routines from outside your main event loop, most often to monitor mouse movements and button states once the user has clicked in some particular part of a window.

Drawing

Contents

Drawing

This chapter shows how you can draw simple graphics and text inside of windows using QuickDraw, the part of the Macintosh Toolbox that performs graphics operations on the user's screen. All Macintosh applications use QuickDraw indirectly whenever they call other Toolbox managers to create and manage the basic graphic user interface elements (such as windows, controls, and menus). Most applications also call QuickDraw directly to define areas in a window and to draw appropriate graphic elements in those areas. The Venn Diagrammer application, for instance, calls QuickDraw to draw the overlapping circles, the tool icons, and the figure and mood selection icons. It also calls QuickDraw to draw all the text displayed in a window.

This chapter begins with a description of QuickDraw, its basic drawing model, and some of the data structures QuickDraw uses. Then it shows how to

- define and draw simple objects such as lines, rectangles, and circles
- define complex graphic objects by combining simple objects
- outline and fill graphic objects
- draw static (that is, noneditable) text in a window

For a complete description of the drawing capabilities of QuickDraw, see the chapter "QuickDraw Drawing" in *Inside Macintosh: Imaging*. For a complete description of the text capabilities of QuickDraw, see the chapter "QuickDraw Text" in *Inside Macintosh: Text*. To learn how to handle editable text, see the chapter "TextEdit" in *Inside Macintosh: Text*.

About QuickDraw

QuickDraw allows you to draw many types of objects on the Macintosh display screen. Some of these objects are illustrated in Figure 5-1.

Figure 5-1   Samples of QuickDraw's abilities

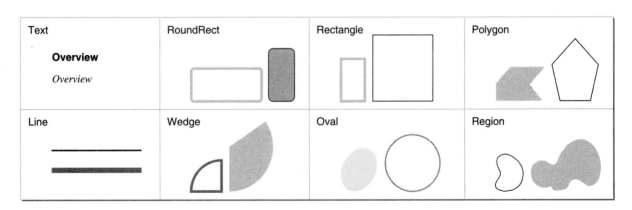

Drawing

As you can see, you can use QuickDraw to draw

- text characters and strings in a number of fonts, sizes, and styles
- straight lines of any length, width, and pattern
- a variety of simple shapes, including rectangles, rounded-corner rectangles, circles, and ovals
- polygons
- arcs of ovals, or wedge-shaped sections filled with a pattern
- any other arbitrary shape or collection of shapes
- bit images, such as icons, cursors, and patterns

This section explains the basic mathematical model employed by QuickDraw and shows how you can define several of these sorts of objects.

Points

QuickDraw measures location and movement in terms of coordinates on a very large plane. The plane is a two-dimensional grid, with integer coordinates ranging from –32767 to 32767, as illustrated in Figure 5-2.

Figure 5-2   The coordinate plane

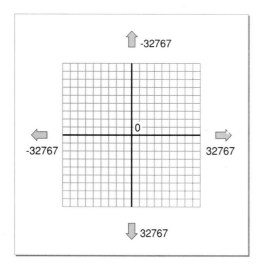

The intersection of a horizontal and a vertical grid line marks a **point** on the coordinate plane. Because all coordinates are limited to simple integers, there are 4,294,836,224 unique points in the QuickDraw plane.

Drawing

You can store the coordinates of a point into a Pascal variable of type `Point`, defined by QuickDraw as a record of two integers:

```
TYPE
   VHSelect = (v,h);

   Point =
   RECORD
      CASE INTEGER OF
         0: (v:   Integer;        {vertical coordinate}
             h:   Integer);       {horizontal coordinate}
         1: (vh:  ARRAY[VHSelect] OF Integer);
   END;
```

The variant part of this record lets you access the vertical and horizontal coordinates of a point either individually or as an array. This book will always use the first way of specifying the coordinates. So, for example, the vertical coordinate of the variable `myPoint` is accessed as `myPoint.v`.

Rectangles

Any two points can define the upper-left and lower-right corners of a **rectangle** on the coordinate plane, as shown in Figure 5-3.

Figure 5-3   A rectangle

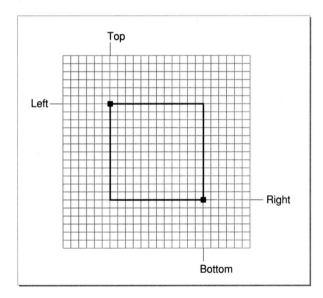

Drawing

You can describe a rectangle using a data structure of type `Rect`, which consists of four integers or two points.

```
TYPE Rect =
   RECORD
      CASE INTEGER OF
         0: (top:       Integer;        {top coordinate}
             left:      Integer;        {left coordinate}
             bottom:    Integer;        {bottom coordinate}
             right:     Integer);       {right coordinate}
         1: (topLeft:   Point;          {upper-left point}
             botRight:  Point);         {lower-right point}
   END;
```

Once again, the record variant allows you to access a variable of type `Rect` either as four boundary coordinates or as two diagonally opposite corner points. This book will always use the first way of specifying a rectangle. So, for example, the top coordinate of the variable `myRect` is accessed as `myRect.top`.

Note

If the bottom coordinate of a rectangle is less than or equal to the top coordinate, or if the right coordinate is less than or equal to the left coordinate, the rectangle is treated as an empty rectangle (that is, one that has no area). ◆

A **pixel** is a physical dot on the screen and corresponds to a rectangle in the QuickDraw coordinate plane that has sides one coordinate long, as shown in Figure 5-4. (This, of course, is the smallest possible rectangle.)

Figure 5-4   Pixels and rectangles

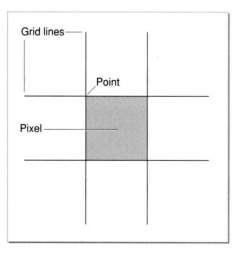

You can think of a pixel as corresponding to the point at the top left of the rectangle. There are many more points in the QuickDraw coordinate plane than there are pixels on the screen. As a result, you'll associate small parts of the coordinate plane with areas on the screen. In general, you don't need to worry about where in that large coordinate plane you're working, because QuickDraw always forces you to work with a particular graphics port, which has its own local coordinate system. (A graphics port is a complete drawing environment that defines where and how graphics operations will take place; see page 92 for more information on graphics ports.)

To draw a line, you can simply move to the desired starting point of the line and draw to the desired end. For example, to draw a line in the current graphics port from point (100,150) to the point (200,250), you could do this:

```
MoveTo(100, 150);
LineTo(200, 250);
```

To draw a rectangle, you need to proceed in a slightly different manner. You first need to define the rectangle in the coordinate plane and then perform some graphical operation on the rectangle. Here's an example:

```
SetRect(myRect, 100, 200, 300, 400);
FrameRect(myRect);
```

These two lines of code define a rectangle and then frame it (that is, draw its outline). Instead of just drawing the rectangle's outline, you could also fill the rectangle with the current pattern (by calling `PaintRect`) or with some other pattern (by calling `FillRect`).

Note
Coordinates are passed to `SetRect` in the order left, top, right, bottom (which is different from the order in the `Rect` data type). The word *litterbug* is a useful mnemonic; it contains the letters l, t, r, and b in the correct order. ◆

QuickDraw does not contain data types that describe circles or ovals. Instead, you draw an oval by defining a rectangle and then asking QuickDraw to draw the oval that fits inside of the rectangle. The oval is completely enclosed within the rectangle, and never includes any pixels lying outside the boundary. If the rectangle is a square, then the oval is a circle.

Regions

One of QuickDraw's most powerful capabilities is the ability to work with **regions** of arbitrary size, shape, and complexity. You define a region by drawing its boundary with QuickDraw operations. The boundary can be any set of lines and shapes (even including other regions) forming one or more closed loops. A region can be concave or convex, can consist of one connected area or many separate ones, and can even have holes in the middle. In Figure 5-5, the region on the left has a hole in it, and the region on the right consists of two disjoint areas.

Figure 5-5   Two regions

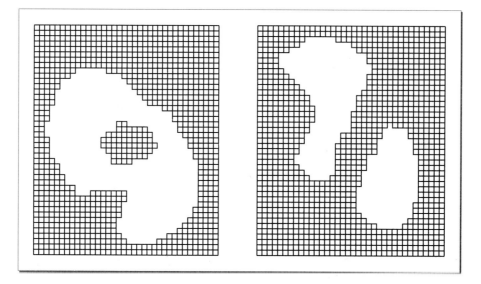

QuickDraw describes a region using a data structure of type `Region`. This structure contains two fixed-length fields followed by a variable-length field.

```
TYPE Region =
    RECORD
        rgnSize:        Integer;        {size in bytes}
        rgnBBox:        Rect;           {enclosing rectangle}
        {more data if not rectangular}
    END;


    RgnPtr      = ^Region;
    RgnHandle   = ^RgnPtr;
```

The `rgnSize` field contains the size, in bytes, of the region variable. The `rgnBBox` field contains a rectangle that completely encloses the region. In general, however, you'll treat the `Region` data structure like a "black box"; you shouldn't need to read the two named fields except in special circumstances.

The Venn Diagrammer application uses a number of regions to pick out the areas defined by the overlapping circles. See "Drawing Shapes" beginning on page 94 for details.

Bit Images

Points, rectangles, and regions are mathematical models—data types that QuickDraw uses for defining areas on the screen—but they can also be graphic elements that actually appear on the screen. A rectangle, for example, can mathematically define a particular visible area, but it can also be an object to be framed, painted, or filled. QuickDraw also defines a number of other graphic elements, including icons, bitmaps, patterns, and other bit images, that have only a direct graphic interpretation. An icon, for instance, defines an image not by mapping an abstract mathematical representation onto the screen pixels but by directly indicating which pixels in a given area are to be black and which are to be white.

IMPORTANT

The discussion in this section applies only to black-and-white bit images, which are the simplest cases. For complete information on color bit images (such as color icons), see *Inside Macintosh: Imaging.* ▲

The Macintosh user interface uses bit images extensively, so QuickDraw contains a number of additional data types describing such direct entities and routines to draw them. The Venn Diagrammer application uses two kinds of bit images: bitmaps and patterns.

A **bitmap** is a data structure that defines a physical bit image in terms of the coordinate plane. A bitmap has three parts: a pointer to a rectangular collection of bits, the row width of that rectangular collection, and a boundary rectangle that gives the bitmap both its dimensions and a coordinate system.

The structure of a bitmap is defined by the `BitMap` data type:

```
TYPE BitMap =
   RECORD
      baseAddr:     Ptr;          {pointer to bit image}
      rowBytes:     Integer;      {row width}
      bounds:       Rect;         {boundary rectangle}
   END;
```

Figure 5-6 shows how these three pieces of information define a particular bitmap.

Figure 5-6  A bitmap

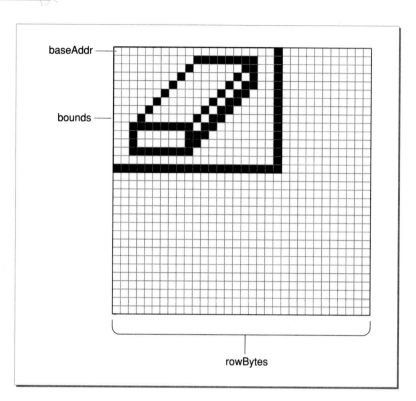

The `baseAddr` field is a pointer to the beginning of the bit image in memory. The `rowBytes` field is the row width, in bytes. (Both `baseAddr` and `rowBytes` must contain even values.) The `bounds` field is the bitmap's bounding rectangle. See "Drawing Bit Images" beginning on page 99 for a description of how to display a bitmap.

Ports and Windows

All drawing takes place in a controlled drawing environment known as a **graphics port.** The graphics port defines a number of drawing parameters, such as the current drawing location, the current font and size used for drawing characters, and so forth. In general, you can think of a graphics port as the window within which you're currently drawing.

A graphics port is defined by the `GrafPort` data structure.

```
TYPE GrafPort =
    RECORD
        device:        Integer;    {device-specific information}
        portBits:      BitMap;     {GrafPort's bit map}
        portRect:      Rect;       {GrafPort's rectangle}
```

```
        visRgn:        RgnHandle;    {visible region}
        clipRgn:       RgnHandle;    {clipping region}
        bkPat:         Pattern;      {background pattern}
        fillPat:       Pattern;      {fill pattern}
        pnLoc:         Point;        {pen location}
        pnSize:        Point;        {pen size}
        pnMode:        Integer;      {pen's transfer mode}
        pnPat:         Pattern;      {pen pattern}
        pnVis:         Integer;      {pen visibility}
        txFont:        Integer;      {font number for text}
        txFace:        Style;        {text's character style}
        txMode:        Integer;      {text's transfer mode}
        txSize:        Integer;      {font size for text}
        spExtra:       Fixed;        {extra space}
        fgColor:       LongInt;      {foreground color}
        bkColor:       LongInt;      {background color}
        colrBit:       Integer;      {color bit}
        patStretch:    Integer;      {used internally}
        picSave:       Handle;       {picture being saved}
        rgnSave:       Handle;       {region being saved}
        polySave:      Handle;       {polygon being saved}
        grafProcs:     QDProcsPtr;   {low-level drawing routines}
    END;


    GrafPtr = ^GrafPort;
```

The fields of a `GrafPort` data structure are maintained by QuickDraw, and you should never write directly into those fields. You can, and often must, read the fields of a `GrafPort` structure. For example, it's often useful to read the `portRect` field of a variable of type `GrafPort`, because it gives the rectangle around the content area of a window. (That information was used in Listing 1-1 on page 3 to center a text string.)

QuickDraw always performs drawing operations on the current graphics port. As a result, you should explicitly set the graphics port before doing any drawing. A safe strategy is to save and later restore the original graphics port upon entry to any routine that affects the screen. Listing 5-1 shows an example.

Listing 5-1   Saving and restoring the current graphics port

```
PROCEDURE DrawInPort(thePort: GrafPtr);
    VAR
        origPort:    GrafPtr;
BEGIN
    GetPort(origPort);
```

```
        SetPort(thePort);

        {Do your drawing (erasing, etc.) here.}

        SetPort(origPort);
    END;
```

Notice that QuickDraw uses the `GrafPtr` data type to refer to graphics ports. For historical reasons, the `GrafPort` data structure is one of the few objects in the Macintosh system software that's referred to by a pointer rather than a handle.

Drawing Shapes

As you've seen, you can draw circles by calling `FrameOval`. The Venn Diagrammer application uses code like this to draw the outlines of the five circles:

```
FOR count := 1 TO 5 DO
    FrameOval(gGeometry^^.circleRects[count]);
```

The rectangles defining the circles are stored in an array of rectangles that is one of the fields of an application-defined data structure of type `MyGeometryRec`. Venn Diagrammer allocates just one of these records when the application first starts up. The global variable `gGeometry` is a handle to that record.

```
VAR
    gGeometry:  MyGeometryHnd;          {handle to a geometry record}
```

Listing 5-2 shows part of the structure of this record.

Listing 5-2   The structure of a record describing a document window's geometry

```
TYPE MyGeometryRec =
    RECORD
        circleRects:    ARRAY[1..5] OF Rect;        {squares for the 5 circles}
        circleRgns:     ARRAY[1..5] OF RgnHandle;   {regions for the 5 circles}
        premiseRgns:    ARRAY[1..8] OF RgnHandle;   {regions for premises}
        concRgns:       ARRAY[1..4] OF RgnHandle;   {regions for conclusion}
        {other fields omitted}
    END;
    MyGeometryPtr = ^MyGeometryRec;
    MyGeometryHnd = ^MyGeometryPtr;
```

Drawing

This record contains all the information needed to perform graphics operations on the Venn diagram in a document window. The fields are initialized at application launch time by the application-defined routine `DoInitGeometry`, shown in Listing 5-3.

Listing 5-3   Initializing the geometry record

```
PROCEDURE DoInitGeometry;
BEGIN
    {Allocate the memory needed to hold the diagram's geometry.}
    gGeometry := MyGeometryHnd(NewHandleClear(sizeof(MyGeometryRec)));

    IF gGeometry = NIL THEN                      {make sure we have the memory}
        DoBadError(eNotEnoughMemory);            {see Listing 9-5 on page 178}

    {Set up the rectangles that define the circles.}
    FOR count := 1 TO 5 DO
        gGeometry^^.circleRects[count] := MyGetIndCircleRect(count);

    {Set up the regions that the circles define.}
    DoSetupCircleRegions;

    {Set up the overlapping regions within the circles.}
    DoSetupOverlapRegions;
END;
```

The `DoInitGeometry` procedure allocates a geometry record and calls other application-defined routines to initialize the fields of that record. First, it calls `MyGetIndCircleRect` to determine the rectangle bounding each of the five circles.

Note

The `MyGetIndCircleRect` function is not defined in this book. You could define such a function in many ways. You could determine in advance where in the window the five rectangles should be and then hard-code that information in constants. Alternatively, you could calculate desirable positions dynamically at run time. The Venn Diagrammer application uses the first method, for speed. ◆

Then `DoInitGeometry` calls two other application-defined routines to set up a number of regions in the window. The first, `DoSetupCircleRegions`, defined in Listing 5-4, creates regions corresponding to the area inside each of the five circles. These regions are used in turn by the `DoSetupOverlapRegions` procedure to calculate the regions of intersection.

Drawing

Listing 5-4   Defining circular regions

```
PROCEDURE DoSetupCircleRegions;
VAR
    count:    Integer;
BEGIN
    FOR count := 1 TO 5 DO
    BEGIN
        gGeometry^^.circleRgns[count] := NewRgn;
        OpenRgn;
        FrameOval(gGeometry^^.circleRects[count]);
        CloseRgn(gGeometry^^.circleRgns[count]);
    END;
END;
```

You create a new region by calling the NewRgn function, which allocates storage in your application heap for a structure of type Region and returns a handle (of type RgnHandle) to that region. The newly created region is empty. To add to the region, you call the OpenRgn procedure and then draw the outline of the area you want enclosed by the region. As you can see, DoSetupCircleRegions indicates the desired area by calling the FrameOval procedure on a circle's defining rectangle. When you're done drawing that outline, you call the CloseRgn procedure, passing it a handle to the region to close.

If you simply want to create a region that's empty, you can call NewRgn, OpenRgn, and CloseRgn without doing any drawing.

```
myRegion := NewRgn;                    {create an empty region}
OpenRgn;
CloseRgn(myRegion);
```

The DoSetupOverlapRegions procedure, defined in Listing 5-5, uses the circular regions defined by DoSetupCircleRegions to define the regions corresponding to the areas defined by the overlapping circles.

Listing 5-5   Defining noncircular regions

```
PROCEDURE DoSetupOverlapRegions;
VAR
    myRegion:    RgnHandle;            {a scratch region}
    count:       Integer;
BEGIN
    FOR count := 1 TO 8 DO            {create new, empty regions}
        BEGIN
            gGeometry^^.premiseRgns[count] := NewRgn;
```

```
        OpenRgn;
        CloseRgn(gGeometry^^.premiseRgns[count]);
    END;


myRegion := NewRgn;                  {create a scratch region}
OpenRgn;
CloseRgn(myRegion);


{Calculate the overlap regions in the premises diagram.}
HLock(Handle(gGeometry));            {lock the handle}
WITH gGeometry^^ DO
    BEGIN
        DiffRgn(circleRgns[1], circleRgns[2], myRegion);
        DiffRgn(myRegion, circleRgns[3], premiseRgns[1]);

        SectRgn(circleRgns[1], circleRgns[2], myRegion);
        DiffRgn(myRegion, circleRgns[3], premiseRgns[2]);

        DiffRgn(circleRgns[2], circleRgns[1], myRegion);
        DiffRgn(myRegion, circleRgns[3], premiseRgns[3]);

        SectRgn(circleRgns[1], circleRgns[3], myRegion);
        DiffRgn(myRegion, circleRgns[2], premiseRgns[4]);

        SectRgn(circleRgns[1], circleRgns[2], myRegion);
        SectRgn(myRegion, circleRgns[3], premiseRgns[5]);

        SectRgn(circleRgns[2], circleRgns[3], myRegion);
        DiffRgn(myRegion, circleRgns[1], premiseRgns[6]);

        DiffRgn(circleRgns[3], circleRgns[1], myRegion);
        DiffRgn(myRegion, circleRgns[2], premiseRgns[7]);
    END;

HUnlock(Handle(gGeometry));          {unlock the handle}
DisposeRgn(myRegion);                {dispose scratch region}
END;
```

The DoSetupOverlapRegions procedure is remarkably straightforward. It initializes the regions in the premises diagram and also creates a temporary scratch region. Then it calculates the seven regions of overlap in that diagram by calling SectRgn and DiffRgn on the circular regions defined in Listing 5-4. The SectRgn procedure takes the intersection of two regions and places it into a third region. The DiffRgn procedure takes the portion of the first region that is outside the second region and places it into the

Drawing

third region. Figure 5-7 shows how the overlap regions are defined by taking intersections and unions of the three circles.

Figure 5-7   Calculating the overlap regions of a Venn diagram

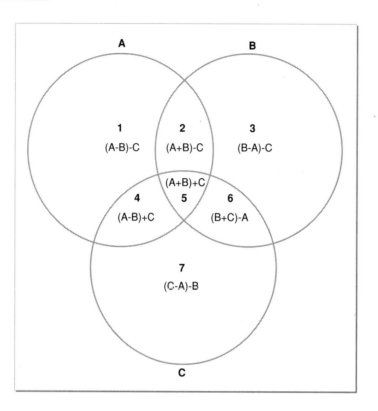

Note

The definition of `DoSetupOverlapRegions` given in Listing 5-5 is not complete. It omits calculations of the conclusion regions and of the fields omitted from the `MyGeometryRec` data structure defined in Listing 5-2. ◆

Now that the Venn Diagrammer application has defined the various regions in the Venn diagram, it's easy to draw in those regions. For instance, to shade the very center of the diagram, you could call the `FillRgn` procedure, as follows:

```
FillRgn(gGeometry^^.premiseRgns[5], gEmptyPats[gEmptyIndex]^^);
```

This fills the specified region with the current emptiness pattern.

Drawing Bit Images

The Venn Diagrammer application uses bit images to draw several parts of a document window, including

- the tool symbols at the top of a document window
- the figure and mood symbols at the bottom of a window
- the existence symbol within the Venn diagram itself

Figure 5-8 shows the location of these items.

Figure 5-8   Bit images in a document window

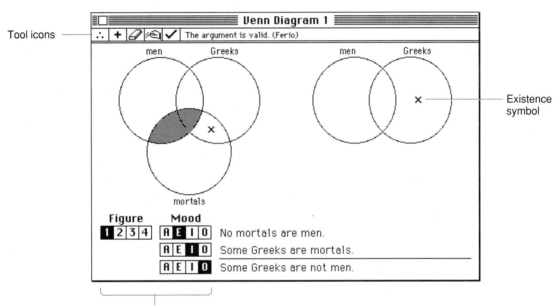

The standard way to draw a bit image is to read into memory the appropriate bit data and then call the `CopyBits` routine to move the data into the desired position in the destination window. The Venn Diagrammer application stores the bit data in resources of type `'ICON'`. Then it calls its own application-defined routine `DoPlotIcon` to move the appropriate portion of the icon into a document window. Notice that none of the bit images in a document window is actually as large as an icon (which is 32 pixels by 32 pixels). Venn Diagrammer uses this strategy because ResEdit provides a simple way to create and edit `'ICON'` resources.

Drawing

When Venn Diagrammer starts up, it reads the necessary icon resources into memory using the code in Listing 5-6.

Listing 5-6   Reading `'ICON'` resources into memory

```
{Get handles to tool icons.}
FOR count := 1 TO kNumTools DO
   gToolsIcons[count] := GetResource('ICON', kToolsIconStart + (count - 1));

{Get handles to available existence-indicating icons.}
FOR count := 1 TO 4 DO
   gExistIcons[count] := GetResource('ICON', kExistID + (count - 1));

{Get handles to mood icons.}
FOR count := 1 TO 4 DO
   gMoodIcons[count] := GetResource('ICON', kMoodIconStart + (count - 1));

{Get handles to figure icons.}
FOR count := 1 TO 4 DO
   gFigureIcons[count] := GetResource('ICON', kFigIconStart + (count - 1));
```

As you can see, the icons in each group are given contiguous resource IDs in the resource file. The handles to each icon are stored in the appropriate array, accessed by global variables.

IMPORTANT

As always, you should make certain that none of the returned handles has the value NIL. For brevity, this check is not shown in Listing 5-6. ▲

To draw the tools area of a window, for example, Venn Diagrammer uses the code shown in Listing 5-7.

Listing 5-7   Drawing the tools area of a document window

```
{Redraw the tool area in the window.}
FOR count := 1 TO kNumTools DO
   BEGIN
      SetRect(myRect, kToolWd * (count - 1), 0, kToolWd * count, kToolHt);
      DoPlotIcon(myRect, gToolsIcons[count], myWindow, srcCopy);
   END;
```

Drawing

This code fragment calls the application-defined routine `DoPlotIcon` to draw the appropriate portion of the icon in the specified rectangle. The `DoPlotIcon` procedure is defined in Listing 5-8.

Listing 5-8   Drawing a portion of an icon

```
PROCEDURE DoPlotIcon (myRect: Rect; myIcon: Handle; myWindow: WindowPtr;
                                    myMode: Integer);
    VAR
       myBitMap:        BitMap;
BEGIN
    myBitMap.baseAddr := myIcon^;
    myBitMap.rowBytes := 4;
    myBitMap.bounds := myRect;
    CopyBits(myBitMap, myWindow^.portBits, myRect, myRect, myMode, NIL);
END;
```

The `DoPlotIcon` procedure plots a portion of an icon by defining a bitmap that includes the desired portion of the icon. (The desired portion of the icon is specified by the `myRect` parameter.) Then `DoPlotIcon` calls the QuickDraw routine `CopyBits` to copy the appropriate bits from their location in memory to the desired location in the specified window.

The `CopyBits` procedure transfers a bit image between two existing bit maps. In this case, the two bitmaps are the bitmapped portion of the icon and the bits in the destination window (which are specified by the `portBits` field of the window's graphics port; see Listing 6-1 on page 112 for details). The `myRect` parameter specifies the rectangle to copy; it's passed to `DoPlotIcon` from the calling routine so that `DoPlotIcon` can be used to plot different parts of the source icon. Finally, `DoPlotIcon` is passed a **transfer mode,** which indicates how the bits are to be drawn in the existing bit image of the destination rectangle. The constant `srcCopy` is passed in Listing 5-7 to indicate that the source bitmap is to overwrite the destination bitmap.

Drawing Text

In addition to the many routines it provides for defining and drawing both simple and complex graphic elements, QuickDraw also provides support for drawing text. You can use QuickDraw to draw characters, words, or other textual elements at any desired size and in any available font. It might seem odd that QuickDraw handles these operations, until you realize that text, like graphics, permeates the Macintosh user interface. Windows, menus, and some controls (for instance, buttons) have titles, which are essential to the user's understanding and manipulation of the application. As a result, it makes sense to treat text fundamentally as a graphic object and to assign basic text-drawing responsibilities to QuickDraw, which manages all graphics within the Macintosh system software.

Although QuickDraw is ultimately responsible for drawing text on the screen, you might need to use other Toolbox managers for other text-handling needs. For example, if you want the user to be able to input and edit some small amount of text, you can use TextEdit. TextEdit provides basic text-editing capabilities, such as cutting, copying, pasting, and entering words and characters. TextEdit calls QuickDraw to display the editable text. Similarly, if your application allows the user to display text in a variety of fonts, you might need to use the Font Manager. The Font Manager supports QuickDraw by providing the character bitmaps it needs to draw text in a specified font, size, and style. For a complete description of TextEdit and the Font Manager, see *Inside Macintosh: Text*.

The Venn Diagrammer application has very minimal text-handling requirements. It does not support any text entry or editing by the user. Instead, it obtains all the text it needs from resources stored in its resource fork. As a result, the Venn Diagrammer application can use basic QuickDraw text-drawing routines to display its text. For example, the Venn Diagrammer application draws the message in a window's status area by calling the application-defined routine DoStatusMesg, defined in Listing 5-9.

Listing 5-9   Retrieving a status message from a resource

```
PROCEDURE DoStatusMesg (myWindow: WindowPtr; myMessageID: Integer);
   VAR
      myText:      Str255;
BEGIN
   GetIndString(myText, rVennD, myMessageID);
   DoStatusText(myWindow, myText);
END;
```

As you can see, the DoStatusMesg routine takes two parameters, a window pointer specifying the window whose status area is to be filled in and an integer specifying the index into an 'STR#' resource. Then DoStatusMesg retrieves the appropriate message text and calls the application-defined procedure DoStatusText to print the message in the window.

Venn Diagrammer calls DoStatusMesg whenever it needs to display a message in the status area. For instance, when the user wants to determine if a syllogism is valid or not, Venn Diagrammer checks the syllogism's validity and then executes the code in Listing 5-10.

_____ **Listing 5-10**   Informing the user of an argument's validity or invalidity

```
IF valid THEN
    BEGIN
        IF gShowNames THEN        {show names of valid syllogisms?}
            BEGIN
                GetIndString(myMesg, rVennD, eArgIsValid);
                DoGetName(myWindow, myName);
                myMesg := concat(myMesg, ' (', myName, ')');
                DoStatusText(myWindow, myMesg);
            END
        ELSE
            DoStatusMesg(myWindow, eArgIsValid);
    END
ELSE
    DoStatusMesg(myWindow, eArgNotValid);
```

This code fragment illustrates why the Venn Diagrammer application defines two different routines, `DoStatusMesg` and `DoStatusText`. The first, `DoStatusMesg`, retrieves the desired message text from a resource and calls the second, `DoStatusText`, to display it on the screen. The application also calls `DoStatusText` at other times, for instance, when it needs to add something to the resource-based message string. In the example shown in Listing 5-10, the application needs to get the name of the valid syllogism, if the user has indicated that this should be done.

The `DoStatusText` procedure is defined in Listing 5-11. Its job is to display the text passed as a parameter in the status area of the specified window.

_____ **Listing 5-11**   Displaying a status message

```
PROCEDURE DoStatusText (myWindow: WindowPtr; myText: Str255);
    VAR
        myRect:     Rect;
        origSize:   Integer;
        origFont:   Integer;
        myHandle:   MyDocRecHnd;
    CONST
        kSlop = 4;
        kSize = 9;
        kFont = applFont;
BEGIN
    IF myWindow <> NIL THEN
        BEGIN
            SetPort(myWindow);
            origSize := myWindow^.txSize;     {remember original size and font}
```

Drawing

```
origFont := myWindow^.txFont;
TextSize(kSize);                       {set desired size and font}
TextFont(kFont);

SetRect(myRect, kToolWd * kNumTools, 0,
                    myWindow^.portRect.right, kToolHt);
EraseRect(myRect);
IF length(myText) > 0 THEN
   BEGIN
      MoveTo(myRect.left + kSlop, myRect.bottom - kSlop);
      DrawString(myText);
   END;

TextSize(origSize);                    {restore original size and font}
TextFont(origFont);

{Remember the last message printed in this window.}
myHandle := MyDocRecHnd(GetWRefCon(myWindow));
myHandle^^.statusText := myText;
   END;
END;
```

The `DoStatusText` procedure first remembers the graphics port's existing font and size, so that it can change and then later restore those values. Then `DoStatusText` sets the desired font and size of the status message by calling the QuickDraw routines `TextFont` and `TextSize`. You should always use these routines—instead of changing the fields of the `grafPort` record—whenever you want to change a graphics port's font and size.

IMPORTANT

Although you should never *change* the fields of a graphics port directly, you sometimes need to *read* those fields directly. In Listing 5-11, the original font and size are determined by reading the appropriate fields (`txFont` and `txSize`) of the graphics port record. This is necessary because QuickDraw doesn't provide routines to read that information from a graphics port record. ▲

Once it's set the desired font and size, the `DoStatusText` procedure calls `SetRect` to define the rectangle into which the text is to be drawn. Then, `DoStatusText` erases that rectangle by calling `EraseRect`. If the string to be displayed consists of at least one character, `DoStatusText` moves to the appropriate spot in the status area and calls the QuickDraw routine `DrawString`, which draws the specified string at the current drawing location in the window.

Finally, `DoStatusText` restores the graphics port's original font and size, and then copies the string just drawn into the `statusText` field of the window's document record. The Venn Diagrammer application needs to remember each window's latest status message so that it can redraw the message whenever necessary (for example, if the message is covered up by another window and then later revealed).

Venn Diagrammer uses similar techniques for all other text drawing it requires. Remember that this application supports only static text (that is, text that cannot be edited) stored in the application's resource fork. To allow the user to enter and edit some text, you need to use more powerful text-handling tools. See *Inside Macintosh: Text* for information about using system software services like the Font Manager and TextEdit to handle editable text. See *Inside Macintosh: Files* for information on storing text and other data in files. Finally, see the chapter "Dialog Manager" in *Inside Macintosh: Macintosh Toolbox Essentials* for information on handling text entry and editing in a dialog box.

Windows

Contents

6

This chapter describes how your application can use the Window Manager to create and manage windows. Windows delineate the space within which the user enters or views information, and every Macintosh application that has a user interface should use windows to communicate with the user. Any piece of information that your application presents to the user should be displayed in a window. Similarly, any piece of information that your application solicits from the user should involve the user performing appropriate actions (such as typing or clicking) in a window.

There are two general kinds of windows: document windows and dialog boxes. Document windows are used primarily to allow the user to enter and manipulate information, such as text, graphics, or other data. Often, but not always, the information in a document window can be stored in a file, from which the user can later retrieve it. Dialog boxes are used for many other purposes, such as alerting the user of unusual occurrences, soliciting information from the user, and displaying various application settings or user preferences.

This chapter focuses on techniques for handling windows in general, with particular emphasis on document windows. It shows how to

- determine the type of a window

- create and display windows

- handle events in windows

- close and remove windows

For specific information about dialog windows, see the chapter "Dialog Boxes" later in this book. For a complete description of the capabilities of the Window Manager and for code samples illustrating more advanced window-handling techniques, see the chapter "Window Manager" in *Inside Macintosh: Macintosh Toolbox Essentials*.

About Windows

A **window** is a user interface element that delimits an area on the screen in which the user can enter or view information. Here "information" is intended quite broadly; for example, an application that draws mazes and allows the user to trace a path through the maze by moving the cursor can reasonably be thought of as displaying information (the maze) and allowing the user to enter information (the desired path through the maze). As a result, virtually any interaction with the user that happens outside the menu bar and menus should occur within a window.

The system software provides a wide array of types of window to accommodate the many uses they can have. Window types are distinguished by their appearance and behavior. Some windows have title bars and others do not. Some windows can be moved around on the screen by the user and others cannot. In your choice of a window type, you should be guided by the behavior your application supports in that window.

Note

You can, if necessary, define your own custom types of windows, with an appearance and behavior unlike the windows provided by the system software. For compatibility reasons, however, this practice is generally discouraged. ◆

As indicated earlier in this chapter, the many types of windows are divided loosely into document windows and dialog boxes. The distinction between windows and dialog boxes is to some degree arbitrary, but in general, you use the Dialog Manager to create and manage dialog boxes and the Window Manager to create and manage document windows. The Dialog Manager essentially just provides a "front-end" to other Toolbox managers, including the Window Manager, the Control Manager, the Event Manager, and TextEdit. The Dialog Manager makes it very easy to create and handle user actions in windows containing controls, text boxes, and other dialog items. However, because dialog boxes are also windows, you might need to use some Window Manager routines as well to manipulate dialog boxes. For example, you can hide a dialog box by calling the `HideWindow` routine (there is no `HideDialog` routine).

When you are designing your application, you need to decide whether to use the Dialog Manager or the Window Manager to create and manage any particular window. For some types of windows, the decision is obvious. For document windows that can contain variable amounts of data and therefore probably require scroll bars and a size box, you'll want to use the Window Manager. For simple windows that contain a message and possibly a few buttons, you'll probably want to use the Dialog Manager. As a dialog box becomes more and more complex, however, you'll want to consider using the Window Manager and other Toolbox managers instead. The Window Manager provides the greatest control over the appearance and behavior of a window. In particular, any time you need to do moderately complex drawing in the window, you should probably use the Window Manager (and QuickDraw) instead of the Dialog Manager.

Note

For a more detailed list of factors that can effect the decision whether to use the Dialog Manager or the Window Manager (and other Toolbox managers) to manage a window, see the chapter "Dialog Manager" in *Inside Macintosh: Macintosh Toolbox Essentials*. ◆

Window Parts

The Window Manager defines and supports a set of standard window elements through which the user can manipulate windows. It's important that your application follow the standard conventions for drawing, moving, resizing, and closing windows. By presenting the standard interface, you make experienced users instantly familiar with many aspects of your application, allowing them to focus on learning its unique features.

The Venn Diagrammer application supports two kinds of windows, a single dialog box for setting general preferences and an unlimited number of document windows for evaluating categorical syllogisms. A sample document window is shown in Figure 6-1.

Windows

Figure 6-1   A Venn diagram window

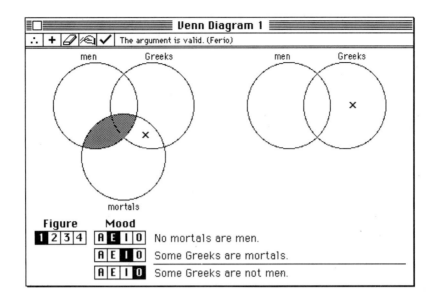

This window contains only two special elements defined by the Window Manager, a title bar and a close box. The **title bar** displays the name of the window and indicates whether it's active or not. The Window Manager displays the title of the window in the center of the title bar, in the system font and system font size. If the system font is in the Roman script system, the title bar is 20 pixels high.

The **close box** offers the user a quick way to close a window. If the user clicks the close box, your application should react exactly as if the user had chosen the Close command from the File menu.

Note
Venn Diagrammer's use of standard window elements is purposely restricted to the title bar and close box. Your application's windows should include as many of the standard window elements as are appropriate. ◆

The window shown in Figure 6-1 also contains a number of elements that are defined and managed by the Venn Diagrammer application. Immediately under the title bar is a row of five tools, which allow the user to manipulate the Venn diagram without leaving the window. To the right of the tools is a status area, where the Venn Diagrammer application displays information and other feedback to the user. In Figure 6-1, the status area contains a message indicating that the syllogism under consideration is valid; the status area also shows the traditional name of that valid syllogism (Ferio).

Underneath the tools area and the status area, the document window contains two sets of overlapping circles, which show the Venn diagram for the syllogism's premises and conclusion. The user can alter the contents of any region of overlap by clicking in that area. Shading indicates that the region is known to be empty; an X indicates that the region is known to contain something; the lack of either shading or an X indicates that the contents of the region are unknown.

The user can alter the syllogism under consideration by changing the figure of the syllogism and the mood of any of the three statements in the syllogism. Any changes in the figure or mood are instantly reflected in the syllogism shown in the bottom center of the window.

Window Records

You've already seen, in skeletal form at least, how to create a window by calling NewWindow (see Listing 1-1 on page 3). When you call NewWindow, the Window Manager creates in your application heap a new **window record** that contains information about the new window. The Window Manager defines a window record using the WindowRecord data structure, shown in Listing 6-1.

Listing 6-1 The WindowRecord data structure

```
TYPE  WindowRecord =
  RECORD
        port:          GrafPort;       {window's graphics port}
        windowKind:    Integer;        {class of the window}
        visible:       Boolean;        {visibility}
        hilited:       Boolean;        {highlighting}
        goAwayFlag:    Boolean;        {presence of close box}
        spareFlag:     Boolean;        {presence of zoom box}
        strucRgn:      RgnHandle;      {handle to structure region}
        contRgn:       RgnHandle;      {handle to content region}
        updateRgn:     RgnHandle;      {handle to update region}
        windowDefProc: Handle;         {handle to window definition }
                                       { function}
        dataHandle:    Handle;         {handle to window state }
                                       { data record}
        titleHandle:   StringHandle;   {handle to window title}
        titleWidth:    Integer;        {title width in pixels}
        controlList:   ControlHandle;  {handle to control list}
        nextWindow:    WindowPeek;     {pointer to next window }
                                       { record in window list}
        windowPic:     PicHandle;      {handle to optional picture}
        refCon:        LongInt;        {storage available to your }
                                       { application}
  END;
```

As you can see, a window record consists of numerous fields that contain information about the window. The first field (`port`) contains the window's graphics port, a drawing environment with its own coordinate system. The graphics port in turn contains information about that drawing environment, such as the location of the port on the screen, the default size and font of any text that is to be drawn in the port, and so forth.

Because many of the operations you'll perform on windows are in reality operations on the window's graphics port, the Window Manager defines the data type `WindowPtr` as a pointer to the window's graphics port.

```
TYPE
    WindowPtr    = GrafPtr;
```

For example, each time you want to draw in a window, you need to make sure that the window is the current drawing port. To do so, you can simply pass the window pointer to the QuickDraw routine `SetPort`.

```
SetPort(myWindow);
```

You can do this because a window pointer is simply a pointer to a graphics port, which is the first field in a window record. Similarly, you can determine the location of the window on the screen by inspecting the `portRect` field of the graphics port. Recall that Listing 1-1 on page 3 centers the text within the window as follows:

```
WITH gWindow^.portRect DO         {set the position of the pen}
    MoveTo(((right - left) DIV 2) - (StringWidth(gString) DIV 2),
              (bottom - top) DIV 2);
```

Usually you don't need to access or directly modify fields in a window record. If you do need to examine the fields of the window record (other than those contained in the window's graphics port), you can use the `WindowPeek` data type:

```
TYPE
    WindowPeek   = ^WindowRecord;
```

A `WindowPeek` data type is a pointer to a window record.

Note
Don't get confused here. A window pointer is a pointer to the window's graphics port, not a pointer to the window record. The `WindowPeek` data type is so called because it lets you "peek" into the fields of the window record beyond the graphics port. ◆

Window Types

The `windowKind` field of a window record indicates the type of window that the window record describes. Your application can, if necessary, read the value in that field to determine how to handle a particular window.

When the Window Manager creates a new window for a desk accessory, it places a negative value (in particular, the reference ID of the desk accessory) in the windowKind field of the window. In all other cases, the Window Manager puts one of two constants into that field:

```
CONST
    dialogKind  = 2;          {dialog or alert window}
    userKind    = 8;          {window created by an application}
```

You can rely on this behavior to determine what kind of window a given window pointer picks out. Listing 6-2 defines a function IsAppWindow that returns TRUE if the application created the specified window by calling a Window Manager routine directly. In the case of the Venn Diagrammer application, this means that the window is a document window.

Listing 6-2   Determining if a window is a document window

```
FUNCTION IsAppWindow (myWindow: WindowPtr): Boolean;
BEGIN
    IF myWindow = NIL THEN
        IsAppWindow := FALSE
    ELSE
        IsAppWindow := WindowPeek(myWindow)^.windowKind = userKind;
END;
```

Notice that IsAppWindow coerces the window pointer myWindow to the type WindowPeek before dereferencing it to examine the windowKind field.

You can define similar functions to identify dialog boxes and desk accessory windows. Listing 6-3 defines a function IsDialogWindow that returns TRUE if your application created the specified window by calling a Dialog Manager routine.

Listing 6-3   Determining if a window is a dialog box

```
FUNCTION IsDialogWindow (myWindow: WindowPtr): Boolean;
BEGIN
    IF myWindow = NIL THEN
        IsDialogWindow := FALSE
    ELSE
        IsDialogWindow := WindowPeek(myWindow)^.windowKind = dialogKind;
END;
```

Finally, Listing 6-4 defines a function IsDAccWindow that returns TRUE if the specified window was created by a desk accessory.

_____ **Listing 6-4**   Determining if a window is a desk accessory window

```
FUNCTION IsDAccWindow (myWindow: WindowPtr): Boolean;
BEGIN
    IF myWindow = NIL THEN
        IsDAccWindow := FALSE
    ELSE
        IsDAccWindow := WindowPeek(myWindow)^.windowKind < 0;
END;
```

These three functions are used extensively throughout the code samples in the remainder of this chapter.

Note

The IsDAccWindow function is provided to help maintain compatibility with previous system software versions. When your application is running in System 7, it receives events only for its own windows and for windows belonging to desk accessories that were launched in its partition. ◆

Creating Windows

The Venn Diagrammer application allows the user to have multiple document windows (that is, multiple Venn diagram windows) on the desktop at the same time. Each different document window probably displays a different syllogism. As a result, the application needs some way to keep track of each window's current settings.

A standard way to do this is to make use of the refCon field in the window record. The refCon field is reserved specifically for use by applications, which can set the field (using the SetWRefCon procedure) to any 4-byte value. Often, applications store a handle to an application-defined data structure that describes the window. This data structure is often known as a **document record.** Given the window pointer, you can retrieve that handle by calling the GetWRefCon function.

The sample code in this book uses a document record of type MyDocRec (shown in Listing 6-5) to store information about the current contents of a Venn diagram window.

_____ **Listing 6-5**   The structure of a document record for the Venn Diagrammer application

```
TYPE MyDocRec =          {information for a document window}
    RECORD
        figure:          Integer;                {the figure of the syllogism}
        mood:            ARRAY[1..3] OF Integer; {the moods of the statements}
        terms:           ARRAY[1..3] OF Str31;   {the three terms}
        statusText:      Str255;                 {most recent status message}
```

```
    userSolution:      MyDiagramState;        {user's diagram state}
    realSolution:      MyDiagramState;        {answer's diagram state}
    isAnswerShowing:   Boolean;               {is the answer showing?}
    isExistImport:     Boolean;               {stmts imply exists subject?}
    needsAdjusting:    Boolean;               {diagram needs adjusting?}
END;
MyDocRecPtr = ^MyDocRec;
MyDocRecHnd = ^MyDocRecPtr;
```

As you can see, the document record used by the Venn Diagrammer application contains fields that describe the current settings of the syllogism in the window, including the figure of the syllogism, the mood of each statement in the syllogism, and the terms used in those statements. The document record also contains fields that maintain information about the current appearance of the window, such as the status message most recently displayed in the window's status area (statusText field) and a Boolean value that indicates whether the answer is visible in the window (isAnswerShowing field). The Venn Diagrammer application uses that Boolean value to determine how to fill in the regions in the overlapping circles. If the value of isAnswerShowing is TRUE, the application displays the correct answer (encoded in the realSolution field); otherwise, the application displays the user's current answer (encoded in the userSolution field).

Note
The structure of the MyDiagramState data type is not shown in this book. ◆

The MyDocRec data structure also contains two other fields containing Boolean values. These specify whether the statements that make up the syllogism are to be interpreted as having existential import or not, and whether the window needs to be checked for automatic adjustment.

IMPORTANT
If a Venn diagram window contained TextEdit fields or controls (such as radio buttons or scroll bars), the document record could be expanded to include handles to those items. Also, if a file were associated with the window, you'd want the document record to include information about that file. In a nutshell, the document record can contain all relevant information about the window that isn't contained in the window record. ▲

The Venn Diagrammer application creates a document record every time it creates a document window, and it stores a handle to the document record in the refCon field of the window record. Listing 6-6 shows the DoCreateWindow routine, which creates a new document window. This function is called when the application is first launched and whenever the user chooses the New command from the File menu.

Listing 6-6   Creating a new Venn diagram window

```
FUNCTION DoCreateWindow: WindowPtr;
   VAR
      myPointer:  Ptr;
      myWindow:   WindowPtr;
      myHandle:   MyDocRecHnd;
BEGIN
   myPointer := NewPtr(sizeof(WindowRecord));
   IF myPointer = NIL THEN
      exit(DoCreateWindow);

   myWindow := GetNewWindow(rVennD, myPointer, WindowPtr(-1));
   IF myWindow <> NIL THEN
      BEGIN
         SetPort(myWindow);
         myHandle := MyDocRecHnd(NewHandleClear(sizeof(MyDocRec)));

         IF myHandle <> NIL THEN
            BEGIN
               HLockHi(Handle(myHandle));      {lock the data high in the heap}
               SetWRefCon(myWindow, LongInt(myHandle));
                                               {attach handle to window record}
               DoSetWindowTitle(myWindow);     {set the window title}

               {Define initial window settings.}
               WITH myHandle^^ DO
                  BEGIN
                     figure := 1;
                     mood[1] := 1;
                     mood[2] := 1;
                     mood[3] := 1;
                     isAnswerShowing := FALSE;
                     isExistImport := gGiveImport;
                  END;
               DoGetRandomTerms(myWindow);
               DoCalcAnswer(myWindow);

               {Position the window and display it.}
               DoPositionWindow(myWindow);
               ShowWindow(myWindow);

            END {IF myHandle <> NIL}
         ELSE
```

```
      BEGIN                              {couldn't get a data record}
          CloseWindow(myWindow);
          DisposePtr(Ptr(myWindow));
          myWindow := NIL;            {so pass back NIL}
      END;
  END;
  DoCreateWindow := myWindow;
END;
```

The DoCreateWindow function first attempts to allocate space in the heap for a window record by calling the Memory Manager's NewPtr function. If no space is available, DoCreateWindow exits and returns NIL to indicate that no new window was created. Otherwise, DoCreateWindow creates the new window, whose size and type are defined in a window resource of type rVennD.

```
CONST
    rVennD       = 131;          {resource ID of document window}
```

If the new window is successfully created, DoCreateWindow next tries to allocate space for a document record. Once again, if the space isn't available, DoCreateWindow takes care to dispose of the new window and return NIL to the calling routine. Otherwise, DoCreateWindow locks the handle to the document record high in the heap and attaches the document record to the window record by calling SetWRefCon.

Note
The document record data is locked at the top of the heap to help prevent heap fragmentation. See the chapter "Introduction to Memory Management" in *Inside Macintosh: Memory* for a discussion of when you need to lock data in the heap. ◆

The DoCreateWindow function next sets up the window's title (by calling the application-defined procedure DoSetWindowTitle) and initializes some of the fields in the document record. Then DoCreateWindow calls two further application-defined procedures (DoGetRandomTerms and DoCalcAnswer) to initialize the terms field and the realSolution field of the document record. (As for the userSolution field, the NewHandleClear function, which sets all bytes in the block to 0, automatically initializes it to encode an empty diagram, according to a clever scheme.)

The application-defined procedure DoPositionWindow sets the original position of the new window according to the user's expectations and good human interface design. Then DoCreateWindow calls the Window Manager procedure ShowWindow to display the window. The ShowWindow procedure generates and update event for the newly displayed window, thereby causing the Venn Diagrammer application to draw the content region of the window.

Note

The procedure `DoPositionWindow` is not defined in this book. For a discussion of how to determine the position of a new window, see the chapter "Window Manager" in *Inside Macintosh: Macintosh Toolbox Essentials*. ◆

Handling Window Events

Your application must be prepared to handle two kinds of window-related events:

- mouse and keyboard events in your application's windows, which are reported by the Event Manager in direct response to user actions

- activate and update events, which are generated by the Window Manager and the Event Manager as an indirect result of user actions

Because Venn Diagrammer does not support text entry, the only relevant keyboard events it needs to handle are keyboard equivalents of menu commands. See the chapter "Menus" in this book for a description of how to handle those events.

This section shows how to handle mouse events as well as update and activate events.

Mouse Events

When your application is active, it receives notice of all mouse-down events in the menu bar, in one of its windows, or in any windows belonging to desk accessories that were launched in its partition. When it receives a mouse-down event, your application should call `FindWindow` to determine where the cursor was when the mouse button was pressed. The `FindWindow` function returns a **part code** that indicates the location of the cursor. These constants define the available part codes:

```
CONST inDesk        = 0;  {none of the following}
      inMenuBar     = 1;  {in menu bar}
      inSysWindow   = 2;  {in desk accessory window}
      inContent     = 3;  {anywhere in content region except size }
                          { box if window is active, }
                          { anywhere including size box if window }
                          { is inactive}
      inDrag        = 4;  {in drag (title bar) region}
      inGrow        = 5;  {in size box (active window only)}
      inGoAway      = 6;  {in close box}
      inZoomIn      = 7;  {in zoom box (window in standard state)}
      inZoomOut     = 8;  {in zoom box (window in user state)}
```

Windows

In addition to returning a part code as its function result, FindWindow also returns in its second parameter a pointer to a window, if the user presses the mouse button while the cursor is in a window. Listing 6-7 show how the Venn Diagrammer application handles mouse-down events.

Listing 6-7   Handling mouse-down events

```
PROCEDURE DoMouseDown (myEvent: EventRecord);
    VAR
        myPart:     Integer;
        myWindow:   WindowPtr;
BEGIN
    myPart := FindWindow(myEvent.where, myWindow);
    CASE myPart OF
        inMenuBar:
            BEGIN
                DoMenuAdjust;
                DoMenuCommand(MenuSelect(myEvent.where));
            END;
        InSysWindow:
            SystemClick(myEvent, myWindow);
        inDrag:
            DoDrag(myWindow, myEvent.where);
        inGoAway:
            DoGoAwayBox(myWindow, myEvent.where);
        inContent:
            BEGIN
                IF myWindow <> FrontWindow THEN
                    SelectWindow(myWindow)
                ELSE
                    DoContentClick(myWindow, myEvent);
            END;
        OTHERWISE
            ;
    END;
END;
```

If the user clicks in the menu bar, DoMouseDown adjusts the menus and calls the application-defined routine DoMenuCommand to handle whatever menu command the user might choose. See the chapter "Menus" in this book for details on handling menu choices.

The FindWindow function returns the part code inSysWindow only when the user presses the mouse button while the cursor is in a window that belongs to a desk accessory launched in your application's partition. You can then call the `SystemClick` procedure, passing it the event record and window pointer. The `SystemClick` procedure makes sure that the event is handled by the appropriate desk accessory. For more information about `SystemClick`, see the chapter "Event Manager" in *Inside Macintosh: Macintosh Toolbox Essentials*.

If the user clicks in a window's drag region (identified by the part code `inDrag`), `DoMouseDown` calls the application-defined routine `DoDrag`, defined in Listing 6-8. The `DoDrag` procedure calls the Window Manager procedure `DragWindow`, which displays an outline of the window, moves the outline as long as the user continues to drag the window, and calls `MoveWindow` to draw the window in its new location when the user releases the mouse button.

Listing 6-8   Dragging a window

```
PROCEDURE DoDrag (myWindow: WindowPtr; mouseloc: Point);
    VAR
        dragBounds: Rect;
BEGIN
    dragBounds := GetGrayRgn^^.rgnBBox;
    DragWindow(myWindow, mouseloc, dragBounds);
END;
```

If the user clicks a window's close box (identified by the part code `inGoAway`), you can call an application-defined procedure to close that window. See "Closing Windows" beginning on page 128 for a discussion of how to close windows.

Finally, the `DoMouseDown` procedure defined in Listing 6-7 handles all user clicks in a window's content region either by selecting the window if it isn't already the frontmost window or by calling the routine `DoContentClick` defined in Listing 6-9.

Listing 6-9   Handling clicks in a window's content region

```
PROCEDURE DoContentClick (myWindow: WindowPtr; myEvent: EventRecord);
    VAR
        myRect:     Rect;                     {temporary rectangle}
        count:      Integer;
BEGIN
    IF NOT IsAppWindow(myWindow) THEN
        exit(DoContentClick);                 {make sure it's a document window}

    SetPort(myWindow);                        {set port to our window}
    GlobalToLocal(myEvent.where);

    {See if the click is in the tools area.}
```

6

Windows

```
        SetRect(myRect, 0, 0, kToolWd * kNumTools, kToolHt);
        IF PtInRect(myEvent.where, myRect) THEN
            BEGIN                    {if so, determine which tool was clicked}
                FOR count := 1 TO kNumTools DO
                    BEGIN
                        SetRect(myRect, (count - 1) * kToolWd, 0,
                                    count * kToolWd, kToolHt);
                        IF PtInRect(myEvent.where, myRect) THEN
                            Leave;       {we found the right tool, so stop looking}
                    END;
                IF DoTrackRect(myWindow, myRect) THEN
                    DoMenuCommand(BitShift(mVennD, 16) +
                            ((kNumTools + 1) - count));   {handle tools selections}
                exit(DoContentClick);
            END;

        {See if the click is in the status area.}
        SetRect(myRect, kToolWd * kNumTools, 0,
                    myWindow^.portRect.right, kToolHt);
        IF PtInRect(myEvent.where, myRect) THEN
            BEGIN
                exit(DoContentClick);
            END;

        {The click must be in somewhere in the rest of the window.}
        DoVennClick(myWindow, myEvent.where);
    END;
```

The general strategy employed in the DoContentClick procedure is to check each part of the content area that is meaningful to the application and determine whether the mouse click occurred there. Then DoContentClick reacts appropriately.

After setting the current drawing port to the specified window, DoContentClick calls the GlobalToLocal procedure to convert the mouse click location from global coordinates to local coordinates. Then DoContentClick checks whether the click occurred in the tools area of the window. If so, DoContentClick handles the tool selection by invoking the corresponding menu command and then exiting.

If the mouse click was in the status area of a window, DoContentClick simply exits. Otherwise, the user must have clicked somewhere in the content area below the tools and status area. In that case, DoContentClick calls the application-defined function DoVennClick to handle the event.

Note

The `DoVennClick` function is not defined in this book, but it's quite simple. It merely checks whether the click occurred in the figure icons, mood icons, or some part of the overlapping circles and, if so, changes the window's document record accordingly and invalidates any affected part of the screen. A portion of `DoVennClick` is shown in Listing 6-10. ◆

Update Events

The Event Manager sends your application an **update event** when part or all of your window's content region needs to be redrawn. Specifically, the Event Manager checks each window's update region every time your application calls `WaitNextEvent` and generates an update event for every window whose update region is not empty.

The Window Manager typically triggers update events when the moving and relayering of windows on the screen requires that one or more windows be redrawn. If the user moves a window that covers part of an inactive window, for example, the Window Manager first redraws the window frame. It then adds the newly exposed area to the window's update region, triggering an update event. In response, your application updates the content region.

Note

Your application can receive update events when it is in either the foreground or the background. In general, however, it doesn't matter whether your update routine is executed in the foreground or the background. ◆

Your application can also trigger update events itself by manipulating the update region. You can add areas to a window's update region by calling the Window Manager procedures `InvalRect` (to add a rectangle to the update region) and `InvalRgn` (to add an arbitrary region to the update region). For example, when the Venn Diagrammer application detects a mouse click in a figure icon, it reacts as shown in Listing 6-10.

Listing 6-10   Handling a click in a figure icon

```
FOR count := 1 TO 4 DO
    BEGIN
        IF PtInRect(myPoint, gFigureRects[count]) THEN
            IF myHandle^^.figure <> count THEN      {new rect differ from prev?}
                BEGIN
                    InvalRect(gFigureRects[myHandle^^.figure]);
                    myHandle^^.figure := count;
                    InvalRect(gFigureRects[myHandle^^.figure]);
                    InvalRect(gTextBoxes[1]);        {invalidate premises}
                    InvalRect(gTextBoxes[2]);
                    DoCalcAnswer(myWindow);          {update the current answer}
```

Windows

```
        DoStatusText(myWindow, '');        {remove any existing message}
      END;

  END;
```

Your general strategy should be to isolate all drawing that occurs in a document window into your application's update routine. Then, within any other routines, you redraw parts of the window, whenever necessary, by invalidating those parts to add them to the window's update region. Listing 6-11 shows the update routine for Venn Diagrammer.

Listing 6-11   Handling update events

```
PROCEDURE DoUpdate (myWindow: WindowPtr);
   VAR
      myHandle:   MyDocRecHnd;
      myRect:     Rect;                {tool rectangle}
      origPort:   GrafPtr;
      origPen:    PenState;
      count:      Integer;
BEGIN
   GetPort(origPort);                  {remember original drawing port}
   SetPort(myWindow);

   BeginUpdate(myWindow);              {clear update region}
   EraseRect(myWindow^.portRect);

   IF IsAppWindow(myWindow) THEN
      BEGIN
         {Draw two lines separating tools area from work area.}
         GetPenState(origPen);        {remember original pen state}
         PenNormal;                   {reset pen to normal state}
         WITH myWindow^ DO
            BEGIN
               MoveTo(portRect.left, portRect.top + kToolHt);
               Line(portRect.right, 0);
               MoveTo(portRect.left, portRect.top + kToolHt + 2);
               Line(portRect.right, 0);
            END;

         {Redraw the tools area in the window.}
         FOR count := 1 TO kNumTools DO
            BEGIN
               SetRect(myRect, kToolWd * (count - 1), 0, kToolWd * count,
                     kToolHt);
```

```
        DoPlotIcon(myRect, gToolsIcons[count], myWindow, srcCopy);
      END;

    {Redraw the status area in the window.}
    myHandle := MyDocRecHnd(GetWRefCon(myWindow));
    DoStatusText(myWindow, myHandle^^.statusText);

    {Draw the rest of the content region.}
    DoVennDraw(myWindow);

      SetPenState(origPen);           {restore previous pen state}
    END; {IF IsAppWindow}

  EndUpdate(myWindow);
  SetPort(origPort);                  {restore original drawing port}
END;
```

In response to an update event, your application calls BeginUpdate, draws the window's contents, and then calls EndUpdate. The BeginUpdate procedure limits the visible region to the intersection of the visible region and the update region. Your application can then update either the visible region or the entire content region—because QuickDraw limits drawing to the visible region, only the parts of the window that actually need updating are drawn. The BeginUpdate procedure also clears the update region. After you've updated the window, you call EndUpdate to restore the visible region in the graphics port to the full visible region.

As you can see in Listing 6-11, the Venn Diagrammer application draws the two lines separating the upper portion of the window's content region and redraws the tools icons. Then it redraws the most recently displayed status message (which it has saved in the window's document record). Finally, DoUpdate calls the application-defined routine DoVennDraw to draw the remainder of the content area (the overlapping circles, the figure and mood icons, the term labels on the circles, and the syllogism itself).

Note
The DoVennDraw routine is not shown in this book, but you've already seen portions of it in the chapter "Drawing" earlier in this book. ◆

Activate Events

The window in which the user is currently working is the **active window.** It's always the frontmost window on the desktop (unless your application supports "floating" windows) and is easily identified by the "racing stripes" in the title bar.

Your application activates and deactivates windows in response to **activate events,** which are generated by the Window Manager to inform your application that a window is becoming active or inactive. Each activate event specifies the window to be changed and the direction of the change (that is, whether it is to be activated or deactivated).

Your application also triggers activate events itself by calling the SelectWindow procedure. When it receives a mouse-down event in an inactive window, for example, your application calls SelectWindow, which brings the selected window to the front, removes the highlighting from the previously active window, and adds highlighting to the selected window (see Listing 6-7 on page 120). The SelectWindow procedure then generates two activate events: the first one tells your application to deactivate the previously active window; the second, to activate the newly active window.

When you receive the event for the previously active window, you need to do whatever is appropriate to make the window's contents appear inactive. Depending on the design of you application, you might need to

- hide the controls and size box

- remove or alter any highlighting of selections in the window

When you receive the event for the newly active window, you

- draw the controls and size box

- restore the content area as necessary, adding the insertion point in its former location and highlighting any previously highlighted selections

If the newly activated window also needs updating, your application also receives an update event, as described in the previous section, "Update Events."

Note

A switch to one of your application's windows from a different application is handled through suspend and resume events, not activate events. See the chapter "Processes" in this book for a description of how your application can handle suspend and resume events. ◆

Listing 6-12 illustrates the application-defined procedure DoActivate, which handles activate events.

Listing 6-12 Handling window activations and deactivations

```
PROCEDURE DoActivate (myWindow: WindowPtr; myModifiers: Integer);
    VAR
        myState:    Integer;                {activation state}
        myControl:  ControlHandle;
BEGIN
    myState := BAnd(myModifiers, activeFlag);

    IF IsDialogWindow(myWindow) THEN
        BEGIN
            myControl := WindowPeek(myWindow)^.controlList;
            WHILE myControl <> NIL DO
                BEGIN
                    HiliteControl(myControl, myState + 255 mod 256);
```

```
            myControl := myControl^^.nextControl;
        END;

    END;

END;
```

The `DoActivate` procedure is passed a window pointer and the `modifiers` field from the event record corresponding to the activate event. The `modifiers` field contains a bit (defined by the `activeFlag` constant) that indicates whether the event specifies window activation or deactivation.

Notice that `DoActivate` does nothing to Venn Diagrammer's document windows, because those windows contain no controls, text, or other items whose visual state might depend on the activation state. For document windows belonging to Venn Diagrammer, the Window Manager handles all the necessary activation and deactivation.

Note

If your application's document windows contain controls (such as scroll bars), your application does need to activate them appropriately. For more information, see the chapter "Control Manager" in *Inside Macintosh: Macintosh Toolbox Essentials.* ◆

However, the Preferences dialog box supported by the Venn Diagrammer application does contain controls, so the `DoActivate` procedure needs to inactivate those controls when the window is deactivated and then reactivate them when the window is activated. The `DoActivate` procedure checks the window's control list and calls the Control Manager procedure `HiliteControl` to perform the necessary activation or deactivation. (The head of the window's control list is stored in the `controlList` field of the window record.) Figure 6-2 shows the Preferences dialog box in its inactive state.

Figure 6-2   An inactive window containing controls

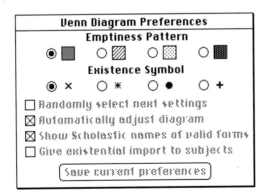

Closing Windows

The user closes a window either by clicking the window's close box (in the upper-left corner of the window) or by choosing the Close command from the File menu. To determine which window to close, you'll proceed in slightly different ways for these two cases. When the user clicks a window's close box, you can get a window pointer for that window by calling the FindWindow function in response to the mouse-down event. When the user chooses a menu command, however, you can't do that; instead, you can call the FrontWindow function to retrieve a pointer to the frontmost window on the screen.

Note

You'll also want to close any windows that might be on the desktop when the user quits your application. You can do that by repeatedly calling FrontWindow until it returns NIL. See Listing 9-4 on page 175. ◆

When the user presses the mouse button while the cursor is in the close box, your application should call the TrackGoAway function to track mouse movement until the user releases the button, as illustrated in Listing 6-13.

Listing 6-13   Handling clicks in the close box

```
PROCEDURE DoGoAwayBox (myWindow: WindowPtr; mouseloc: Point);
BEGIN
    IF TrackGoAway(myWindow, mouseloc) THEN
        DoCloseWindow(myWindow);
END;
```

If TrackGoAway returns FALSE, the user released the button while the cursor was outside the close box, and your application should do nothing. If TrackGoAway returns TRUE, your application should invoke its own procedure for closing a window.

Listing 6-14 illustrates an application-defined function that closes a window. Notice that the effect of this function varies according to which kind of window it's being asked to close. If the user wants to close a dialog window, DoCloseWindow simply hides the window; this strategy leaves the data structures associated with the dialog box in memory, in expectation that the user might open the dialog box again. If the user wants to close a desk accessory window, DoCloseWindow calls the Desk Manager routine CloseDeskAcc to close that desk accessory.

Listing 6-14   Closing a window

```
PROCEDURE DoCloseWindow (myWindow: WindowPtr);
BEGIN
    IF myWindow <> NIL THEN
        IF IsDialogWindow(myWindow) THEN        {this is a dialog window}
            HideWindow(myWindow)
        ELSE IF IsDAccWindow(myWindow) THEN     {this is a DA window}
            CloseDeskAcc(WindowPeek(myWindow)^.windowKind)
        ELSE IF IsAppWindow(myWindow) THEN      {this is a document window}
            DoCloseDocWindow(myWindow);
END;
```

If the window to be closed is a document window, DoCloseWindow calls the
application-defined procedure DoCloseDocWindow defined in Listing 6-15 to deallocate
the document record, close the window, and then deallocate the window record.

Listing 6-15   Closing a Venn diagram window

```
PROCEDURE DoCloseDocWindow (myWindow: WindowPtr);
    VAR
        myHandle:    MyDocRecHnd;
BEGIN
    IF myWindow = NIL THEN
        exit(DoCloseDocWindow)                  {ignore NIL windows}
    ELSE
        BEGIN
            myHandle := MyDocRecHnd(GetWRefCon(myWindow));
            DisposeHandle(Handle(myHandle));
            CloseWindow(myWindow);              {close the window}
            DisposePtr(Ptr(myWindow));          {and release the storage}
        END;
END;
```

The DoCloseDocWindow procedure retrieves a handle to the document record from the
window record. Then it calls DisposeHandle to free the memory occupied by the
document record. Next DoCloseDocWindow closes the window by calling the Window
Manager procedure CloseWindow and deallocates the window record by calling
DisposePtr.

Note

When you create a window, if you allow the Window Manager to allocate memory for the window record (by passing NIL as the second parameter to GetNewWindow), then you should call the DisposeWindow procedure to close the window, instead of calling CloseWindow and DisposePtr. ◆

Dialog Boxes

Contents

This chapter describes how your application can use the Dialog Manager to create and manage dialog boxes. You can use dialog boxes to alert the user to unusual situations or to solicit information from the user. The Venn Diagrammer application uses one modeless dialog box and two modal dialog boxes.

This chapter shows how to

■ create resources describing dialog boxes and the items in dialog boxes

■ open those resources to display a dialog box

■ define application-specific dialog items

■ handle events associated with both modeless and modal dialog boxes

Most Macintosh applications support a number of dialog boxes and provide more complete event handling in those dialog boxes than is illustrated in this chapter. For example, the dialog boxes supported by the Venn Diagrammer application do not contain text fields. For a complete description of the capabilities of the Dialog Manager and for code samples illustrating more advanced dialog handling, see the chapter "Dialog Manager" in *Inside Macintosh: Macintosh Toolbox Essentials*.

About Dialog Boxes

A **dialog box** is a window that's used for some special, limited purpose. In the simplest case, you can use a dialog box just to display information to the user. The information might be a report of some error, a greeting, or a progress bar showing what percentage of some operation has completed. Figure 7-1 shows a simple modal dialog box of this ilk; this is the box Venn Diagrammer displays when the user chooses the About Venn Diagrammer command from the Apple menu.

Figure 7-1   An About box

This kind of dialog box is said to be **modal:** it puts the user in the state or "mode" of being able to work only inside the dialog box. To dismiss the dialog box, the user must click one or the other of the two buttons.

Dialog Boxes

The system software distinguishes a special category of modal dialog boxes, called **alert boxes.** You'll use alert boxes to report errors or to give warnings to the user. Figure 7-2 shows an alert box. (Venn Diagrammer displays this alert box if it cannot read the resources it uses to create menus; see Listing 8-1 on page 155.)

Figure 7-2   An alert box

Other types of dialog boxes both display information to the user and allow the user to enter or change information. You might, for instance, use a dialog box of this sort in an application that allows users to specify a word to be searched for. The Venn Diagrammer application displays the modeless dialog shown in Figure 7-3 when the user chooses the Preferences command from the Venn menu.

Figure 7-3   A Preferences dialog box

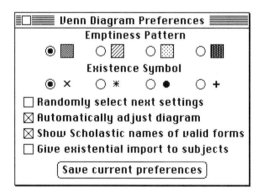

This modeless dialog box contains a **button,** four **checkboxes,** and eight **radio buttons.** It also contains eight application-defined items—the icons used to show the available existence symbols and emptiness patterns.

In contrast to the modal dialog boxes shown in Figure 7-1 and Figure 7-2, the dialog box shown in Figure 7-3 is said to be **modeless:** the user can switch to another window or perform other actions without dismissing the dialog box. The user doesn't have to change any preferences settings or click any buttons to be able to switch to a document window or pull down a menu. Moreover, clicking a button in the modeless dialog box should not dismiss it; instead, the dialog box should remain on the desktop so that the user can continue to see the information displayed in it or repeat any actions it permits.

IMPORTANT

To give users maximum control and minimum frustration, you should, whenever possible, implement your dialog boxes as modeless dialog boxes. ▲

The distinctive feature of dialog boxes—as opposed to windows—is that they are very easy to create and manage. The Dialog Manager looks in dialog resources to find descriptions of the dialog box and the items in it. Then the Dialog Manager draws the dialog box and handles user actions in the dialog box accordingly. This can be especially useful for managing dialog boxes that contain editable text fields. The Dialog Manager calls TextEdit to handle all the standard text-editing operations such as cutting, pasting, and copying.

To create a dialog box, you first need to define a **dialog resource** and a dialog **item list.** The dialog resource specifies, among other things, the rectangle on the screen in which the dialog box is drawn, a **window definition ID** indicating the type of dialog box to draw, and a resource ID of the dialog item list. A dialog resource is of type `'DLOG'`. See Figure 3-2 on page 58 for the ResEdit form of a dialog resource and Listing 3-1 on page 57 for the Rez form of the same dialog resource. Both of these correspond to the dialog box in Figure 7-3.

One of the main pieces of information in a dialog resource is the resource ID of a dialog item list (a resource of type `'DITL'`). The item list specifies the items—such as buttons and static text—to display in an alert box or a dialog box. (Once again, you can specify an item list graphically using a utility like ResEdit or textually in the Rez resource description language.) The Dialog Manager uses the item list both to draw the dialog box and also to handle user actions in dialog boxes. It reports user actions to your application by specifying the **item number** of the relevant item. An item's number is simply its rank in the item list. In Listing 7-1, the Venn Diagrammer application defines a number of constants to keep track of the numbers of the items in its Preferences dialog box.

Listing 7-1   Dialog item numbers

```
iEmpty1Radio            = 1;
iEmpty2Radio            = 2;
iEmpty3Radio            = 3;
iEmpty4Radio            = 4;
iEmpty1Icon             = 5;
iEmpty2Icon             = 6;
iEmpty3Icon             = 7;
iEmpty4Icon             = 8;
iExist1Radio            = 9;
iExist2Radio            = 10;
```

Dialog Boxes

```
iExist3Radio              = 11;
iExist4Radio              = 12;
iExist1Icon               = 13;
iExist2Icon               = 14;
iExist3Icon               = 15;
iExist4Icon               = 16;
iGetNextRandomly          = 19;
iAutoAdjust               = 20;
iShowSchoolNames          = 21;
iUseExistImport           = 22;
iSaveVennPrefs            = 23;
```

Note

Notice that several item numbers (namely, 17 and 18) are missing from this list. They are the item numbers of the two text labels "Emptiness Pattern" and "Existence Symbol." Venn Diagrammer ignores those item numbers because clicking them has no effect. ◆

Dialog boxes can contain various sorts of items, such controls (buttons, checkboxes, and radio buttons) and fields for entering and editing text. The Dialog Manager recognizes these constants for dialog box items:

```
CONST
    ctrlItem    = 4;   {add this to the next four constants}
    btnCtrl     = 0;   {standard button control}
    chkCtrl     = 1;   {standard checkbox control}
    radCtrl     = 2;   {standard radio button}
    resCtrl     = 3;   {control defined in a control resource}
    helpItem    = 1;   {help balloons}
    statText    = 8;   {static text}
    editText    = 16;  {editable text}
    iconItem    = 32;  {icon}
    picItem     = 64;  {QuickDraw picture}
    userItem    = 0;   {application-defined item}
```

Several Dialog Manager routines return these constants to your application. For instance, you can get information about a particular dialog item by calling the GetDialogItem routine:

```
GetDialogItem(myDialog, itemNum, myType, myHand, myRect);
```

Suppose, for example, that itemNum has the value specified by the constant iSaveVennPrefs. Then on return from the procedure call, myType will contain the value ctrlItem+btnCtrl, indicating that the specified item is a standard button control.

As you can see, a dialog box can contain standard user interface elements like buttons, checkboxes, icons, and even arbitrary pictures. If you need to include other kinds of elements in a dialog box, you can create application-defined items. Because the Dialog Manager uses the constant `userItem` to designate these items, they're often called **user items.** The Venn Diagrammer application employs eight user items in the Preferences dialog box, to draw the four emptiness patterns and the four existence symbols.

When you use any application-defined user items in a dialog box, your application needs to tell the Dialog Manager how to draw the items and what to do in response to user selections of those items. See "Setting Up Application-Defined Items" beginning on page 139 for instructions on implementing user items in a dialog box.

Note
Most dialog boxes don't need to contain user items. The Venn Diagrammer application uses them because it needs to draw bit images (not entire icons) in the dialog box. ◆

Using Modeless Dialog Boxes

To display a modeless dialog box, you can create the dialog box by calling `GetNewDialog`. Then you can respond to user actions in the dialog box by intercepting dialog-related events in your main event loop and handling those events. The Dialog Manager calls the Control Manager to draw any controls you've put in the dialog box and handle user actions in them. If the dialog box contains any application-defined user items, you need to provide the Dialog Manager with a drawing procedure so that it knows how to draw the items. You also need to handle user actions for any such application-defined items yourself.

Creating a Modeless Dialog Box

You can create a modeless dialog box by calling `GetNewDialog` and passing it the resource ID of an appropriate `'DLOG'` resource. The Venn Diagrammer application supports only one modeless dialog box, in which the user can set various application preferences. Venn Diagrammer displays that dialog box after the user chooses the Preferences command from the Venn menu.

```
iGetVennPrefs:
    DoModelessDialog(rVennDPrefsDial, gPrefsDialog);
```

As you can see, Venn Diagrammer simply calls the application-defined procedure `DoModelessDialog`, passing it a resource ID specifying the dialog box to open and a global variable in which to return the dialog pointer created by `GetNewDialog`. Listing 7-2 defines the `DoModelessDialog` procedure.

Listing 7-2   Creating a modeless dialog box

```
PROCEDURE DoModelessDialog (myKind: Integer; VAR myDialog: DialogPtr);
   VAR
      myPointer:  Ptr;
BEGIN
   IF myDialog = NIL THEN                   {the dialog box doesn't exist yet}
      BEGIN
         myPointer := NewPtr(sizeof(DialogRecord));
         IF myPointer = NIL THEN
            exit(DoModelessDialog);

         myDialog := GetNewDialog(myKind, myPointer, WindowPtr(-1));
         IF myDialog <> NIL THEN
            BEGIN
               DoSetupUserItems(myKind, myDialog);     {set up user items}
               DoSetupCtrlValues(myDialog);            {set up initial values}
            END;
      END
   ELSE
      BEGIN
         ShowWindow(myDialog);
         SelectWindow(myDialog);
         SetPort(myDialog);
      END;
END;
```

The `DoModelessDialog` procedure first determines whether the specified dialog box has already been created, by checking the value of the global variable passed to it. If the variable contains any value other than `NIL`, the dialog box already exists (but is perhaps hidden or obscured by other windows). If so, `DoModelessDialog` simply makes the dialog box visible (by calling `ShowWindow`), makes it the active window (by calling `SelectWindow`), and establishes it as the current graphics port (by calling `SetPort`).

If, however, the specified dialog box doesn't exist yet, then `DoModelessDialog` allocates memory for a new dialog record and (if successful) calls `GetNewDialog`, passing it the appropriate resource ID. If `GetNewDialog` returns successfully (as indicated by a returned dialog pointer whose value isn't `NIL`), `DoModelessDialog` then calls two application-defined routines, `DoSetupUserItems` and `DoSetupCtrlValues`, to tell the Dialog Manager how draw the user items in the dialog box and to set the correct initial values for the dialog box's radio buttons and checkboxes.

Setting Up Application-Defined Items

Whenever a modeless dialog box contains application-defined user items, you need to tell the Dialog Manager how to draw them. You do this by calling the Dialog Manager procedure SetDialogItem for each application-defined item in the dialog box. Listing 7-3 shows the DoSetupUserItems procedure called by DoModelessDialog (defined in Listing 7-2).

Listing 7-3   Setting up application-defined dialog items

```
PROCEDURE DoSetupUserItems (myKind: Integer; VAR myDialog: DialogPtr);
    VAR
        myType:     Integer;
        myHand:     Handle;
        myRect:     Rect;
        count:      Integer;
        origPort:   GrafPtr;
BEGIN
    GetPort(origPort);
    SetPort(myDialog);

    CASE myKind OF
        rVennDPrefsDial:
            FOR count := 1 TO kVennPrefsItemCount DO
                IF count IN [iExist1Icon..iExist4Icon,
                                iEmpty1Icon..iEmpty4Icon] THEN
                BEGIN
                    GetDialogItem(myDialog, count, myType, myHand, myRect);
                    SetDialogItem(myDialog, count, myType, @DoUserItem, myRect);
                END;
        OTHERWISE
            ;
    END;

    SetPort(origPort);
END;
```

The DoSetupUserItems procedure simply selects the relevant application-defined items, retrieves information about each item (by calling GetDialogItem), and then calls SetDialogItem to associate a particular application-defined drawing procedure with each item. As you can see, the drawing procedure (DoUserItem) is the same for each user item in the Preferences dialog box. This is possible because the Dialog

Manager passes the drawing procedure the dialog pointer and item number when it wants a particular item to be drawn. Listing 7-4 defines the Venn Diagrammer procedure that draws user items.

Listing 7-4   Drawing application-defined dialog items

```
PROCEDURE DoUserItem (myDialog: DialogPtr; myItem: Integer);
   VAR
      myType:     Integer;
      myHand:     Handle;
      myRect:     Rect;
      origPort:   GrafPtr;
BEGIN
   GetPort(origPort);
   SetPort(myDialog);

   GetDialogItem(myDialog, myItem, myType, myHand, myRect);

   IF myDialog = gPrefsDialog THEN
      CASE myItcm OF
         iExist1Icon..iExist4Icon:
            BEGIN
               DoPlotIcon(myRect, GetIcon(kExistID + myItem - iExist1Icon),
                            myDialog, srcCopy);
            END;
         iEmpty1Icon..iEmpty4Icon:
            BEGIN
               DoPlotIcon(myRect, GetIcon(kEmptyID + myItem - iEmpty1Icon),
                            myDialog, srcCopy);
               FrameRect(myRect);
            END;
         OTHERWISE
            ;
      END; {CASE}

   SetPort(origPort);                    {restore original port}
END;
```

The DoUserItem procedure is also fairly simple. It makes sure that the dialog pointer passed to it picks out the Preferences dialog box. Then it calls the application-defined procedure DoPlotIcon (defined in Listing 5-8 on page 101) to draw the appropriate part of an icon in the item rectangle. If the emptiness patterns are being drawn, DoUserItem also draws a box around the pattern (by calling FrameRect).

Handling User Actions in a Modeless Dialog Box

The Venn Diagrammer application calls its `DoHandleDialogEvent` function for each event it retrieves from the Event Manager. Its strategy is to determine if the returned event applies to a dialog box. If so, `DoHandleDialogEvent` handles the event and returns `TRUE` to indicate that it did so; otherwise, `DoHandleDialogEvent` just returns `FALSE` to indicate that it didn't handle the event. Listing 7-5 defines `DoHandleDialogEvent`. (See Listing 4-4 on page 77 to see when `DoHandleDialogEvent` is called.)

Listing 7-5   Handling events in a modeless dialog box

```
FUNCTION DoHandleDialogEvent (myEvent: EventRecord): Boolean;
    VAR
        eventHandled:       Boolean;            {did we handle the event?}
        myDialog:           DialogPtr;
        myItem:             Integer;
BEGIN
    eventHandled := FALSE;
    IF FrontWindow <> NIL THEN
        IF IsDialogEvent(myEvent) THEN
            IF DialogSelect(myEvent, myDialog, myItem) THEN
                BEGIN
                    eventHandled := TRUE;
                    SetPort(myDialog);

                    IF myDialog = gPrefsDialog THEN
                        BEGIN
                            CASE myItem OF
                                iEmpty1Radio..iEmpty4Radio:
                                    gEmptyIndex := myItem;
                                iEmpty1Icon..iEmpty4Icon:
                                    gEmptyIndex := myItem - 4;
                                iExist1Radio..iExist4Radio:
                                    gExistIndex := myItem - iEmpty4Icon;
                                iExist1Icon..iExist4Icon:
                                    gExistIndex := myItem - (iEmpty4Icon + 4);
                                iGetNextRandomly:
                                    gStepRandom := NOT gStepRandom;
                                iAutoAdjust:
                                    gAutoAdjust := NOT gAutoAdjust;
                                iShowSchoolNames:
                                    gShowNames := NOT gShowNames;
                                iUseExistImport:
```

```
                    gGiveImport := NOT gGiveImport;
                iSaveVennPrefs:
                    DoSavePrefs;
                OTHERWISE
                    ;
            END;

            DoSetupCtrlValues(myDialog);        {update values}
        END;
    END;


    DoHandleDialogEvent := eventHandled;
END;
```

The `DoHandleDialogEvent` function calls the Dialog Manager's `IsDialogEvent` function to determine whether at the time of the event the frontmost window is a dialog box. If not, then `DoHandleDialogEvent` just exits and returns the value `FALSE`. If, however, the event did occur while a dialog box was active, then the event might apply to that dialog box. To determine whether it does apply, `DoHandleDialogEvent` calls the Dialog Manager's `DialogSelect` function, which handles most of the events relating to a dialog box. For example, if the event is an update or activate event for the dialog box, `DialogSelect` updates or activates the dialog box and returns `FALSE` (to indicate that no further processing is required by the calling application).

If the event involves an enabled item in the dialog box, `DialogSelect` returns a function result of `TRUE`. In the `myItem` parameter, it returns the item number of the item selected by the user. In the `myDialog` parameter, it returns a pointer to the dialog record for the dialog box where the event occurred. In all other cases, the `DialogSelect` function returns `FALSE`. When `DialogSelect` returns `TRUE`, you should do whatever is appropriate as a response to the event involving that item in that particular dialog box; when it returns `FALSE`, you should do nothing.

The `DoHandleDialogEvent` function uses a very simple technique for handling user selections of items in the Preferences dialog box. As you can see, it sets the appropriate application global variables for clicks of the radio buttons, and it toggles the appropriate global variables for clicks of the checkboxes. Then `DoHandleDialogEvent` calls the application-defined procedure `DoSetupCtrlValues` to change the values of those controls, turning the radio buttons and checkboxes off or on, as appropriate. Listing 7-6 gives the definition of `DoSetupCtrlValues`.

Listing 7-6   Setting the state of radio buttons and checkboxes

```
PROCEDURE DoSetupCtrlValues (myDialog: DialogPtr);
    VAR
        count:      Integer;
        myType:     Integer;
```

```
    myHand:      Handle;
    myRect:      Rect;
    origPort:    GrafPtr;
BEGIN
  IF myDialog = NIL THEN
    exit(DoSetupCtrlValues);

  GetPort(origPort);                  {save the current graphics port}
  SetPort(myDialog);                  {always do this before drawing}
  ShowWindow(myDialog);

  IF myDialog = gPrefsDialog THEN
    BEGIN
      FOR count := 1 TO kVennPrefsItemCount DO
        BEGIN
          GetDialogItem(myDialog, count, myType, myHand, myRect);
          IF myType = ctrlItem + radCtrl THEN
            CASE count OF
              iExist1Radio..iExist4Radio:
                SetCtlValue(ControlHandle(myHand),
                  ORD(gExistIndex = count - (iExist1Radio - 1)));
              iEmpty1Radio..iEmpty4Radio:
                SetCtlValue(ControlHandle(myHand),
                  ORD(gEmptyIndex = count - (iEmpty1Radio - 1)));
            OTHERWISE
              ;
            END;
          IF myType = ctrlItem + chkCtrl THEN
            CASE count OF
              iGetNextRandomly:
                SetCtlValue(ControlHandle(myHand),
                            ORD(gStepRandom = TRUE));
              iShowSchoolNames:
                SetCtlValue(ControlHandle(myHand),
                            ORD(gShowNames = TRUE));
              iUseExistImport:
                SetCtlValue(ControlHandle(myHand),
                            ORD(gGiveImport = TRUE));
              iAutoAdjust:
                SetCtlValue(ControlHandle(myHand),
                            ORD(gAutoAdjust = TRUE));
            OTHERWISE
              ;
```

```
            END;
        END;
    END;


    SetPort(origPort);                    {restore the previous graphics port}
END;
```

The `DoSetupCtrlValues` procedure simply calls the Control Manager procedure `SetCtlValue` to set the value of each control in the dialog box according to the value of some global variable. This makes it easy to toggle checkboxes and to group radio buttons in such a way that exactly one radio button in each group is on.

IMPORTANT

The strategy for handling dialog box events described in this section might not be the best or most efficient strategy for your application. For a more complete discussion of handling dialog box events, see the chapter "Dialog Manager" in *Inside Macintosh: Macintosh Toolbox Essentials.* ▲

Using Modal Dialog Boxes

Remember that a modal dialog box puts the user into the state or "mode" of being able to work only inside the dialog box. The user cannot move the dialog box and can dismiss it only by clicking its buttons (perhaps after supplying some necessary information).

Note

The Dialog Manager also provides **movable modal dialog boxes;** these are modal dialog boxes that contain a title bar so that the user can drag the dialog box. You should use movable modal dialog boxes whenever the user might need to move a modal dialog box to see what it obscures or whenever you want allow the user to switch to another application while the dialog box is displayed. ◆

In general, it's easier to create and handle simple modal dialog boxes than it is to create and handle modeless dialog boxes. The reason is that the Dialog Manager provides special routines that you can call to display alerts and other simple dialog boxes. The Dialog Manager also provides the `ModalDialog` procedure, which you can call to manage all user actions in modal dialog boxes.

IMPORTANT

Ease of implementation is not a sufficient reason for using modal dialog boxes instead of modeless ones. You should avoid using modal dialog boxes except when absolutely necessary. ▲

Displaying a Modal Dialog Box

Listing 7-7 shows a standard way to display a modal dialog box. It defines the procedure DoAboutBox, which is called after the user chooses the About Venn Diagrammer command from the Apple menu.

Listing 7-7   Displaying a modal dialog box

```
PROCEDURE DoAboutBox (myWindow: WindowPtr);
    VAR
        myWindow:    WindowPtr;
        myDialog:    DialogPtr;
        myItem:      Integer;
BEGIN
    myWindow := FrontWindow;
    IF myWindow <> NIL THEN
        DoActivate(myWindow, 1 - activeFlag);

    myDialog := GetNewDialog(rAboutDial, NIL, WindowPtr(-1));
    IF myDialog <> NIL THEN
        BEGIN
            SetPort(myDialog);
            DoDefaultButton(myDialog);

            REPEAT
                ModalDialog(@MyModalFilter, myItem);
            UNTIL myItem = iOK;

            DisposeDialog(myDialog);
            SetPort(myWindow);
        END;
END;
```

When you display a modal dialog box, you should first deactivate any existing front window. The DoAboutBox procedure retrieves a window pointer to the front window and passes that pointer to the application-defined activate routine DoActivate. Then DoAboutBox calls GetNewDialog to open the dialog box specified by the resource ID rAboutDial:

```
CONST
    rAboutDial = 7000;            {resource ID of About dialog}
```

If GetNewDialog returns a dialog pointer whose value is not NIL, then DoAboutBox calls SetPort to establish the new dialog box as the current drawing port. Then it calls the application-defined procedure DoDefaultButton (defined in Listing 7-8) to draw a

Dialog Boxes

thick border around the default button. This indicates that the user can dismiss the dialog box by pressing the Return key or the Enter key.

Listing 7-8   Outlining the default button of a modal dialog box

```
PROCEDURE DoDefaultButton (myDialog: DialogPtr);
    VAR
        myType:     Integer;
        myHand:     Handle;
        myRect:     Rect;
BEGIN
    GetDialogItem(myDialog, iOK, myType, myHand, myRect);
    DoOutlineControl(myHand);
END;
```

The `DoDefaultButton` procedure simply calls the application-defined procedure `DoOutlineControl` to outline the dialog item whose item number is 1 (identified by the constant `iOK`). See page 200 for a definition of `DoOutlineControl`.

At this point, the modal dialog box is displayed on the screen. The `DoAboutBox` procedure loops indefinitely, repeatedly calling `ModalDialog` until the user clicks the OK button. The `ModalDialog` procedure handles all mouse, keystroke, and update events that occur inside the dialog box until an event involving an enabled dialog item occurs. When that happens, `ModalDialog` exits and returns the dialog item number in the second parameter. Your application can then do whatever is appropriate in response to an event in that item. In `DoAboutBox`, `ModalDialog` is called repeatedly until a click in the OK button occurs. At that time, the modal dialog is removed from the screen, and `DoAboutBox` calls `SetPort` to reinstate the original drawing port.

Defining a Modal Dialog Filter Function

The actions of `ModalDialog` are guided by the **modal dialog filter function** whose address is passed in its first parameter. If you pass `NIL` as the first parameter to the `ModalDialog` procedure, you'll get the standard event filtering provided by the Dialog Manager. The standard event filter function returns `TRUE` and causes `ModalDialog` to return item number 1 (the number of the default button) when the user presses the Return or the Enter key.

For most modal dialog boxes, the standard modal dialog filter function is too simple. Your application should define a modal dialog filter function that performs the following tasks:

■ return `TRUE` and the item number for the default button if the user presses the Return key or the Enter key

■ return `TRUE` and the item number for the Cancel button if the user presses the Escape key or the Command-period combination

- allow background applications to receive update events and return FALSE when they do

- return FALSE for all other events that your event filter doesn't handle

Listing 7-9 defines a modal dialog filter function that accomplishes these tasks. In addition, the filter function MyModalFilter handles any disk-inserted events that occur while the modal dialog box is displayed.

Listing 7-9   A modal dialog filter function

```
FUNCTION MyModalFilter (myDialog: DialogPtr; VAR myEvent: EventRecord;
                        VAR myItem: Integer): Boolean;
    VAR
        myType:     Integer;
        myHand:     Handle;
        myRect:     Rect;
        myKey:      Char;
        myIgnore:   LongInt;
BEGIN
    MyModalFilter := FALSE;                {assume we don't handle the event}

    CASE myEvent.what OF
        updateEvt:
            BEGIN
                IF WindowPtr(myEvent.message) <> myDialog THEN
                    DoUpdate(WindowPtr(myEvent.message));
                                           {update the window behind}
            END;
        keyDown, autoKey:
            BEGIN
                myKey := char(BAnd(myEvent.message, charCodeMask));

                {if Return or Enter pressed, do default button}
                IF (myKey = kReturn) OR (myKey = kEnter) THEN
                    BEGIN
                        GetDialogItem(myDialog, iOK, myType, myHand, myRect);
                        HiliteControl(ControlHandle(myHand), 1);
                                    {make button appear to have been pressed}
                        Delay(kVisualDelay, myIgnore);
                        HiliteControl(ControlHandle(myHand), 0);
                        MyModalFilter := TRUE;
                        myItem := iOK;
                    END;
```

```
        {if Escape or Cmd-. pressed, do Cancel button}
        IF (myKey = kEscape)
            OR ((myKey = kPeriod)
                    AND (BAnd(myEvent.modifiers, CmdKey) <> 0)) THEN
            BEGIN
                GetDialogItem(myDialog, iCancel, myType, myHand, myRect);
                HiliteControl(ControlHandle(myHand), 1);
                            {make button appear to have been pressed}
                Delay(kVisualDelay, myIgnore);
                HiliteControl(ControlHandle(myHand), 0);
                MyModalFilter := TRUE;
                myItem := iCancel;
            END;
        END;
    diskEvt:
        BEGIN
            DoDiskEvent(myEvent);
            MyModalFilter := TRUE;               {show we've handled the event}
        END;
    OTHERWISE
        ;
    END; {CASE}
END;
```

An interesting part of `MyModalFilter` is the way it intercepts key-down events and translates them into button clicks. When, for instance, it detects that the Return key was pressed, it calls `GetDialogItem` to retrieve a handle to the first item in the item list (by convention, the OK button). Then `MyModalFilter` calls `HiliteControl` to invert the state of the button, waits for a specified number of ticks, and then calls `HiliteControl` once again to restore the button to its original state. Finally, it sets the function result and the variable parameter `myItem`, thus informing the calling routine that the event was handled.

Menus

Contents

This chapter describes how your application can use the Menu Manager to create and manage menus. Menus provide a simple and standard method for the user to view or choose from a list of commands and settings that your application provides. Every Macintosh application that has a user interface should support pull-down menus (that is, menus that the user "pulls down" by pressing the mouse button when the cursor is over the menu title in the menu bar).

This chapter shows how to

- create menu and menu bar resources

- open those resources to display the menu bar

- handle user clicks in the menu bar

- handle user choices of menu items

- handle keyboard equivalents of menu commands

- enable and disable menu items

Most Macintosh applications provide more menu handling than is illustrated in this chapter. For example, you might want to use pop-up menus in a window or dialog box. For a complete description of the capabilities of the Menu Manager and for code samples illustrating more advanced menu-handling techniques, see the chapter "Menu Manager" in *Inside Macintosh: Macintosh Toolbox Essentials*.

About Menus

A **menu** is a user interface element that your application can create to allow the user to view or choose an item from a list of commands and options that your application provides. For example, the sample application Venn Diagrammer provides a menu (shown in Figure 8-1) that contains a list of commands for manipulating Venn diagrams.

Figure 8-1 A typical pull-down menu

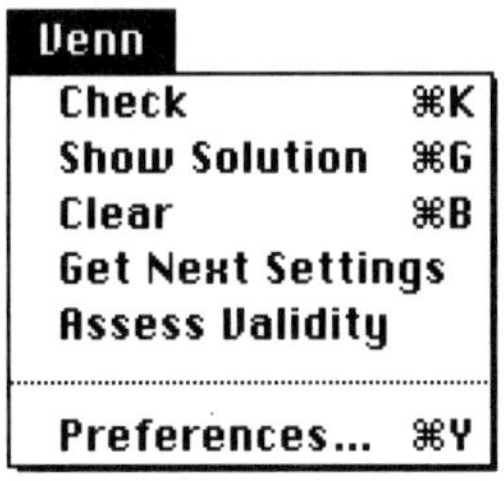

This kind of menu is known as a **pull-down menu,** because the user "pulls down" the menu by clicking the **menu title** (the word "Venn" in the menu bar). A pull-down menu always has associated with it one or more **menu items,** rectangles containing text and other characteristics that identify a command that the user can choose to perform an action. The menu shown in Figure 8-1 contains six menu items and one **divider** (the gray line used to separate the first five items from the last one). In addition, four of the menu items in that menu have **keyboard equivalents** associated with them. The user can invoke the menu command by pressing the appropriate combination of characters on the keyboard. For example, the user can make the Preferences dialog box appear by pressing the combination Command-Y.

Note

This chapter shows how to create and handle pull-down menus only.
The word "menu" should therefore be understood to mean "pull-down menu." ◆

The Menu Manager provides routines that allow you to create your application's **menu bar** and menus, and to handle user actions in the menu bar and in individual menus. You'll call these routines when you detect that a mouse-down event has occurred in the menu bar or when you detect that the user has typed a keyboard equivalent of a menu command. You'll also call the Menu Manager to perform other operations on menus, such as changing menu item text or enabling and disabling menu items.

All Macintosh applications should support at least three standard menus: the Apple menu, the File menu, and the Edit menu. In addition, you'll want to support other menus that contain commands and options specific to your application. The Venn Diagrammer application supports only one application-specific menu along with the three standard menus.

Creating Menus

The easiest way to define menu titles and commands is to use a resource editor like ResEdit to create resources describing your application's menu bar and the individual menus. It's also possible to define your menu bar and menu items internally in your application, but you can make your application significantly easier to localize by isolating that information in resources.

Note

As you learned in the chapter "Resources," you can also create resources using the Rez resource-description language and a resource compiler. This chapter shows how to use ResEdit to create menu-related resources. ◆

Creating a Menu Resource

You can define the menu title and characteristics of each individual menu item in a **menu resource** (a resource of type 'MENU'). Figure 8-2 shows the appearance of ResEdit's 'MENU' resource editor.

Menus

Figure 8-2   Defining a `'MENU'` resource

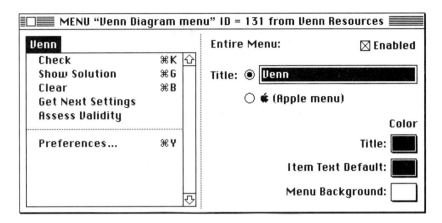

As you can see, the menu title is currently selected. ResEdit allows you to change the menu title text or to designate this menu as the Apple menu. This window also lets you set the menu as initially enabled or disabled. In most cases, you'll want to have your menus initially enabled. The Venn Diagrammer application, however, disables the Edit menu because it does not support any text editing.

To edit the text of a menu command, you can click it. ResEdit highlights the selected command and changes the controls in the right side of the window, as shown in Figure 8-3.

Figure 8-3   Editing a menu command

You can use the controls in the right side of the window to change the menu item text, the keyboard equivalent, the menu's mark, and several other items. You can also designate the menu item as initially enabled or disabled. Once again, you'll probably want most items to be initially enabled. You can disable and reenable menu items dynamically during your application's execution; see "Handling Menu Choices" beginning on page 156 for details.

Creating a Menu Bar Resource

You can define the order and resource IDs of the menus in your application in a **menu bar resource** (a resource of type 'MBAR'). You should define your 'MBAR' resource in such a way that the Apple menu is the first menu in the menu bar. You should define the next two menus as the File and Edit menus, followed by any other menus that your application uses. You do not need to define the Keyboard, Help, or Application menus in your 'MBAR' resource; the Menu Manager automatically adds them to your application's menu bar if your application calls the GetNewMBar function and your menu bar includes an Apple menu or if your application inserts the Apple menu into the current menu list using the InsertMenu procedure.

You can use ResEdit to create an 'MBAR' resource. Figure 8-4 shows the 'MBAR' resource window for the Venn Diagrammer application.

Figure 8-4   An 'MBAR' resource in ResEdit

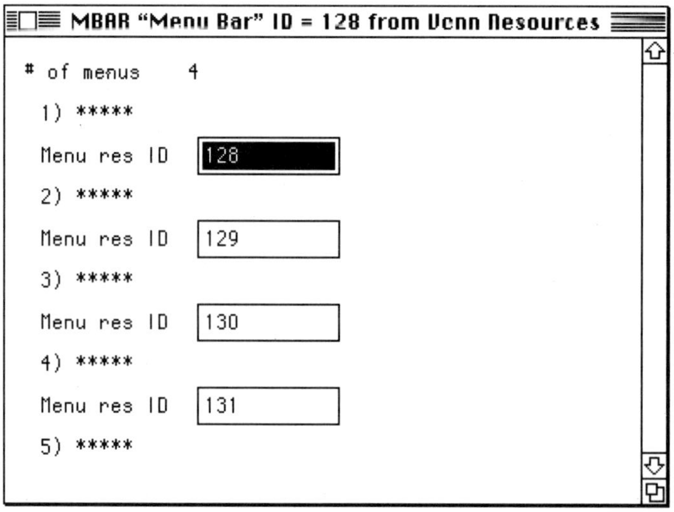

An 'MBAR' resource is simply a list of the **menu IDs,** in the order you want the corresponding menu titles to appear from left to right in the menu bar.

Setting Up the Menu Bar and Menus

One of the very first things you need to do when your application starts running is set up your menu bar and menus. You can do this by calling the Menu Manager function GetNewMBar, which reads a specified 'MBAR' resource from your application's resource fork and inserts each menu described there into the menu bar. You can define a constant that indicates which 'MBAR' resource to open.

```
CONST
    rMenuBar = 128;                      {menu bar resource ID}
```

Listing 8-1 shows a standard way to call GetNewMBar.

Listing 8-1   Setting up the menu bar and menus

```
PROCEDURE DoSetupMenus;
    VAR
        menuBar:     Handle;
BEGIN
    menuBar := GetNewMBar(rMenuBar);
    IF menuBar = NIL THEN
        DoBadError(eCantFindMenus);

    SetMenuBar(menuBar);
    DisposeHandle(menuBar);
    AppendResMenu(GetMenuHandle(mApple), 'DRVR');
    DrawMenuBar;
END;
```

The routine DoSetupMenus creates the application's menu bar by reading in the definition from the 'MBAR' resource with resource ID rMenuBar. The GetNewMBar function returns a handle to the menu bar information stored in that resource and in the 'MENU' resources whose IDs are contained in the 'MBAR' resource. Notice that DoSetupMenus makes sure that the value of the returned handle isn't NIL; if it is, you shouldn't continue.

Note

Checking that GetNewMBar returns handle with a non-NIL value is probably overkill. It's extremely unlikely that the Menu Manager will have a problem reading your menu-related resources or finding enough free memory to hold the menu list to which menuBar is a handle. Nonetheless, it's best to make sure, because passing AppendResMenu a handle whose value is NIL is likely to cause your application to crash. As a result, DoSetupMenus calls the application-defined routine DoBadError (defined in Listing 9-5 on page 178) to alert the user of the problem and terminate the application. If the application can't even put up its menu bar, there's no point in continuing to run. (See Figure 7-2 on page 134 for the alert box displayed if the menu resources can't be found.) ◆

If `GetNewMBar` returns a handle with a non-`NIL` value, then `DoSetupMenus` calls the procedure `SetMenuBar` to install the individual menus into the menu bar. At that point, you no longer need the handle and you can dispose of it (by calling the Memory Manager routine `DisposeHandle`). Next `DoSetupMenus` calls the `AppendResMenu` procedure to add the items in the Apple Menu Items folder to the Apple menu. Finally, the `DoSetupMenus` procedure displays the menu bar by calling the `DrawMenuBar` procedure.

Handling Menu Choices

Your application is informed of user menu choices in a slightly roundabout fashion. First, your application receives a mouse-down event indicating that the user has clicked in the menu bar. At that time, you should call the Menu Manager function `MenuSelect` to determine which menu and menu item, if any, the user chose. When you call `MenuSelect`, the Menu Manager pulls down the appropriate menu and tracks all subsequent mouse movement in the menu. When the user releases the mouse button, `MenuSelect` exits and returns to your application a long integer that indicates which menu and item the user chose. The high-order word of that long integer contains the menu number, and the low-order word contains the menu item number.

To coordinate the menu numbers and menu item numbers with the menus and menu items as defined in your `'MBAR'` and `'MENU'` resources, you'll probably want to define a set of constants, as shown in Listing 8-2.

Listing 8-2   Defining menu numbers and menu item numbers

```
CONST
     mApple        = 128;              {resource ID of Apple menu}
     iAbout        = 1;                {our About... dialog}

     mFile         = 129;             {resource ID of File menu}
     iNew          = 1;
     iClose        = 2;
     iQuit         = 4;

     mEdit         = 130;             {resource ID of Edit menu}
     iUndo         = 1;
     iCut          = 3;
     iCopy         = 4;
     iPaste        = 5;
     iClear        = 6;

     mVenn         = 131;             {resource ID of Venn menu}
```

Menus

```
iCheckVenn      = 1;
iDoVenn         = 2;
iClearVenn      = 3;
iNextTask       = 4;
iCheckArg       = 5;
iGetVennPrefs   = 7;
```

Note

The divider in a menu counts as a menu item, even though the user can't choose it. ◆

In general, you'll define a routine like DoMenuCommand shown in Listing 8-3 to handle all menu choices. Both your mouse-down event handler (Listing 6-9 on page 121) and your key-down event handler (Listing 8-5 on page 160) call MenuSelect. It is passed either the result of MenuSelect (for menu selections) or MenuKey (for keyboard equivalents of menu selections).

Listing 8-3   Handling menu selections

```
PROCEDURE DoMenuCommand (menuAndItem: LongInt);
    VAR
        myMenuNum:  Integer;
        myItemNum:  Integer;
        myResult:   Integer;
        myDAName:   Str255;
        myWindow:   WindowPtr;
BEGIN
    myMenuNum := HiWord(menuAndItem);
    myItemNum := LoWord(menuAndItem);
    GetPort(myWindow);

    CASE myMenuNum OF
        mApple:
            CASE myItemNum OF
                iAbout:
                    BEGIN
                        DoAboutBox;
                    END;
                OTHERWISE
                    BEGIN
                        GetMenuItemText(GetMenuHandle(mApple), myItemNum,
                                        myDAName);
                        myResult := OpenDeskAcc(myDAName);
                    END;
```

```
        END;
mFile:
    BEGIN
        CASE myItemNum OF
            iNew:
                myWindow := DoCreateWindow;
            iClose:
                DoCloseWindow(FrontWindow);
            iQuit:
                DoQuit;
            OTHERWISE
                ;
        END;
    END;
mEdit:
    BEGIN
        IF NOT SystemEdit(myItemNum - 1) THEN
            ;
    END;
mVennD:
    BEGIN
        myWindow := FrontWindow;
        CASE myItemNum OF
            iCheckVenn:
                DoVennCheck(myWindow);
            iDoVenn:
                DoVennAnswer(myWindow);
            iClearVenn:
                DoVennClear(myWindow);
            iNextTask:
                DoVennNext(myWindow);
            iCheckArg:
                DoVennAssess(myWindow);
            iGetVennPrefs:
                DoModelessDialog(rVennDPrefsDial, gPrefsDialog);
            OTHERWISE
                ;
        END;
    END;

OTHERWISE
    ;
```

```
  END;
  HiliteMenu(0);
END;
```

The DoMenuCommand procedure is passed a long integer that encodes the menu number and item number of the chosen item. As you can see, DoMenuCommand consists mainly of a CASE statement that branches on the menu number. Each menu number, in turn, consists mainly of a CASE statement that branches on the menu item number. In this simple way, you can handle all menus and all menu items.

Most of the innermost branches just call application-defined routines to handle the appropriate menu item choice. (For example, if the user chooses Quit from the File menu, then DoMenuCommand calls the application-defined routine DoQuit.) The code that handles choices in the Apple menu (Listing 8-4) is slightly different, however.

Listing 8-4   Handling Apple menu selections

```
iAbout:
    BEGIN
        DoAboutBox;
    END;
OTHERWISE
    BEGIN
        GetMenuItemText(GetMenuHandle(mApple), myItemNum, myDAName);
        myResult := OpenDeskAcc(myDAName);
    END;
```

If the user chooses the command About Venn Diagrammer (picked out by the constant iAbout), then DoMenuCommand calls the application-defined routine DoAboutBox (see Listing 7-7 on page 145). Otherwise, the user must have chosen a desk accessory or other item in the Apple menu. In that case, DoMenuCommand retrieves the name of the desk accessory (by calling GetMenuItemText) and passes that name to the OpenDeskAcc function.

Because Venn Diagrammer doesn't support any text editing, it simply calls the system software routine SystemEdit to handle user choices in the Edit menu. SystemEdit checks whether the frontmost window belongs to a desk accessory; if so, it passes the menu choice to the desk accessory and returns TRUE. The parameter to SystemEdit is interpreted so you can pass the item number less 1 of the standard Edit menu commands.

Before exiting, DoMenuCommand calls the Menu Manager procedure HiliteMenu to undo the menu title highlighting provided automatically by MenuSelect or MenuKey.

Handling Keyboard Equivalents

Keyboard equivalents of menu commands allow the user to invoke a menu command from the keyboard. You can determine if the user chose the keyboard equivalent of a menu command by examining the event record for a key-down event. If the user pressed the Command key in combination with another character, you can then determine if this combination maps to a known **Command-key equivalent** by calling the Menu Manager function MenuKey. Listing 8-5 shows the Venn Diagrammer application's DoKeyDown procedure, which handles key-down events and determines if a keyboard equivalent was pressed.

Listing 8-5   Handling Command-key equivalents

```
PROCEDURE DoKeyDown (myEvent: EventRecord);
    VAR
        myKey:        char;
BEGIN
    myKey := chr(BAnd(myEvent.message, charCodeMask));
    IF (BAnd(myEvent.modifiers, CmdKey) <> 0) THEN
        BEGIN
            DoMenuAdjust;
            DoMenuCommand(MenuKey(myKey));
        END;
END;
```

The DoKeyDown procedure first extracts the pressed key from the message field of the event record and then examines the modifiers field to determine whether the Command key was also pressed. If so, the application first adjusts its menus and then calls the DoMenuCommand procedure defined in Listing 8-3 on page 157. In turn, DoKeyDown passes to DoMenuCommand the value returned from the MenuKey function. If the key combination pressed by the user is not the keyboard equivalent of any currently enabled menu item, then MenuKey sets the high-order word of its return value to 0.

Note

The Venn Diagrammer application does not accept any text input from the user. As a result, the DoKeyDown procedure shown in Listing 8-5 doesn't need an ELSE clause to handle keypresses in which the Command key is not held down. ◆

Several keyboard equivalents (listed in Table 8-1) are reserved for common commands in the File and Edit menus. If your application supports these commands, you should assign these equivalents to the specified commands. Otherwise, you should ignore these keyboard equivalents.

Menus

Table 8-1   Reserved keyboard equivalents

Keys	Command	Menu
⌘-A	Select All	Edit
⌘-C	Copy	Edit
⌘-N	New	File
⌘-O	Open...	File
⌘-P	Print...	File
⌘-Q	Quit	File
⌘-S	Save	File
⌘-V	Paste	Edit
⌘-W	Close	File
⌘-X	Cut	Edit
⌘-Z	Undo	Edit

IMPORTANT

You should never assign the keyboard equivalents listed in Table 8-1 to other menu commands. This helps ensure predictable behavior among all applications. ▲

Adjusting Menus

At any given time during the execution of your application, it's likely that some of the commands in your menus will not be appropriate. For example, if the front window is a dialog window, then any menu commands that manipulate only document windows should be disabled. Similarly, if the desktop shows no windows belonging to your application, then the Close command in the File menu should be disabled. When a menu item is disabled, it is drawn in a dimmed text and is not highlighted when the cursor passes over it. This disabling prevents the user from choosing those commands.

An easy way to achieve this effect is to call an application-defined routine that adjusts the menus according to the current application context just before you call either `MenuSelect` or `MenuKey`. Listing 8-6 shows the version of `DoMenuAdjust` used by the Venn Diagrammer application.

Listing 8-6   Adjusting menus

```
PROCEDURE DoMenuAdjust;
   VAR
      myWindow:    WindowPtr;
      myMenu:      MenuHandle;
      count:       Integer;
```

```
BEGIN
    myWindow := FrontWindow;

    IF myWindow = NIL THEN
        DisableMenuItem(GetMenuHandle(mFile), iClose)
    ELSE
        EnableMenuItem(GetMenuHandle(mFile), iClose);

    myMenu := GetMenuHandle(mVennD);
    IF IsAppWindow(myWindow) THEN
        FOR count := 1 TO kNumTools DO
            EnableMenuItem(myMenu, count)
    ELSE
        FOR count := 1 TO kNumTools DO
            DisableMenuItem(myMenu, count);

    IF IsDAccWindow(myWindow) THEN
        EnableMenuItem(GetMenuHandle(mEdit), 0)
    ELSE
        DisableMenuItem(GetMenuHandle(mEdit), 0);
    DrawMenuBar;
END;
```

The DoMenuAdjust procedure calls FrontWindow to get a pointer to the frontmost window belonging to the Venn Diagrammer application. If there is no window belonging to the Venn Diagrammer application, DoMenuAdjust disables the Close menu command in the File menu. Conversely, if there is a window belonging to the application, DoMenuAdjust enables the Close command.

If the front window is a document window, then DoMenuAdjust enables all the document-specific commands in the Venn menu; otherwise, it disables all those commands. (DoMenuAdjust retrieves the menu handle by calling GetMenuHandle and passes that handle to EnableMenuItem or DisableMenuItem.)

You can disable or enable an entire menu by passing DisableMenuItem or EnableMenuItem the value 0 in place of a menu item number. This is the strategy that DoMenuAdjust follows for the Edit menu. Venn Diagrammer does no editing of its own, so DoMenuAdjust makes certain to enable the Edit menu only when a desk accessory window is frontmost. When you call DisableMenuItem or EnableMenuItem in this way, however, you also need to call the Menu Manager procedure DrawMenuBar to update the menu bar's appearance.

Processes

Contents

Processes

Your application is usually only one of several applications that a user has open at one time. Your application must therefore share the available system resources such as the central processing unit (CPU) and the available random-access memory (RAM). The Macintosh Operating System uses a very simple and elegant method for your application to coordinate its actions with those of other open applications. The Process Manager sends events, through the Event Manager, to your application informing it of impending changes in your application's processing status. Your application needs to respond to those events in the appropriate way to ensure the smooth operation of all open applications.

This chapter describes what you need to do to ensure that your application operates smoothly in the Macintosh Operating System. It describes how your application is launched and how the Operating System controls access to the CPU and other system resources to create a cooperative multitasking environment in which your application and any other open applications execute. This environment is managed primarily by the Process Manager, which is responsible for launching processes, scheduling their use of the available system resources, and handling their termination. This chapter shows how to

- indicate the desired size of your application's memory partition
- suspend your application's execution when another application needs the CPU
- resume execution when your application regains control of the CPU
- terminate your application when the user quits or when a serious error occurs
- determine what software and hardware features are available on a particular machine

For a complete description of the cooperative multitasking environment, see the chapter "Process Manager" in *Inside Macintosh: Processes*. For a complete description of how to handle suspend and resume events, see the chapter "Event Manager" in *Inside Macintosh: Macintosh Toolbox Essentials*.

About Processes

The Macintosh Operating System, the Finder, and several other system software components work together to provide a **multitasking environment** in which a user can have multiple applications open at once and can switch between open applications as desired. To run in this environment, however, your application must follow certain rules governing its use of the available system resources. Because the smooth operation of all applications depends on their cooperation, this environment is known as a **cooperative multitasking environment.**

Note
The cooperative multitasking environment is available in system software versions 7.0 and later, and when the MultiFinder option is enabled in earlier system software versions. ◆

Processes

Although a number of documents and applications can be open at the same time, only one application is the active application. The **active application** is the application currently interacting with the user; its icon appears at the right side of the menu bar. The active application displays its menu bar and is responsible for highlighting the controls of its frontmost window. In Figure 9-1, Venn Diagrammer is the active application. Windows of other applications are visible on the desktop behind the frontmost window.

Figure 9-1   The desktop with several applications open

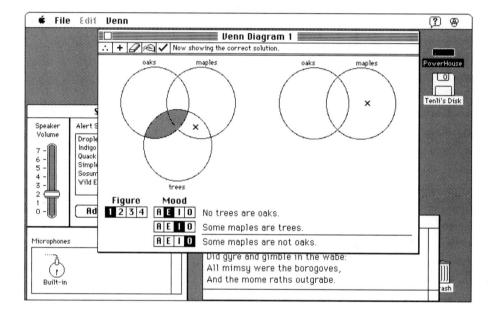

The Operating System schedules the processing of all applications and desk accessories, known collectively as **processes.** When a user opens an application, the Operating System loads the application code into memory and schedules the application to run at the next available opportunity, usually when the current process relinquishes the CPU. In most cases, the application runs immediately (or so it appears to the user).

When your application is first launched, it is the **foreground process.** Usually the foreground process has control of the CPU and other system resources, but it can agree to relinquish control of the CPU if there are no events (other than null events) pending for it. A process that is open but that isn't currently the foreground process is said to be a **background process.**

A background process can receive processing time when the foreground process makes an event call (that is, calls `WaitNextEvent` or `EventAvail`) and there are no events pending for that foreground process. The Process Manager sends a null event to the background process, thereby informing it that it is now the current process and can perform whatever background processing it desires. The background process should make an event call periodically in order to relinquish the CPU and ensure a timely return to foreground processing when necessary.

The CPU is available only to the current application, whether it is running in the foreground or the background. The application can be interrupted only by hardware interrupts, which are transparent to the application. However, to give processing time to background applications and to allow the user to interact with your application and others, you must periodically call the Event Manager's `WaitNextEvent` or `EventAvail` function to allow your application to relinquish control of the CPU for short periods. By using these event routines in your application, you allow the user to interact not only with your application but also with other applications.

The method by which the available processing time is distributed among multiple processes is known as **context switching** (or just **switching**). All switching occurs at a well-defined time, namely, when an application calls `WaitNextEvent`. When a context switch occurs, the Process Manager allocates processing time to a process other than the one that had been receiving processing time. Two types of context switching may occur: major and minor.

A **major switch** is a complete context switch: an application's windows are moved from the back to the front, or vice versa. In a major switch, two applications are involved, the one being switched to the foreground and the one being switched to the background. The Process Manager switches the A5 worlds of both applications, as well as the relevant low-memory environments. If those applications can handle suspend and resume events, they are so notified at the time that a major switch occurs.

A **minor switch** occurs when the Process Manager gives time to a background process without bringing the background process to the front. The two processes involved in a minor switch can be two background processes or a foreground process and a background process. As in a major switch, the Process Manager switches the A5 worlds and the low-memory environments of the two processes. However, the order of windows is not switched, and neither process receives either suspend or resume events.

When the frontmost window is an alert box or modal dialog box, major switching does not occur, although minor switching can. To determine whether major switching can occur, the Operating System checks (among other things) whether the window definition procedure of the frontmost window is `dBoxProc`, because the type `dBoxProc` is specifically reserved for alert boxes and modal dialog boxes. (If the frontmost window is a movable modal dialog box, major switching can still occur.)

Note
Your application can also be switched out if it calls a system software routine that internally makes an event call. For example, when your application calls `ModalDialog`, a minor switch can occur. ◆

Specifying Processing Options

To take full advantage of the cooperative multitasking environment provided by the Macintosh system software, you need to inform the Operating System about the processing capabilities and requirements of your application. You need to indicate, for example, the partition size your application needs in order to execute most effectively. You also need to indicate whether your application can do any processing while it is in the background. If it cannot do any background processing, there's no use in having the Process Manager give your application access to the CPU while it's in the background.

You specify these and other processing options to the Operating System by including in your application's resource fork a resource of type `'SIZE'`, known as its **size resource.** The size resource contains several long integers and many flag bits, which together give the Process Manager the information it needs to launch your application and control its processing.

IMPORTANT

Every application executing in system software version 7.0 and later, as well as every application executing in system software version 6.0 with MultiFinder, should contain a size resource. ▲

A `'SIZE'` resource consists of a 16-bit flags field, followed by two 32-bit size fields. The flags field specifies operating characteristics of your application, and the size fields indicate the minimum and preferred partition sizes for your application. The **minimum partition size** is the actual limit below which your application will not run. The **preferred partition size** is the memory size at which your application can run most effectively. The Operating System attempts to secure this preferred amount of memory when your application is launched. If that amount of memory is unavailable, your application is placed into the largest contiguous block available, provided that it is larger than the specified minimum size.

Note

If the amount of available memory is between the minimum and the preferred sizes, the Finder displays a dialog box asking if the user wants to run the application using the amount of memory available. If your application does not have a `'SIZE'` resource, it is assigned a default partition size of 512 KB, and the Process Manager uses a default value of `FALSE` for all specifications normally defined by constants in the flags field. ◆

When you define a `'SIZE'` resource, you should give it a resource ID of –1. A user can modify the preferred size in the Finder's information window for your application. If the user does alter the partition size, the Operating System creates a new `'SIZE'` resource having a resource ID of 0 in your application's resource fork. At application launch time, the Process Manager looks for a `'SIZE'` resource with ID 0; if this resource is not found, the Process Manager uses your original `'SIZE'` resource (with ID –1). This new `'SIZE'` resource is also created when the user modifies any of the other settings in the resource.

Listing 9-1 shows the Rez input for a sample 'SIZE' resource.

Listing 9-1   The Rez input for a sample 'SIZE' resource

```
resource 'SIZE' (-1) {
    reserved,                        /*reserved*/
    acceptSuspendResumeEvents,       /*accepts suspend and resume events*/
    reserved,                        /*reserved*/
    cannotBackground,                /*can't use background null events*/
    doesActivateOnFGSwitch,          /*activates own windows in */
                                     /* response to OS events*/
    backgroundAndForeground,         /*application has a user interface*/
    dontGetFrontClicks,              /*don't return mouse events */
                                     /* in front window on resume*/
    ignoreAppDiedEvents,             /*doesn't want app-died events*/
    is32BitCompatible,               /*works with 24- or 32-bit addr*/
    notHighLevelEventAware,          /*can't use high-level events*/
    onlyLocalHLEvents,               /*can't use remote high-level events*/
    notStationeryAware,              /*can't use stationery documents*/
    dontUseTextEditServices,         /*can't use inline input services*/
    reserved,                        /*reserved*/
    reserved,                        /*reserved*/
    reserved,                        /*reserved*/
    kPrefSize * 1024,                /*preferred memory size*/
    kMinSize * 1024                  /*minimum memory size*/
};
```

The 'SIZE' resource specification in Listing 9-1 indicates, among other things, that the application accepts suspend and resume events, does no processing in the background, activates or deactivates any windows as necessary in response to operating-system events, has a user interface, and doesn't want to receive any mouse event associated with a resume event that was caused by the user clicking in the application's front window. In this example, the Rez input file must define values for the constants kPrefSize and kMinSize; for example, if kPrefSize is set to 50, the preferred partition size is 50 KB.

Note

See the chapter "Event Manager" in *Inside Macintosh: Macintosh Toolbox Essentials* for a more complete description of the 'SIZE' resource. ◆

The numbers you specify as your application's preferred and minimum partition sizes depend on the particular memory requirements of your application. Your application's memory requirements depend in turn on the size of your application's A5 world, heap, and stack. (See the chapter "Memory" earlier in this book for details about these areas of your application's partition.)

You can usually make a fairly reliable estimate of the size of your application's A5 world by determining the size of your application's global variables and its jump table (whose size you can determine by looking at the size of your compiled application's `CODE` resource with ID 0). You can also make a good guess about the size of your application's static heap objects—objects that are always present during the execution of your application (for example, code segments, Toolbox data structures for window records, and so on).

It's a little bit more work to determine the amount of space you'll need to reserve for dynamic heap objects. These include objects created on a per-document basis (which may vary in size proportionally with the document itself) and objects required for specific commands or functions. Perhaps the best advice to follow in determining your application's minimum and preferred partition sizes is to experiment with reasonable values and make sure that there is always enough memory to meet reasonable requests from the user. You can also use tools such as MacsBug's heap-exploring commands to help empirically determine your application's dynamic memory requirements.

Handling Suspend and Resume Events

Your application receives suspend and resume events as a result of changes in its processing status. When your application is in the foreground and the Process Manager wants to switch it into the background, the Process Manager sends it a **suspend event.** This is a signal to your application to prepare to be switched out. Your application isn't actually switched out immediately. Instead, the Process Manager gives your application a chance to handle the suspend event. Your application is switched out at the *next* event call it makes. Similarly, the application that is about to be switched into the foreground is sent a **resume event** once it's actually switched. The resume event is a signal to that application that it can resume normal foreground processing.

Upon receiving a suspend event, your application should deactivate the front window, remove the highlighting from any selections, and hide any floating windows. Your application should also convert any private scrap into the global scrap, if necessary. If your application shows a window that displays the Clipboard contents, you should hide this window also, because the user might change the contents of the Clipboard before returning to your application. Your application can also do anything else necessary to get ready for a major switch. Then your application should call `WaitNextEvent` to relinquish the processor and allow the Operating System to schedule other processes for execution.

Processes

Upon receiving a resume event, your application should activate the front window and restore any windows to the state the user left them in at the time of the previous suspend event. For example, your application should show scroll bars, restore any selections that were previously in effect, and show any floating windows. Your application should copy the contents of the Clipboard and convert the data back to its private scrap, if necessary. If your application shows a window that displays the Clipboard contents, you can update the contents of the window after reading in the scrap. Your application can then resume interacting with the user.

Responding to a suspend or resume event usually involves activating or deactivating windows. If you set the acceptSuspendResumeEvents flag and the doesActivateOnFGSwitch flag in your application's 'SIZE' resource, your application is responsible for activating or deactivating its windows when it handles suspend and resume events.

Listing 9-2 defines the routine called by the Venn Diagrammer application to handle operating-system events.

Listing 9-2   Handling operating-system events

```
PROCEDURE DoOSEvent (myEvent: EventRecord);
    VAR
        myWindow:    WindowPtr;
BEGIN
    CASE BSR(myEvent.message, 24) OF
        mouseMovedMessage:
            BEGIN
                DoIdle(myEvent);                     {right now, do nothing}
            END;
        suspendResumeMessage:
            BEGIN
                myWindow := FrontWindow;
                IF (BAnd(myEvent.message, resumeFlag) <> 0) THEN
                    DoActivate(myWindow, activeFlag)        {activate window}
                ELSE
                    DoActivate(myWindow, 1 - activeFlag);   {deactivate window}
            END;
        OTHERWISE
            ;
    END;
END;
```

The procedure DoOSEvent is called by the main event loop (Listing 4-4 on page 77) whenever the what field of an event record contains the constant osEvt. You need to inspect the message field of that event record to determine what kind of operating-system event you've received. Table 9-1 shows the information contained in the bits of the message field.

Table 9-1   The bits in the message field of an operating-system event record

Bit	Contents
0	0 if a suspend event 1 if a resume event
1	0 if Clipboard conversion is not required 1 if Clipboard conversion is required
2–23	Reserved
24–31	suspendResumeMessage if a suspend or resume event mouseMovedMessage if a mouse-moved event

As you can see, you need to inspect bits 24–31 to determine what kind of operating-system event you've received. Those eight bits contain one of two constants:

```
CONST
    suspendResumeMessage     = $01;      {suspend or resume event}
    mouseMovedMessage        = $FA;      {mouse-moved event}
```

If the event is a suspend or resume event, you then need to examine bit 0 to determine whether that event is a suspend or resume event. (Bits 0 and 1 are meaningful only if bits 24–31 indicate that the event is a suspend or resume event.) You can use the resumeFlag constant to determine whether the event is a suspend or resume event. If the event is a resume event, you can use the convertClipboardFlag constant to determine whether Clipboard conversion from the Clipboard to your application's scrap is required.

```
CONST
    resumeFlag               = 1;   {resume event}
    convertClipboardFlag     = 2;   {Clipboard conversion required}
```

The procedure DoOSEvent defined in Listing 9-2 first checks what kind of event it has received. If the event is a mouse-moved event, DoOSEvent ignores the event, treating it like a null event. If the event is a suspend or resume event, DoOSEvent then activates or deactivates the front window, depending on whether the event is a resume or a suspend event.

Processes

Note

Because the Venn Diagrammer application doesn't support cutting or pasting, it doesn't need to worry about converting the Clipboard. ◆

Handling Null Events

Recall that the Event Manager sends your application a null event when there are no other events to report. The `WaitNextEvent` function reports a null event by returning a function result of `FALSE` and by setting the `what` field of the event record to `nullEvt`.

When your application receives a null event, it can perform idle processing. Your application should do only minimal processing in response to a null event, so that other processes can use the CPU and so that the foreground process (or your application, when it is in the foreground) can respond promptly to the user. For example, if your application is in the foreground when it receives a null event, you can make the insertion point blink in the active window (if your application supports text entry).

If your application receives a null event in the background, it can perform tasks or do other processing while in the background. However, your application should not perform any tasks that would slow down the responsiveness of the foreground process. Your application also should not interact with the user if it is in the background.

Note

Remember that your application receives null events while it is in the background only if you've set the `canBackground` flag in your application's `'SIZE'` resource. If you don't want your application to receive null events when it is in the background, you should set the `cannotBackground` flag. ◆

The Venn Diagrammer application uses null events in a somewhat interesting way. Whenever the application receives a null event, it calls the application-defined procedure `DoIdle`, which checks to see whether the user wants it to automatically adjust the Venn diagram and whether the diagram might need adjusting. If both of these are true, then `DoIdle` calls the application-defined procedure `DoVennIdle` to perform the automatic adjustment. The `DoIdle` procedure is defined in Listing 9-3.

Listing 9-3   Handling null events

```
PROCEDURE DoIdle (myEvent: EventRecord);
    VAR
        myWindow:   WindowPtr;
        myHandle:   MyDocRecHnd;
BEGIN
    myWindow := FrontWindow;
    IF IsAppWindow(myWindow) THEN
        IF gAutoAdjust THEN
```

```
BEGIN
    myHandle := MyDocRecHnd(GetWRefCon(myWindow));
    IF myHandle^^.needsAdjusting THEN
        DoVennIdle(myWindow);
    END;
END;
```

The document record contains the field needsAdjusting, which is set to TRUE each time the user clicks anywhere within the Venn diagram circles. If the user's preference is for automatic diagram adjustment, then DoIdle calls the application-defined procedure DoVennIdle to adjust the diagram. Figure 9-2 shows the state of a diagram needing adjustment, and Figure 9-3 shows the same diagram after DoVennIdle has adjusted the diagram.

Note
The DoVennIdle procedure is not defined in this book. In addition to determining whether and how to adjust the diagram, DoVennIdle resets the needsAdjusting field of the document record to FALSE. ◆

Figure 9-2   A Venn diagram before automatic adjusting

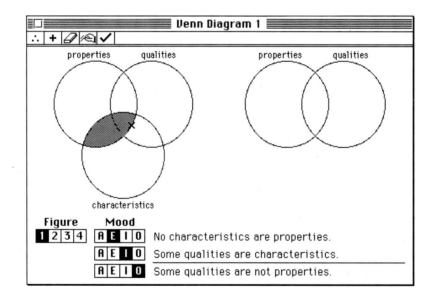

Figure 9-3   A Venn diagram after automatic adjusting

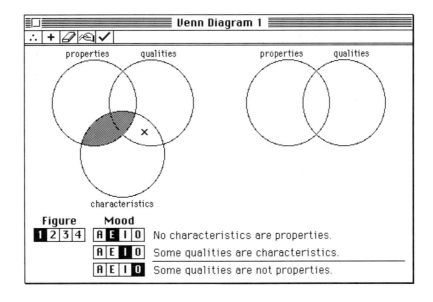

Quitting an Application

Eventually the user will quit your application, usually by choosing Quit from the File menu (or by pressing the usual keyboard equivalent, Command-Q). At that time, you should close all windows, release any memory you still are holding, and exit your main event loop. Listing 9-4 shows the `DoQuit` routine called by the Venn Diagrammer application when the user chooses Quit from the File menu.

Listing 9-4   Quitting your application

```
PROCEDURE DoQuit;
   VAR
      myWindow:    WindowPtr;
BEGIN
   myWindow := FrontWindow;                {close all windows}
   WHILE myWindow <> NIL DO
      BEGIN
         DoUpdate(myWindow);               {force redrawing window}
         DoCloseWindow(myWindow);
         myWindow := FrontWindow;
```

```
      END;
    gDone := TRUE;                            {set flag to exit main event loop}
  END;
```

The `DoQuit` procedure simply closes all windows belonging to the application and then sets the application global variable `gDone` to indicate that the user has finished using the application. Recall that the main event loop (Listing 4-4 on page 77) terminates when `gDone` is `TRUE`.

Note
The Process Manager automatically deallocates your application partition and closes all windows when your application terminates. As a result, the Venn Diagrammer application could simply have set `gDone` to `TRUE` in response to the Quit command. However, `DoQuit` illustrates how to close all windows because your version of `DoCloseWindow` might need to prompt the user to save any unsaved data in document windows currently on the desktop. ◆

Handling Errors

Occasionally, a system software routine might be unable to perform the service you've requested of it. You might, for instance, pass `GetResource` a resource specification that doesn't apply to any resource in any of the open resource files. Or, the user might have opened so many document windows that there simply isn't enough space in your application's heap to open another one. In these situations, you need to determine that an error has occurred and react to it in some appropriate manner.

The system software has several ways of informing your application that a requested service is not possible. Many functions return a result code that indicates whether the function completed successfully, and if not, what the reason for failure was. These functions return a result of type `OSErr`. Here's an example:

```
myResult := FindFolder(kOnSystemDisk, kPreferencesFolderType,
                          kDontCreateFolder, myVRefNum, myDirID);
IF myResult = noErr THEN
    ...
ELSE
    ...;
```

Other routines—mainly procedures and functions that return other types of results—don't return a result code directly. To find out whether these kinds of routines were successful, you need to call an additional system software routine. For example, some Resource Manager procedures don't directly indicate if the resource operation was successful or not. To find that out, you can call the `ResError` function. The `DoSavePrefs` routine (defined in Listing 3-6 on page 66) uses this strategy to update a preferences resource:

Processes

```
RmveResource(myHandle);
IF ResError = noErr THEN
   AddResource(myPrefData, kPrefResType, kPrefResID, myName);
IF ResError = noErr THEN
   WriteResource(myPrefData);
```

Similarly, the Resource Manager routine `Get1Resource` returns a handle to the specified resource data. If for some reason the resource cannot be opened, the function returns a handle whose value is `NIL`. You can inspect the returned value to determine whether it's safe to proceed.

```
myHandle := Get1Resource(kPrefResType, kPrefResID);
IF myHandle <> NIL THEN
   ...;
```

You could also call `ResError` to determine if `Get1Resource` succeeded. In other words, the following lines are equivalent to the preceding ones:

```
myHandle := Get1Resource(kPrefResType, kPrefResID);
IF ResError <> noErr THEN
   ...;
```

The Memory Manager provides the `MemError` function, which works much as `ResError` does. For Memory Manager functions that return a value, you can either inspect the returned value or call `MemError` to determine if the function completed successfully.

This book has used a fairly simple strategy for detecting and reacting to the normal kinds of problems. When calling a function that returns a pointer or handle, Venn Diagrammer checks that the value of that pointer or handle isn't `NIL`. If it is `NIL`, Venn Diagrammer usually just skips any code that uses that pointer or handle.

IMPORTANT

Venn Diagrammer's error-handling strategy is far too simple for most applications, and it runs afoul of good human interface principles. For example, if the `DoCreateWindow` function (defined in Listing 6-6 on page 117) cannot allocate the memory it needs, it exits and returns a `NIL` window pointer to the calling routine. The net result is that no new window is created, in spite of the user's desire to create one. At the very least, `DoCreateWindow` should inform the user that a new window could not be created because sufficient memory was not available. ▲

Occasionally, an application might run into some more serious problem during its execution that renders further processing impossible or undesirable. For example, if the Venn Diagrammer application isn't able to allocate enough memory for the data structure it uses to maintain information about a document window's geometry, there's no point in continuing to run, because the application won't be able to draw anything in any document windows. In that case, the application should gracefully terminate its own execution. (See Listing 5-3 on page 95.)

To do this, the Venn Diagrammer application defines the `DoBadError` procedure and calls it whenever there is a problem serious enough to warrant such drastic action. The `DoBadError` procedure is defined in Listing 9-5.

Listing 9-5   Handling serious errors

```
PROCEDURE DoBadError (myError: Integer);
VAR
    myItem:      Integer;
    myMessage:   Str255;
BEGIN
    SetCursor(arrow);                               {set arrow cursor}
    GetIndString(myMessage, kErrorStrings, myError);
    ParamText(myMessage, '', '', '');
    myItem := Alert(rErrorAlert, NIL);              {display message}
    ExitToShell;                                    {terminate execution}
END;
```

The application passes `DoBadError` an index into a resource of type `'STR#'` that contains messages indicating the types of serious errors. First `DoBadError` sets the cursor to the standard arrow cursor (this step is necessary only if your application ever changes the cursor). Then `DoBadError` retrieves the appropriate message from the application's resource fork and calls the Dialog Manager routine `ParamText` to substitute the message into the alert box text. After that, `DoBadError` displays the alert box by calling the Dialog Manager routine `Alert`. (See Figure 7-2 on page 134 for an example of this alert box.) Finally, `DoBadError` calls the Process Manager procedure `ExitToShell` to terminate the application immediately.

Checking the Operating Environment

Calling `ExitToShell` is the preferred way to terminate your application if for some reason you don't want to return to your main event loop. You might also want to call `DoBadError` to terminate your application before you even get to the main event loop. This might happen if your application requires system software routines that aren't available in all operating environments. In general, if your application uses any system software routines that aren't available in all operating environments, you need to make sure that they are available in the current environment. Otherwise, your application will crash.

For example, the Venn Diagrammer application uses the `FindFolder` function to find the Preferences folder containing the application's preferences file (see Listing 3-3 on page 62). Because `FindFolder` was introduced in system software version 7.0, Venn Diagrammer will crash if it calls `FindFolder` when running in an earlier system software version.

To avoid crashing in environments that don't support the `FindFolder` function, the Venn Diagrammer application makes sure that the function is available before calling it. It calls the `Gestalt` function to see if `FindFolder` is present, as shown in Listing 9-6.

Listing 9-6   Checking that `FindFolder` is present

```
FUNCTION IsFindFolder: Boolean;
VAR
    myResult:   OSErr;
    myFeature:  LongInt;
BEGIN
    IsFindFolder := FALSE;          {assume it's not available}
    myResult := Gestalt(gestaltFindFolderAttr, myFeature);
    IF myResult = noErr THEN
        IsFindFolder := BTST(myFeature, gestaltFindFolderPresent);
END;
```

The `Gestalt` function is part of the Gestalt Manager, which you can use to determine what software and hardware features are available in the current operating environment. When passed the `gestaltFindFolderAttr` selector code, the `Gestalt` function fills in the long integer passed in its second parameter (`myFeature`) with a bit field that encodes information about the features of the `FindFolder` function. Currently only one bit is defined, specified using the constant `gestaltFindFolderPresent`. If that bit is set, then `FindFolder` is present in the operating environment. The Venn Diagrammer application calls `IsFindFolder` as follows (see Listing 3-3 on page 62):

```
IF IsFindFolder THEN
    myResult := FindFolder(kOnSystemDisk, kPreferencesFolderType,
                           kDontCreateFolder, myVRefNum, myDirID);
```

Note

For complete details about using the `Gestalt` function to determine the features of the current operating environment, see the chapter "Gestalt Manager" in *Inside Macintosh: Operating System Utilities*. ◆

If `FindFolder` function isn't available, Venn Diagrammer looks in the **default directory** instead of in the Preferences folder for the user's preferences file. This isn't the best strategy possible, but it's good enough for a simple application like Venn Diagrammer. More generally, however, you need to decide what the base system software requirements of your application are and how you want to react if necessary services aren't available. In some cases, working around a problem isn't so easy. In those cases, informing the user that your software won't run in the current system configuration and then exiting is probably the right thing to do.

A second way to determine the availability of a particular system software routine is to test directly for the existence of the routine by inspecting its trap number (a number that identifies each system software routine), using the technique illustrated in Listing 9-7.

Processes

You should use this method to test for the existence of routines not included in managers about which Gestalt can report.

Listing 9-7   Determining whether a trap is available

```
FUNCTION NumToolboxTraps: Integer;
BEGIN
    IF NGetTrapAddress(_InitGraf, ToolTrap) =
                        NGetTrapAddress($AA6E, ToolTrap) THEN
        NumToolboxTraps := $200
    ELSE
        NumToolboxTraps := $400;
END;


FUNCTION GetTrapType (theTrap: Integer): TrapType;
CONST
    TrapMask = $0800;
BEGIN
    IF BAND(theTrap, TrapMask) > 0 THEN
        GetTrapType := ToolTrap
    ELSE
        GetTrapType := OSTrap;
END;


FUNCTION TrapAvailable (theTrap: Integer): Boolean;
VAR
    tType:        TrapType;
BEGIN
    tType := GetTrapType(theTrap);
    IF tType = ToolTrap THEN
    BEGIN
        theTrap := BAND(theTrap, $07FF);
        IF theTrap >= NumToolboxTraps THEN
            theTrap := _Unimplemented;
    END;
    TrapAvailable := NGetTrapAddress(theTrap, tType) <>
                        NGetTrapAddress(_Unimplemented, ToolTrap);
END;
```

Listing 9-8 shows how to use the `TrapAvailable` function defined in Listing 9-7 to determine whether the `WaitNextEvent` function is available.

Listing 9-8   Checking for the availability of the `WaitNextEvent` function

```
FUNCTION WNEAvailable: Boolean;
CONST
    _WaitNextEvent     = $A860;     {trap number of WaitNextEvent}
BEGIN
    WNEAvailable :=  TrapAvailable(_WaitNextEvent);
END;
```

The `NumToolboxTraps` function relies on the fact that the `InitGraf` trap (trap number $A86E) is always implemented. If the trap dispatch table is large enough (that is, has more than $200 entries), then $AA6E always points to either `_Unimplemented` or something else, but never to `InitGraf`. As a result, you can check the size of the trap dispatch table by checking to see if the address of trap $A86E is the same as $AA6E.

After receiving the information about the size of the dispatch table, the `TrapAvailable` function first checks to see if the trap to be tested has a trap number greater than the total number of traps available on the machine. If so, it sets the `theTrap` variable to `_Unimplemented` before testing it against the `_Unimplemented` trap. See the discussion of the trap dispatch table utilities in *Inside Macintosh: Operating System Utilities* for complete details on trap numbers and the trap dispatch table.

IMPORTANT

There's one final twist in this story. Your software development system might provide glue routines that mimic the operation of some system software routines, thereby allowing you to call them in earlier system software versions. (For instance, MPW versions 3.2 and later provide glue that allows you to call `FindFolder` in system software versions prior to 7.0.) However, you cannot in general use `Gestalt` or the technique shown in Listing 9-7 to test for the availability of routines provided as glue. Instead, you'll need to consult the documentation for your development system to find out what glue routines it provides. ▲

Going Further

If you've made it this far, you've learned quite a bit about putting a Macintosh application together. You've seen how to create and manage menus, windows, dialog boxes, and preference files. You know how to get information about the user's actions, and you know how to respond to many of those actions. You also know, at least in overview, how your application shares the available system resources with the Operating System and other open applications. Congratulations; that's a lot to learn in less than 200 pages.

No doubt, however, you want to learn more. The Venn Diagrammer application fails to implement a number of very fundamental elements of a typical Macintosh application. It provides no text-input or editing capabilities, no support for user drawing, no support for color, and virtually no support for the many important features introduced in System 7. The following section briefly describes some of these capabilities and refers you to the *Inside Macintosh* books that give more information about implementing those capabilities.

This afterword also provides some hints on writing your application so that it is compatible with all existing Macintosh computers and system software versions and so that it can be easily localized to different languages. This afterword ends with a list of additional developer services provided by Apple Computer, Inc.

Implementing Further Features

Venn Diagrammer succeeds in its basic goal, which is to illustrate how to implement many of the essential user interface components of a typical Macintosh application and to introduce the very simplest features of the Operating System. It shows how to do basic drawing in a window and how to handle many user actions. Best of all, it's a real application that does useful, albeit limited, work.

It's important to realize that although some parts of the source code presented throughout this book are purposely simplified, other parts are not. The code for handling dialog boxes, for instance, is designed to be easily amplified to handle other modeless dialog boxes. The basic event loop and the menu-handling code are also quite typical of what you'd find in a commercial Macintosh application. The Venn Diagrammer source code is not intended as a shell on which to base your application, but chances are you'll do at least a few things in the same way.

Still, the Venn Diagrammer source code fails to illustrate how to implement a number of important Macintosh features. Here's a moderately complete list of what's missing and where you can look to get the information you need to add these features to your application:

- **Windows.** The document windows created by the Venn Diagrammer application are of fixed size, so they don't need to contain zoom boxes, size boxes, or scroll bars. In all likelihood, however, your application will allow the user to enter and edit information (such as text or graphics) that will usually not fit in a fixed-size window. As a result, you will probably want to include support for these window elements. To learn how to handle zoom and size boxes, see the chapter "Window Manager" in *Inside Macintosh: Macintosh Toolbox Essentials*. To learn how to implement scroll bars, see the chapter "Control Manager" in that same book.

- **Menus.** The Macintosh system software provides support for several kinds of menus in addition to the standard "pull-down" menus used by the Venn Diagrammer application. A very useful adaptation of the pull-down menu is the **pop-up menu,** which you can put in dialog boxes and document windows. Moreover, both pop-up menus and pull-down menus can contain **hierarchical menus,** where an entire menu is attached to a menu item. For information about these additional kinds of menus, see the chapter "Menu Manager" in *Inside Macintosh: Macintosh Toolbox Essentials*. That chapter also shows how to modify a menu item's text and style, how to add a mark to a menu item, and how to associate an icon with a menu item. Because pop-up menus are actually very complex controls, you'll also need to read the chapter "Control Manager" in *Inside Macintosh: Macintosh Toolbox Essentials* to learn how to handle pop-up menus.

- **Text.** Most Macintosh applications support some form of text entry and editing, even if just to solicit some piece of information from the user in a dialog box. The system software includes TextEdit, which you can use to provide basic text-handling capabilities for your application. Although TextEdit was originally designed to handle edit fields in a dialog box, you can also use it for other purposes. For example, if you're writing a spreadsheet application, you might use TextEdit to handle small amounts of text. TextEdit is not, however, suitable for large amounts of text (greater than about 32,000 characters). If you're writing a word-processing application, you'll need to write your own custom text-handling routines. To learn how to handle text entry and editing in dialog boxes, see the chapter "Dialog Manager" in *Inside Macintosh: Macintosh Toolbox Essentials*. To learn how to use TextEdit directly, see the chapter "TextEdit" in *Inside Macintosh: Text*. This latter book also describes a number of other text-related facilities provided by the Macintosh system software, such as support for multiple fonts and non-Roman character sets.

- **Files.** The Venn Diagrammer application can create, read, and write resource files only (which contain the user's preferences). Most applications allow the user to create and edit information of arbitrary size, and they store that information in a file's data fork. The data fork can contain any kind of information you care to put there. You read and write data from a file's data fork using the File Manager, and you present the standard user interface for opening and saving files using the Standard File Package. The chapter "Introduction to File Management" in *Inside Macintosh: Files* shows how to use these and other services to implement the typical File menu commands (Open, Save, Save As, Revert, and so forth). Other chapters in that book provide more detailed information about the structure of the file system used on Macintosh computers and about the system software managers you can use to manipulate objects in the file system. For more complete information on reading and writing resource files, see the chapter "Resource Manager" in *Inside Macintosh: More Macintosh Toolbox*.

■ **Icons.** To learn how to define icons for your application and its document files, see the chapter "Finder Interface" in *Inside Macintosh: Macintosh Toolbox Essentials*.

■ **Help.** Every application should include the resources necessary to allow the Help Manager to display help balloons after the user has chosen the Show Balloons command from the Help menu. Usually you can add support for help balloons simply by adding resources to your application's resource fork, without having to change or recompile its source code. In some cases, however, you might also need to modify the source code to provide help balloons. For complete details on implementing help balloons, see the chapter "Help Manager" in *Inside Macintosh: More Macintosh Toolbox*.

■ **Printing.** One of the easiest features to add to the Venn Diagrammer application is the capability to print a Venn diagram window. Printing essentially involves just drawing the window into a special graphics port called a printing graphics port. Before doing that, however, you need to present the standard dialog boxes to set up a page and to send a print job to a printer. If, as is usually the case, there are multiple pages to be printed, you'll want to structure your printing code into a printing loop. A complete printing loop is provided in the chapter "QuickDraw Printing Manager" in *Inside Macintosh: Imaging*. That chapter also shows how to handle a number of other printing-related tasks.

■ **Memory.** The Venn Diagrammer application is surprisingly naive in its management of the memory in its own partition. For the most part, it simply tries to allocate the memory it needs for some particular operation, and if it fails to get that memory, it just does the safest thing it can to work around that failure. You'll want to implement a much more robust scheme to manage the memory you're allocated when your application starts up. You need to make sure that your application's memory requirements don't consume too much of your partition, because many system software routines (especially many QuickDraw routines) also use memory in your application partition. For a simple but effective memory-management strategy, see the chapter "Introduction to Memory Management" in *Inside Macintosh: Memory*. For some advice on how to segment your application's executable code to minimize its memory footprint, see the chapter "Segment Manager" in *Inside Macintosh: Processes*.

- **Interapplication Communication.** To take full advantage of the cooperative multitasking environment provided in system software versions 7.0 and later, your application should be able to communicate effectively with other open applications. The system software provides several ways in which you can interact with other applications. You can support the publish and subscribe capabilities of the Edition Manager (described earlier in "Interapplication Communication" beginning on page 14) and you can support high-level events such as Apple events. For complete details on how to communicate and share data with other applications, see the book *Inside Macintosh: Interapplication Communication*.

- **Sound.** You can enhance the perceived quality of your application by appropriately including sounds in its user interface. When, for example, the user asks the Venn Diagrammer application to check the user's diagram, the application might play some agreeable sound if the diagram is correct and some discordant sound otherwise. Sound can provide user feedback that is not achievable using text and graphics alone. Other applications are more directly involved with recording or producing sound. To learn how to add sound capabilities to your application, see the chapter "Introduction to Sound" in *Inside Macintosh: Sound*.

- **Color.** Like sound, color might be either an enhancement to or a fundamental feature of your application. For example, Venn Diagrammer might allow the user to fill empty regions with colored patterns. You can use QuickDraw to draw shapes, regions, and even text in any color supported by the available video devices. For complete information on supporting color in your application, see the appropriate chapters in *Inside Macintosh: Imaging*.

IMPORTANT

You don't have to read all of the books mentioned in this list to develop a Macintosh application. Which of the many *Inside Macintosh* books you'll need depends on the particular requirements of your application. (The Venn Diagrammer application, for instance, draws mainly on four books only: *Inside Macintosh: Macintosh Toolbox Essentials*, *Inside Macintosh: More Macintosh Toolbox*, *Inside Macintosh: Memory*, and *Inside Macintosh: Imaging*.) Moreover, you don't necessarily have to read all of a chapter to get started using a certain manager. Most chapters in *Inside Macintosh* contain advanced material that is likely to be of interest only to developers with very specialized needs. ▲

Maintaining Compatibility

Compatibility is the ability of an application to execute properly in different operating environments. Compatibility is important if you want to write software that runs, with little or no modification, on all members of the Macintosh family and in all system software versions.

The key to achieving compatibility is not to depend on things that may change. *Inside Macintosh* contains numerous warnings about which information is likely to change. As the Operating System and Toolbox evolve to accommodate the needs of developers and users, many of their elements will vary. Whenever possible, Apple Computer strives to add features without altering existing programming interfaces. In general, you can assume that Operating System and Toolbox routines are less likely to change than data structures. Therefore, you should never directly manipulate data structures that are internal to a manager or system software routine, even if their structure is documented. Instead, you should manipulate those structures only indirectly, by calling Operating System and Toolbox routines that achieve the desired effect. In particular, you should never alter any portion of a data structure marked as unused or reserved.

Another key to writing compatible code is to code defensively. Do not assume that users perform actions in a particular order, and do not assume that function and procedure calls always succeed. You should always test the return values of routines for errors, as illustrated in most of the code samples presented in this book.

Here are some more specific guidelines to keep in mind as you write your application:

- Never address hardware directly; whenever possible, use the routines provided by the various device drivers and managers to send data to the available hardware. The addresses of memory-mapped hardware are always subject to change, as is the hardware itself. More important, direct access to such hardware is not possible in every operating environment. In multi-user systems like A/UX, for instance, the operating system manipulates all hardware; applications simply cannot write directly to hardware addresses.

- Avoid writing directly to the screen. Use QuickDraw routines whenever possible to draw on the screen. If you absolutely must write directly to the screen, do not assume that the screen is a fixed size or that it is in a fixed location. The location, size, and bit depth of the screen differ in various machines.

■ Don't rely on system global variables. Many of these variables are documented in *Inside Macintosh*, but many are not. In particular, you must avoid undocumented system global variables because they are most likely to change. But you should try to avoid even well-known system global variables because they may not be available in all environments or in the future. In general, you can avoid using system global variables by using available routines that return the same information. (For example, the `TickCount` function returns the same value that is contained in the system global variable `Ticks`.)

Making Your Application Localizable

Localization is the process of adapting an application to a specific language, culture, and region. By planning ahead and making localization relatively painless, you'll ensure that your product is ready for international markets in the future. This section provides a brief overview of what you need to do to make it easy to localize your application. For the complete account of writing software that is compatible with Macintosh computers throughout the world, see *Inside Macintosh: Text* and *Guide to Macintosh Software Localization*.

The key to easy localization is to store region-dependent information used by your application as resources (rather than within the application's code). Text seen by the user can then be translated without modifying the code. In addition, storing such information in resources means that your application can be adapted for a different area of the world simply by substituting the appropriate resources. Make sure that at least the following kinds of information are stored in resources:

■ all text, including special characters and delimiters

■ menus and keyboard equivalents for menu commands (if available)

■ character, word, phrase, and text translation tables

■ address formats, including zip codes and telephone numbers

When you create resources for your applications, remember the following key points:

■ text needs room to grow (up, down, and sideways)
  □ translated text is often 50 percent larger than the U.S. English text
  □ diacritical marks, widely used outside the United States, may extend up to the ascent line
  □ some system fonts contain characters that extend to *both* the ascent and descent lines

■ text location within a window should be easy to change

Using Developer Services

In addition to the *Inside Macintosh* library of books, Apple Computer provides a number of other services that you can use to learn more about programming for Macintosh computers and simplify your software development process. Apple's goal in making these services available is to provide you with the resources you need to create outstanding Macintosh applications. These services include

- books and other technical publications

- programming languages and tools

- programming classes and self-paced training materials

- conferences and workshops

- technical support

Most of these products and services are available to anyone interested in programming for Macintosh computers. You can get information about them by contacting APDA, Apple's source for developer tools. See the Preface (page xv) for details on contacting APDA.

Some of the services just listed—in particular, technical support and invitations to some developer conferences and workshops—are provided only to members of the Apple Associates and Partners Program. For information about Apple's support programs for commercial developers, call the Developer Hotline at (408) 974-4897. These programs are available to developers in the United States and Canada only.

Technical Publications

Apple provides a number of technical publications that can assist you in writing Macintosh applications. Here's a brief description of three books that you'll probably need right now:

- *Macintosh Human Interface Guidelines*. A complete description of the Apple Desktop Interface and an indispensable set of guidelines governing the appearance and behavior of Macintosh applications. You will need this book to ensure that your application conforms to those guidelines.

- *Technical Introduction to the Macintosh Family*. A general introduction to the family of Macintosh computers, with emphasis on the features that make it a desirable platform for application developers. This book also provides details on Macintosh hardware and on A/UX, Apple's version of the UNIX® operating system.

■ *Guide to Macintosh Software Localization.* A guide to the process of localizing application software for Macintosh computers around the world. You'll want to read this book for essential information about making your product marketable worldwide.

If you are an Apple Associate or Partner, you'll automatically receive a subscription to *develop, The Apple Technical Journal*. This magazine is intended to complement other reference materials like *Inside Macintosh*. It doesn't try to replace or reword those books; instead, it's designed to help you understand them by illustrating some of the techniques they describe. For subscription information, contact

develop
Apple Computer, Inc.
P.O. Box 531
Mount Morris, IL 61054-7858

Telephone	800-877-5548 (United States)
	815-734-6309 (All other countries)
Fax	815-734-4205
AppleLink	DEV.SUBS

Training

Apple Developer University offers a broad range of Macintosh programming instruction through hands-on classes and self-paced training products. Classes are offered in Cupertino, at Apple training facilities worldwide, on an on-site basis, and through selected third-party University and Corporate trainers.

Developer University provides expert instruction for all levels of Macintosh programmers. These course teach programmers to produce fast, efficient code that takes maximum advantage of the Macintosh Toolbox and Operating System.

Apple Developer University is open to all individuals worldwide who have an interest in mastering leading-edge technology. To reserve your place in a class, schedule an on-site training class, or for more information, contact

Apple Developer University Training Registrar
Apple Computer, Inc.
20525 Mariani Avenue
M/S 75-6U
Cupertino, CA 95014

Telephone	408-974-6215 (United States)
Fax	408-974-0544
AppleLink	DEVUNIV

Technical Support

If you are an Apple Associate or Partner, you'll have access to various levels of technical support from Apple. Both Associates and Partners receive monthly mailings that include a newsletter, Apple II and Macintosh Technical Notes, pertinent Developer Programs information, and the latest news relating to Apple products. Mailings also usually include the latest developer CD-ROM, which contains system software, programming utilities, code samples illustrating how to use various parts of the Macintosh system software, and the latest on-line technical documentation.

In addition, Apple Partners receive discounts on Apple equipment and technical assistance from the staff of Apple's Developer Technical Support department.

Appendixes

The following five appendixes provide complete source code listings of the parts of the Venn Diagrammer application whose operations are explained in this book. For clarity, the source code is divided into five parts:

- Appendix A, "Constants, Types, and Variables", beginning on page 195, defines the constants, data types, and global variables used by the Venn Diagrammer application

- Appendix B, "Utility Routines", beginning on page 199, defines a number of utility procedures and functions used by the remaining code samples

- Appendix C, "Dialog Code", beginning on page 205, defines a handful of procedures that manage dialog boxes

- Appendix D, "Resource Code", beginning on page 211, shows how to read and write a simple set of application preferences

- Appendix E, "User Interface Code", beginning on page 217, shows the code that manages the basic application setup, event handling, and user interface

Code that is specific to handling Venn diagrams (such as the procedures that handle the first five menu commands in the Venn menu) is not shown in this book.

IMPORTANT

As explained in the preface to this book, this code is provided for explanatory purposes only. The code listed in these appendixes might not be appropriate for the particular needs of your application. ▲

Constants, Types, and Variables

This appendix defines most of the constants, data types, and global variables used by the Venn Diagrammer application.

```
UNIT Global;
INTERFACE

    CONST
        {menu constants (resource IDs and menu command numbers)}
        rMenuBar      = 128;                    {menu bar resource ID}

        mApple        = 128;                    {resource ID of Apple menu}
        iAbout        = 1;                      {our About... dialog}

        mFile         = 129;                    {resource ID of File menu}
        iNew          = 1;
        iClose        = 2;
        iQuit         = 4;

        mEdit         = 130;                    {resource ID of Edit menu}
        iUndo         = 1;
        iCut          = 3;
        iCopy         = 4;
        iPaste        = 5;
        iClear        = 6;

        mVennD        = 131;                    {resource ID of Venn menu}
        iCheckVenn    = 1;
        iDoVenn       = 2;
        iClearVenn    = 3;
        iNextTask     = 4;
        iCheckArg     = 5;
        iGetVennPrefs = 7;

        kNumTools     = 5;

        rVennD        = mVennD;      {resource ID of Venn diagram window}

        {dialog boxes and their associated items}
        rAboutDial    = 7000;                       {resource ID of About dialog}
```

Constants, Types, and Variables

```
iOK                = 1;                          {OK button}
iCancel            = 2;                          {Cancel button}


rVennDPrefsDial = 3040;      {resource ID of Preferences dialog}
iEmpty1Radio             = 1;            {dialog item numbers}
iEmpty2Radio             = 2;
iEmpty3Radio             = 3;
iEmpty4Radio             = 4;
iEmpty1Icon              = 5;
iEmpty2Icon              = 6;
iEmpty3Icon              = 7;
iEmpty4Icon              = 8;
iExist1Radio             = 9;
iExist2Radio             = 10;
iExist3Radio             = 11;
iExist4Radio             = 12;
iExist1Icon              = 13;
iExist2Icon              = 14;
iExist3Icon              = 15;
iExist4Icon              = 16;
iGetNextRandomly         = 19;
iAutoAdjust              = 20;
iShowSchoolNames         = 21;
iUseExistImport          = 22;
iSaveVennPrefs           = 23;
kVennPrefsItemCount      = 23;


kVisualDelay       = 8;      {ticks to invert a button to simulate press}
kCntlActivate      = 0;      {enabled control's hilite state}
kCntlDeactivate    = $FF;    {disabled control's hilite state}


kToolHt            = 14;     {height of a tool icon}
kToolWd            = 21;     {width of a tool icon}


kVennToolsIconStart = 768; {base resource ID of tools icons}
kExistID           = 2000;  {first (of four) icons showing existence}
kEmptyID           = 3000;  {first (of four) patterns showing emptiness}


{Text strings printed in a Venn diagram window.}
rMiscStrings       = 1004;  {resource ID of 'STR#' for text items}
kShowAnswerText    = 1;      {in Venn menu}
kShowUserText      = 2;      {in Venn menu}
kAllText           = 3;
```

Constants, Types, and Variables

```
kNoText              = 4;
kSomeText            = 5;
kAreText             = 6;
kAreNotText          = 7;
kFigureText          = 8;
kMoodText            = 9;

{Venn Diagram window status messages: 'STR#' resource ID = rVennD}
eDiagramCorrect      = 1;
eDiagramIncorrect    = 2;
eHereIsSolution      = 3;
eHereIsYourWork      = 4;
eCannotEditAnswer    = 5;
eCannotEraseAnswer   = 6;
eArgIsValid          = 7;
eArgNotValid         = 8;
eExistNotPossible    = 9;

rErrorAlert          = 129;    {res ID of 'ALRT' resource for error mesgs}
kErrorStrings        = 1005;   {res ID of 'STR#' resource for error mesgs}
eCantFindMenus       = 1;      {can't read menu bar resource}
eNotEnoughMemory     = 2;      {insufficient memory for operation}

{constants defining several keyboard characters}
kEnter               = char(3);      {the enter character}
kReturn              = char(13);     {the return character}
kEscape              = char(27);     {the escape character}
kPeriod              = '.';          {the period character}

TYPE
    {record to hold the current settings of a Venn Diagram window}
    MyDocRec =
        RECORD               {information about a document window}
            figure:          Integer;           {the figure of the syllogism}
            mood:            ARRAY[1..3] of Integer;
                                                {the moods of the statements}
            terms:           ARRAY[1..3] of Str31;    {the three terms}
            statusText:      Str255;            {most recent status message}
            userSolution:    MyDiagramState;    {user's diagram state}
            realSolution:    MyDiagramState;    {answer's diagram state}
            isAnswerShowing: Boolean;           {is the answer showing?}
            isExistImport:   Boolean;           {stmts imply exists subject?}
            needsAdjusting:  Boolean;           {diagram needs adjusting?}
```

Constants, Types, and Variables

```
        END;
    MyDocRecPtr = ^MyDocRec;
    MyDocRecHnd = ^MyDocRecPtr;


    VAR
        gNumDocWindows:       Integer;      {the number of open document windows}
        gPrefsDialog:         DialogPtr;    {pointer to Preferences dialog window}
        gAppsResourceFile:    Integer;      {reference number of app's res file}
        gPreferencesFile:     Integer;      {reference number of app's prefs file}
        gToolsIcons:          ARRAY[1..kNumTools] of Handle;
                                            {handles to tools icons}
        gEmptyPats:           ARRAY[1..4] of PatHandle;
                                            {handles to emptiness patterns}
        gExistIcons:          ARRAY[1..4] of Handle;
                                            {handles to existence symbols}
        gMoodIcons:           ARRAY[1..4] of Handle;
                                            {handles to mood icons}
        gFigureIcons:         ARRAY[1..4] of Handle;
                                            {handles to figure icons}
        gExistIndex:          Integer;      {rank of icon showing existence}
        gEmptyIndex:          Integer;      {rank of icon showing emptiness}
        gStepRandom:          Boolean;      {generate next setup randomly?}
        gAutoAdjust:          Boolean;      {automatically adjust the diagram?}
        gGiveImport:          Boolean;      {do subjects have existential import?}
        gShowNames:           Boolean;      {do we show names of valid forms?}

IMPLEMENTATION
END. {UNIT Global}
```

Utility Routines

This appendix defines a number of utility procedures and functions that are called by other parts of the Venn Diagrammer application.

```
UNIT Utilities;
INTERFACE
   USES
      Global;

   PROCEDURE DoPlotIcon (myRect: Rect; myIcon: Handle; myWindow: WindowPtr;
                         myMode: Integer);
   PROCEDURE DoOutlineControl (myControl: univ ControlHandle);
   PROCEDURE DoDefaultButton (myDialog: DialogPtr);
   FUNCTION IsDAccWindow (myWindow: WindowPtr): Boolean;
   FUNCTION IsAppWindow (myWindow: WindowPtr): Boolean;
   FUNCTION IsDialogWindow (myWindow: WindowPtr): Boolean;
   PROCEDURE DoPositionWindow (myWindow: WindowPtr);
   PROCEDURE DoSetWindowTitle (myWindow: WindowPtr);
   FUNCTION DoTrackRect (myWindow: WindowPtr; myRect: Rect): Boolean;
   PROCEDURE DoStatusText (myWindow: WindowPtr; myText: Str255);
   PROCEDURE DoStatusMesg (myWindow: WindowPtr; myMessage: Integer);
   PROCEDURE DoBadError (myError: Integer);
   FUNCTION IsFindFolder: Boolean;
   FUNCTION MyRandom (last: Integer): Integer;

IMPLEMENTATION

{DoPlotIcon: plot a piece of an icon in a specified rectangle}
   PROCEDURE DoPlotIcon (myRect: Rect; myIcon: Handle; myWindow: WindowPtr;
                         myMode: Integer);
      VAR
         myBitMap:   BitMap;
   BEGIN
      myBitMap.baseAddr := myIcon^;
      myBitMap.rowBytes := 4;
      myBitMap.bounds := myRect;
      CopyBits(myBitMap, myWindow^.portBits, myRect, myRect, myMode, NIL);
   END;
```

Utility Routines

```
{DoOutlineControl: draw bold outline around a control}
    PROCEDURE DoOutlineControl (myControl: UNIV ControlHandle);
        VAR
            myOval:         Integer;
            myRect:         Rect;
            origPen:        PenState;
            origPort:       GrafPtr;
    BEGIN
        IF myControl <> NIL THEN
            BEGIN
                GetPort(origPort);
                SetPort(myControl^^.contrlOwner);
                GetPenState(origPen);
                PenNormal;

                myRect := myControl^^.contrlRect;
                InsetRect(myRect, -4, -4);
                myOval := ((myRect.bottom - myRect.top) DIV 2) + 2;

                IF (myControl^^.contrlHilite = kCntlActivate) THEN
                    PenPat(black)
                ELSE
                    PenPat(gray);
                PenSize(3, 3);
                FrameRoundRect(myRect, myOval, myOval);
                SetPenState(origPen);                    {restore previous pen state}
                SetPort(origPort);
            END;
    END;


{DoDefaultButton: draw bold outline around default button in a dialog}
{this procedure assumes that the default button is item number 1 (i.e., iOK)}
    PROCEDURE DoDefaultButton (myDialog: DialogPtr);
        VAR
            myType:         Integer;
            myHand:         Handle;
            myRect:         Rect;
    BEGIN
        GetDialogItem(myDialog, iOK, myType, myHand, myRect);
        DoOutlineControl(myHand);
    END;


{IsDAccWindow: determine if specified window belongs to a desk accessory}
```

Utility Routines

```pascal
FUNCTION IsDAccWindow (myWindow: WindowPtr): Boolean;
BEGIN
    IF myWindow = NIL THEN
        IsDAccWindow := FALSE
    ELSE
        IsDAccWindow := WindowPeek(myWindow)^.windowKind < 0;
END;


{IsAppWindow: determine if specified window belongs to my app}
    FUNCTION IsAppWindow (myWindow: WindowPtr): Boolean;
    BEGIN
        IF myWindow = NIL THEN
            IsAppWindow := FALSE
        ELSE
            IsAppWindow := WindowPeek(myWindow)^.windowKind = userKind;
    END;


{IsDialogWindow: determine if specified window is a dialog}
    FUNCTION IsDialogWindow (myWindow: WindowPtr): Boolean;
    BEGIN
        IF myWindow = NIL THEN
            IsDialogWindow := FALSE
        ELSE
            IsDialogWindow := WindowPeek(myWindow)^.windowKind = dialogKind;
    END;


{DoPositionWindow: set the position of a new window}
    PROCEDURE DoPositionWindow (myWindow: WindowPtr);
    BEGIN
    END;


{DoSetWindowTitle: construct a title for a new window}
    PROCEDURE DoSetWindowTitle (myWindow: WindowPtr);
        VAR
            myName:     Str255;
            myRank:     Str255;
    BEGIN
        GetWTitle(myWindow, myName);
        gNumDocWindows := gNumDocWindows + 1;
        NumToString(gNumDocWindows, myRank);
        myName := concat(myName, ' ', myRank);
        SetWTitle(myWindow, myName);
    END;
```

Utility Routines

```
{DoTrackRect: do "TrackBox" for a random rectangle}
{this is used to process clicks in a window tool}
   FUNCTION DoTrackRect (myWindow: WindowPtr; myRect: Rect): Boolean;
      VAR
         myIgnore:   LongInt;
         myPoint:    Point;
   BEGIN
      InvertRect(myRect);   {invert the rectangle}
      REPEAT
         Delay(kVisualDelay, myIgnore)
      UNTIL NOT StillDown;               {keep inversion until mouse is released}
      InvertRect(myRect);

      GetMouse(myPoint);                 {get mouse location in local coordinates}
      DoTrackRect := PtInRect(myPoint, myRect);
   END;


{DoStatusText: print a message in a window's status area}
   PROCEDURE DoStatusText (myWindow: WindowPtr; myText: Str255);
      VAR
         myRect:     Rect;
         origSize:   Integer;
         origFont:   Integer;
         myHandle:   MyDocRecHnd;
      CONST
         kSlop = 4;
         kSize = 9;
         kFont = applFont;
   BEGIN
      IF myWindow <> NIL THEN
         BEGIN
            SetPort(myWindow);
            origSize := myWindow^.txSize; {remember original size and font}
            origFont := myWindow^.txFont;
            TextSize(kSize);                {set desired size and font}
            TextFont(kFont);

            SetRect(myRect, kToolWd * kNumTools, 0,
                           myWindow^.portRect.right, kToolHt);
            EraseRect(myRect);
            IF length(myText) > 0 THEN
               BEGIN
```

```
                    MoveTo(myRect.left + kSlop, myRect.bottom - kSlop);
                    DrawString(myText);
                END;

            TextSize(origSize);              {restore original size and font}
            TextFont(origFont);

            {Remember the last message printed in this window.}
            myHandle := MyDocRecHnd(GetWRefCon(myWindow));
            myHandle^^.statusText := myText;
        END;
    END;


{DoStatusMesg: call DoStatusText, getting the text from a resource}
    PROCEDURE DoStatusMesg (myWindow: WindowPtr; myMessageID: Integer);
        VAR
            myText:     Str255;
    BEGIN
        GetIndString(myText, rVennD, myMessageID);
        DoStatusText(myWindow, myText);
    END;


{DoBadError: inform the user of fatal errors, then terminate the app}
    PROCEDURE DoBadError (myError: Integer);
        VAR
            myItem:     Integer;
            myMessage:  Str255;
    BEGIN
        SetCursor(arrow);                           {set arrow cursor}
        GetIndString(myMessage, kErrorStrings, myError);
        ParamText(myMessage, '', '', '');
        myItem := Alert(rErrorAlert, NIL);          {display message}
        ExitToShell;                                {terminate execution}
    END;


{IsFindFolder: is the FindFolder function available?}
    FUNCTION IsFindFolder: Boolean;
    VAR
        myResult:   OSErr;
        myFeature:  LongInt;
    BEGIN
        IsFindFolder := FALSE;          {assume it's not available}
        myResult := Gestalt(gestaltFindFolderAttr, myFeature);
```

Utility Routines

```
        IF myResult = noErr THEN
            IsFindFolder := BTST(myFeature, gestaltFindFolderPresent);
    END;


{MyRandom: generate a reasonably random number between 0 and last}
    FUNCTION MyRandom (last: Integer): Integer;
    BEGIN
        MyRandom := ABS(Random) MOD SUCC(last);
    END;
END.
```

Dialog Code

This appendix defines several procedures used by the Venn Diagrammer application to manage dialog boxes.

```
UNIT Dialog;                {routines to handle dialog boxes}
INTERFACE
   USES
      Global, Utilities, Preferences, VennProcs;

      PROCEDURE DoSetupUserItems (myKind: Integer; VAR myDialog: DialogPtr);
      PROCEDURE DoSetupCtrlValues (myDialog: DialogPtr);
      PROCEDURE DoUserItem (myDialog: DialogPtr; myItem: Integer);
      PROCEDURE DoModelessDialog (myKind: Integer; VAR myDialog: DialogPtr);
      FUNCTION DoHandleDialogEvent (myEvent: EventRecord): Boolean;


IMPLEMENTATION


{DoSetupUserItems: set up application-defined ("user") items in a dialog box}
   PROCEDURE DoSetupUserItems (myKind: Integer; VAR myDialog: DialogPtr);
      VAR
         myType:     Integer;
         myHand:     Handle;
         myRect:     Rect;
         count:      Integer;
         origPort:   GrafPtr;
   BEGIN
      GetPort(origPort);
      SetPort(myDialog);

      CASE myKind OF
         rVennDPrefsDial:
            FOR count := 1 TO kVennPrefsItemCount DO
               IF count IN [iExist1Icon..iExist4Icon,
                              iEmpty1Icon..iEmpty4Icon] THEN
               BEGIN
                  GetDialogItem(myDialog, count, myType, myHand, myRect);
                  SetDialogItem(myDialog, count, myType, @DoUserItem,
                                                            myRect);
               END;
         OTHERWISE
```

Dialog Code

```
                  ;
         END;


         SetPort(origPort);
    END;


{DoSetupCtrlValues: install initial values in a dialog}
    PROCEDURE DoSetupCtrlValues (myDialog: DialogPtr);
        VAR
            count:      Integer;
            myType:     Integer;
            myHand:     Handle;
            myRect:     Rect;
            origPort:   GrafPtr;
    BEGIN
        IF myDialog = NIL THEN
            exit(DoSetupCtrlValues);


        GetPort(origPort);                    {save the current graphics port}
        SetPort(myDialog);                    {always do this before drawing}
        ShowWindow(myDialog);


        IF myDialog = gPrefsDialog THEN
            BEGIN
                FOR count := 1 TO kVennPrefsItemCount DO
                    BEGIN
                        GetDialogItem(myDialog, count, myType, myHand,
                                      myRect);
                        IF myType = ctrlItem + radCtrl THEN
                            CASE count OF
                                iExist1Radio..iExist4Radio:
                                    SetCtlValue(ControlHandle(myHand),
                                        ORD(gExistIndex = count - (iExist1Radio - 1)));
                                iEmpty1Radio..iEmpty4Radio:
                                    SetCtlValue(ControlHandle(myHand),
                                        ORD(gEmptyIndex = count - (iEmpty1Radio - 1)));
                            OTHERWISE
                                ;
                            END;
                        IF myType = ctrlItem + chkCtrl THEN
                            CASE count OF
                                iGetNextRandomly:
                                    SetCtlValue(ControlHandle(myHand),
```

Dialog Code

```
                                            ORD(gStepRandom = TRUE));
                        iShowSchoolNames:
                            SetCtlValue(ControlHandle(myHand),
                                        ORD(gShowNames = TRUE));
                        iUseExistImport:
                            SetCtlValue(ControlHandle(myHand),
                                        ORD(gGiveImport = TRUE));
                        iAutoAdjust:
                            SetCtlValue(ControlHandle(myHand),
                                        ORD(gAutoAdjust = TRUE));
                    OTHERWISE
                        ;
                    END;
                END;
            END;

        SetPort(origPort);                  {restore the previous graphics port}
    END;


{DoUserItem: handle drawing of application-defined items in a dialog box}
    PROCEDURE DoUserItem (myDialog: DialogPtr; myItem: Integer);
        VAR
            myType:     Integer;
            myHand:     Handle;
            myRect:     Rect;
            origPort:   GrafPtr;
    BEGIN
        GetPort(origPort);
        SetPort(myDialog);

        GetDialogItem(myDialog, myItem, myType, myHand, myRect);

        IF myDialog = gPrefsDialog THEN
            CASE myItem OF
                iExist1Icon..iExist4Icon:
                    BEGIN
                        DoPlotIcon(myRect,
                                GetIcon(kExistID + myItem - iExist1Icon),
                                myDialog, srcCopy);
                    END;
                iEmpty1Icon..iEmpty4Icon:
                    BEGIN
                        DoPlotIcon(myRect,
```

Dialog Code

```
                                GetIcon(kEmptyID + myItem - iEmpty1Icon),
                            myDialog, srcCopy);
                    FrameRect(myRect);
                END;
            OTHERWISE
                ;
        END; {CASE}


    SetPort(origPort);              {restore original port}
    END;


{DoModelessDialog: put up a modeless dialog box}
    PROCEDURE DoModelessDialog (myKind: Integer; VAR myDialog: DialogPtr);
        VAR
            myPointer:  Ptr;
    BEGIN
        IF myDialog = NIL THEN          {the dialog box doesn't exist yet}
            BEGIN
                myPointer := NewPtr(sizeof(DialogRecord));
                IF myPointer = NIL THEN
                    exit(DoModelessDialog);

                myDialog := GetNewDialog(myKind, myPointer, WindowPtr(-1));
                IF myDialog <> NIL THEN
                    BEGIN
                        DoSetupUserItems(myKind, myDialog);     {set up user items}
                        DoSetupCtrlValues(myDialog);            {set up initial values}
                    END;
            END
        ELSE
            BEGIN
                ShowWindow(myDialog);
                SelectWindow(myDialog);
                SetPort(myDialog);
            END;
    END;


{DoHandleDialogEvent: handle events in modeless dialog boxes}
    FUNCTION DoHandleDialogEvent (myEvent: EventRecord): Boolean;
        VAR
            eventHandled:       Boolean;        {did we handle the event?}
            myDialog:           DialogPtr;
            myItem:             Integer;
```

Dialog Code

```
BEGIN
    eventHandled := FALSE;
    IF FrontWindow <> NIL THEN
        IF IsDialogEvent(myEvent) THEN
            IF DialogSelect(myEvent, myDialog, myItem) THEN
                BEGIN
                    eventHandled := TRUE;
                    SetPort(myDialog);

                    IF myDialog = gPrefsDialog THEN
                        BEGIN
                            CASE myItem OF
                                iEmpty1Radio..iEmpty4Radio:
                                    gEmptyIndex := myItem;
                                iEmpty1Icon..iEmpty4Icon:
                                    gEmptyIndex := myItem - 4;
                                iExist1Radio..iExist4Radio:
                                    gExistIndex := myItem - iEmpty4Icon;
                                iExist1Icon..iExist4Icon:
                                    gExistIndex := myItem - (iEmpty4Icon + 4);
                                iGetNextRandomly:
                                    gStepRandom := NOT gStepRandom;
                                iAutoAdjust:
                                    gAutoAdjust := NOT gAutoAdjust;
                                iShowSchoolNames:
                                    gShowNames := NOT gShowNames;
                                iUseExistImport:
                                    gGiveImport := NOT gGiveImport;
                                iSaveVennPrefs:
                                    DoSavePrefs;
                                OTHERWISE
                                    ;
                            END;

                            DoSetupCtrlValues(myDialog);        {update values}
                        END;
                END;

    DoHandleDialogEvent := eventHandled;
END;

END.
```

Resource Code

This appendix defines the routines used by the Venn Diagrammer application to create, read, and write the resources it uses to store the user's preferences. The application expects to find those resources in a file named "Venn Diagrammer Preferences" in the Preferences folder in the currently-active System folder. If no such file is found, the application creates a new file of the desired name in that location; then it copies into that file a default set of preferences settings that is contained in the application's resource file.

```
UNIT Preferences;
INTERFACE
   USES
      Folders, Global, Utilities;

   CONST
      kPrefResType =      'PRFN';   {type of preferences resource}
      kPrefResID =        259;      {resource ID of preferences resource}

   TYPE
      {structure of a resource that contains Venn diagram preferences}
      MyPrefsRec = RECORD
         autoDiag:   Boolean;      {do we automatically fix the diagram?}
         showName:   Boolean;      {do we show names of valid arguments?}
         isImport:   Boolean;      {do subjects have existential import?}
         isRandom:   Boolean;      {do we select next setting randomly?}
         emptyInd:   Integer;      {index of the desired emptiness pattern}
         existInd:   Integer;      {index of the desired existence symbol}
      END;
      MyPrefsPtr = ^MyPrefsRec;
      MyPrefsHnd = ^MyPrefsPtr;

   FUNCTION DoCopyResource (rType: ResType; rID: Integer; source: Integer;
                            dest: Integer): OSErr;
   PROCEDURE DoReadPrefs;
   PROCEDURE DoSavePrefs;

IMPLEMENTATION

{DoCopyResource}
{copy a resource from one open resource file [source] to another [dest];}
{make sure not to alter the current resource file }
```

```
{ and to preserve resource attributes}
    FUNCTION DoCopyResource (rType: ResType; rID: Integer; source: Integer;
                            dest: Integer): OSErr;
        VAR
            myHandle:   Handle;               {handle to resource to copy}
            myName:     Str255;               {name of resource to copy}
            myAttr:     Integer;              {resource attributes}
            myType:     ResType;              {ignored; used for GetResInfo}
            myID:       Integer;              {ignored; used for GetResInfo}
            myResult:   OSErr;
            myCurrent:  Integer;                {current resource file on entry}
    BEGIN
        myCurrent := CurResFile;              {remember current resource file}
        UseResFile(source);                   {set the source resource file}
        myHandle := Get1Resource(rType, rID); {open the source resource}
        IF myHandle <> NIL THEN
            BEGIN
                GetResInfo(myHandle, myID, myType, myName); {get res name}
                myAttr := GetResAttrs(myHandle);            {get res attributes}
                DetachResource(myHandle);     {so we can copy the resource}
                UseResFile(dest);             {set destination resource file}
                IF ResError = noErr THEN
                    AddResource(myHandle, rType, rID, myName);
                IF ResError = noErr THEN
                    SetResAttrs(myHandle, myAttr);{set res attributes of copy}
                IF ResError = noErr THEN
                    ChangedResource(myHandle);    {mark resource as changed}
                IF ResError = noErr THEN
                    WriteResource(myHandle);      {write resource data}
            END;

        DoCopyResource := ResError;           {return result code}
        ReleaseResource(myHandle);            {get rid of resource data}
        UseResFile(myCurrent);                {restore original resource file}
    END;


{DoCreatePrefsFile:}
{Create a preferences file in the specified location.}
{The initial settings are just those in the app's resource file.}
    FUNCTION DoCreatePrefsFile (myVRefNum: Integer; myDirID: LongInt;
                                myName: Str255): Integer;
        VAR
            myResNum:   Integer;
```

```
        myResult:    OSErr;
        myID:        Integer;     {resource ID of resource in app's res fork}
        myHandle:    Handle;      {handle to resource in app's res fork}
        myType:      ResType;     {ignored; used for GetResInfo}
    BEGIN
      myResult := noErr;
      HCreateResFile(myVRefNum, myDirID, myName);
      IF ResError = noErr THEN
        BEGIN
          myResNum := HOpenResFile(myVRefNum, myDirID, myName, fsCurPerm);
          IF myResNum <> -1 THEN
            BEGIN
              UseResFile(gAppsResourceFile);
              myHandle := Get1Resource(kPrefResType, kPrefResID);
              IF ResError = noErr THEN
                BEGIN
                  GetResInfo(myHandle, myID, myType, myName);
                  myResult := DoCopyResource(kPrefResType, myID,
                                        gAppsResourceFile, myResNum);
                END
              ELSE
                BEGIN
                  CloseResFile(myResNum);
                  myResult := HDelete(myVRefNum, myDirID, myName);
                  myResNum := -1;
                END;
            END;

          DoCreatePrefsFile := myResNum;
        END;
    END; {DoCreatePrefsFile}


{DoReadPrefs:}
{Open the application's global preferences file and read indicated settings.}
    PROCEDURE DoReadPrefs;
      VAR
        myVRefNum:   Integer;
        myDirID:     LongInt;
        myName:      Str255;       {name of this application}
        myPrefs:     Handle;       {handle to actual preferences data}
        myResNum:    Integer;      {reference number of opened resource file}
        myResult:    OSErr;
      CONST
```

D

Resource Code

Resource Code

```
        kNameID = 4000;              {resource ID of 'STR#' with filename}
BEGIN
   {Determine the name of the preferences file.}
   GetIndString(myName, kNameID, 1);

   {Figure out where the preferences file is.}
   IF IsFindFolder THEN
      myResult := FindFolder(kOnSystemDisk, kPreferencesFolderType,
                             kDontCreateFolder, myVRefNum, myDirID)
   ELSE
      myResult := -1;

   IF myResult <> noErr THEN
      BEGIN
         myVRefNum := 0;          {use default volume}
         myDirID := 0;            {use default directory}
      END;

   {Open the preferences resource file.}
   myResNum := HOpenResFile(myVRefNum, myDirID, myName, fsCurPerm);

   {If no preferences file successfully opened, create one }
   { by copying default preferences in app's resource file.}
   IF myResNum = -1 THEN
      myResNum := DoCreatePrefsFile(myVRefNum, myDirID, myName);

   IF myResNum <> -1 THEN           {if we successfully opened the file...}
      BEGIN
         UseResFile(myResNum);    {make the new resource file current one}
         myPrefs := Get1Resource(kPrefResType, kPrefResID);
         IF myPrefs = NIL THEN
            exit(DoReadPrefs);
         WITH MyPrefsHnd(myPrefs)^^ DO
            BEGIN                    {read the preferences settings}
               gAutoAdjust := autoDiag;
               gShowNames := showName;
               gGiveImport := isImport;
               gStepRandom := isRandom;
               gEmptyIndex := emptyInd;
               gExistIndex := existInd;
            END;

   {Make sure some preferences globals make sense.}
```

```
        IF NOT (gExistIndex IN [1..4]) THEN
            gExistIndex := 1;
        IF NOT (gEmptyIndex IN [1..4]) THEN
            gEmptyIndex := 1;


        {Reinstate the application's resource file.}
        UseResFile(gAppsResourceFile);
      END;


    gPreferencesFile := myResNum;              {remember its resource ID}
  END; {DoReadPrefs}


{DoSavePrefs:}
{Save the current preference settings.}
  PROCEDURE DoSavePrefs;
    VAR
        myPrefData: Handle;     {handle to new resource data}
        myHandle:   Handle;     {handle to resource to replace}
        myName:     Str255;     {name of resource to copy}
        myAttr:     Integer;    {resource attributes}
        myType:     ResType;    {ignored; used for GetResInfo}
        myID:       Integer;    {ignored; used for GetResInfo}
  BEGIN
    {Make sure we have an open preferences file.}
    IF gPreferencesFile = -1 THEN
        exit(DoSavePrefs);

    myPrefData := NewHandleClear(sizeof(MyPrefsRec));
    HLock(myPrefData);
    WITH MyPrefsHnd(myPrefData)^^ DO
        BEGIN
            autoDiag := gAutoAdjust;
            showName := gShowNames;
            isImport := gGiveImport;
            isRandom := gStepRandom;
            emptyInd := gEmptyIndex;
            existInd := gExistIndex;
        END;

    UseResFile(gPreferencesFile);                        {use preferences file}
    myHandle := Get1Resource(kPrefResType, kPrefResID);
    IF myHandle <> NIL THEN
        BEGIN
```

Resource Code

```
        GetResInfo(myHandle, myID, myType, myName);   {get res name}
        myAttr := GetResAttrs(myHandle);              {get res attributes}
        RmveResource(myHandle);
        IF ResError = noErr THEN
            AddResource(myPrefData, kPrefResType, kPrefResID, myName);
        IF ResError = noErr THEN
            WriteResource(myPrefData);
    END;

    HUnlock(myPrefData);
    ReleaseResource(myPrefData);
    UseResFile(gAppsResourceFile);                {restore app's resource file}

  END; {DoSavePrefs}

END. {UNIT Preferences}
```

User Interface Code

This appendix shows the source code that manages the basic setup and user interface for the Venn Diagrammer application.

```pascal
PROGRAM VennDiagrammer;
   USES
      Global, Utilities, Dialog, Preferences, VennProcs;


   VAR
      gDone:      Boolean;


{DoInitManagers: initialize Toolbox Managers}
   PROCEDURE DoInitManagers;
   BEGIN
      MaxApplZone;                    {extend heap zone to limit}
      MoreMasters;                    {get 64 more master pointers}

      InitGraf(@thePort);             {initialize QuickDraw}
      InitFonts;                      {initialize Font Manager}
      InitWindows;                    {initialize Window Manager}
      InitMenus;                      {initialize Menu Manager}
      TEInit;                         {initialize TextEdit}
      InitDialogs(NIL);               {initialize Dialog Manager}

      FlushEvents(everyEvent, 0);     {clear event queue}
      InitCursor;                     {initialize cursor to arrow}
   END;


{DoSetupMenus: set up the menu bar}
   PROCEDURE DoSetupMenus;
      VAR
         menuBar:     Handle;
   BEGIN
      menuBar := GetNewMBar(rMenuBar);
      IF menuBar = NIL THEN
         DoBadError(eCantFindMenus);

      SetMenuBar(menuBar);
      DisposeHandle(menuBar);
      AppendResMenu(GetMenuHandle(mApple), 'DRVR');
```

217

```
            DrawMenuBar;
        END;


{DoUpdate: update a window}
    PROCEDURE DoUpdate (myWindow: WindowPtr);
        VAR
            myHandle:   MyDocRecHnd;
            myRect:     Rect;                  {tool rectangle}
            origPort:   GrafPtr;
            origPen:    PenState;
            count:      Integer;
    BEGIN
        GetPort(origPort);                 {remember original drawing port}
        SetPort(myWindow);

        BeginUpdate(myWindow);             {clear update region}
        EraseRect(myWindow^.portRect);

        IF IsAppWindow(myWindow) THEN
            BEGIN
                {Draw two lines separating tools area from work area.}
                GetPenState(origPen);      {remember original pen state}
                PenNormal;                 {reset pen to normal state}
                WITH myWindow^ DO
                    BEGIN
                        MoveTo(portRect.left, portRect.top + kToolHt);
                        Line(portRect.right, 0);
                        MoveTo(portRect.left, portRect.top + kToolHt + 2);
                        Line(portRect.right, 0);
                    END;

                {Redraw the tools area in the window.}
                FOR count := 1 TO kNumTools DO
                    BEGIN
                        SetRect(myRect, kToolWd * (count - 1), 0, kToolWd * count,
                                kToolHt);
                        DoPlotIcon(myRect, gToolsIcons[count], myWindow, srcCopy);
                    END;

                {Redraw the status area in the window.}
                myHandle := MyDocRecHnd(GetWRefCon(myWindow));
                DoStatusText(myWindow, myHandle^^.statusText);
```

```
                {Draw the rest of the content region.}
                DoVennDraw(myWindow);


                SetPenState(origPen);              {restore previous pen state}
            END; {IF IsAppWindow}


        EndUpdate(myWindow);
        SetPort(origPort);                         {restore original drawing port}
    END;


{DoCreateWindow: create a new window}
    FUNCTION DoCreateWindow: WindowPtr;
        VAR
            myPointer:   Ptr;
            myWindow:    WindowPtr;
            myHandle:    MyDocRecHnd;
    BEGIN
        myPointer := NewPtr(sizeof(WindowRecord));
        IF myPointer = NIL THEN
            exit(DoCreateWindow);


        myWindow := GetNewWindow(rVennD, myPointer, WindowPtr(-1));
        IF myWindow <> NIL THEN
            BEGIN
                SetPort(myWindow);
                myHandle := MyDocRecHnd(NewHandleClear(sizeof(MyDocRec)));


                IF myHandle <> NIL THEN
                    BEGIN
                        HLockHi(Handle(myHandle));
                                            {lock the data high in the heap}
                        SetWRefCon(myWindow, LongInt(myHandle));
                                            {attach data handle to window record}


                        DoSetWindowTitle(myWindow);        {set the window title}


                        {Define initial window settings.}
                        WITH myHandle^^ DO
                            BEGIN
                                figure := 1;
                                mood[1] := 1;
                                mood[2] := 1;
                                mood[3] := 1;
```

```
                    isAnswerShowing := FALSE;
                    isExistImport := gGiveImport;
                 END;
              DoGetRandomTerms(myWindow);
              DoCalcAnswer(myWindow);

              {Position the window and display it.}
              DoPositionWindow(myWindow);
              ShowWindow(myWindow);

           END {IF myHandle <> NIL}
         ELSE
           BEGIN                            {couldn't get a data record}
                 CloseWindow(myWindow);
                 DisposePtr(Ptr(myWindow));
                 myWindow := NIL;         {so pass back NIL}
           END;
        END;

     DoCreateWindow := myWindow;
   END;


{DoCloseDocWindow: dispose a document window and all its data structures}
   PROCEDURE DoCloseDocWindow (myWindow: WindowPtr);
      VAR
         myHandle:    MyDocRecHnd;
   BEGIN
      IF myWindow = NIL THEN
         exit(DoCloseDocWindow)                {ignore NIL windows}
      ELSE
         BEGIN
            myHandle := MyDocRecHnd(GetWRefCon(myWindow));
            DisposeHandle(Handle(myHandle));
            CloseWindow(myWindow);             {close the window}
            DisposePtr(Ptr(myWindow));         {and release the storage}
         END;
   END;


{DoCloseWindow: close a window}
   PROCEDURE DoCloseWindow (myWindow: WindowPtr);
   BEGIN
      IF myWindow <> NIL THEN
         IF IsDialogWindow(myWindow) THEN        {this is a dialog window}
```

```
                HideWindow(myWindow)
            ELSE IF IsDAccWindow(myWindow) THEN    {this is a DA window}
                CloseDeskAcc(WindowPeek(myWindow)^.windowKind)
            ELSE IF IsAppWindow(myWindow) THEN     {this is a document window}
                DoCloseDocWindow(myWindow);
    END;


{DoDrag: handle window dragging}
    PROCEDURE DoDrag (myWindow: WindowPtr; mouseloc: Point);
        VAR
            dragBounds: Rect;
    BEGIN
        dragBounds := GetGrayRgn^^.rgnBBox;
        DragWindow(myWindow, mouseloc, dragBounds);
    END;


{DoGoAwayBox: process a click in close box}
    PROCEDURE DoGoAwayBox (myWindow: WindowPtr; mouseloc: Point);
    BEGIN
        IF TrackGoAway(myWindow, mouseloc) THEN
            DoCloseWindow(myWindow);
    END;


{DoQuit: quit the program}
    PROCEDURE DoQuit;
        VAR
            myWindow:   WindowPtr;
    BEGIN
        myWindow := FrontWindow;            {close all windows}
        WHILE myWindow <> NIL DO
            BEGIN
                DoUpdate(myWindow);         {force redrawing window}
                DoCloseWindow(myWindow);
                myWindow := FrontWindow;
            END;
        gDone := TRUE;                      {set flag to exit main event loop}
    END;


{DoActivate: handle activate and deactivate events for the specified window}
    PROCEDURE DoActivate (myWindow: WindowPtr; myModifiers: Integer);
        VAR
            myState:    Integer;            {activation state}
            myControl: ControlHandle;
```

User Interface Code

```
    BEGIN
        myState := BAnd(myModifiers, activeFlag);

        IF IsDialogWindow(myWindow) THEN
            BEGIN
                myControl := WindowPeek(myWindow)^.controlList;
                WHILE myControl <> NIL DO
                    BEGIN
                        HiliteControl(myControl, myState + 255 mod 256);
                        myControl := myControl^^.nextControl;
                    END;
            END;
    END;


{DoDiskEvent: handle disk-inserted events}
    PROCEDURE DoDiskEvent (myEvent: EventRecord);
        VAR
            myResult:   Integer;
            myPoint:    Point;
    BEGIN
        IF HiWord(myEvent.message) <> noErr THEN
            BEGIN
                SetPt(myPoint, 100, 100);
                myResult := DIBadMount(myPoint, myEvent.message);
            END;
    END;


{MyModalFilter: a basic modal dialog filter function}
    FUNCTION MyModalFilter (myDialog: DialogPtr; VAR myEvent: EventRecord;
                            VAR myItem: Integer): Boolean;
        VAR
            itemType:   Integer;
            itemHand:   Handle;
            itemRect:   Rect;
            myKey:      Char;
            myIgnore:   LongInt;
    BEGIN
        MyModalFilter := FALSE;                 {assume we don't handle the event}

        CASE myEvent.what OF
            updateEvt:
                BEGIN
                    IF WindowPtr(myEvent.message) <> myDialog THEN
```

```
                    DoUpdate(WindowPtr(myEvent.message));
                                        {update the window behind}
        END;
    keyDown, autoKey:
        BEGIN
            myKey := char(And(myEvent.message, charCodeMask));

            {if Return or Enter pressed, do default button}
            IF (myKey = kReturn) OR (myKey = kEnter) THEN
                BEGIN
                    GetDItem(myDialog, iOK, itemType, itemHand, itemRect);
                    HiliteControl(ControlHandle(itemHand), 1);
                                {make button appear to have been pressed}
                    Delay(kVisualDelay, myIgnore);
                    HiliteControl(ControlHandle(itemHand), 0);
                    MyModalFilter := TRUE;
                    myItem := iOK;
                END;

            {if Escape or Cmd-. pressed, do Cancel button}
            IF (myKey = kEscape)
                OR ((myKey = kPeriod)
                    AND (BAnd(myEvent.modifiers, CmdKey) <> 0)) THEN
                BEGIN
                    GetDItem(myDialog, iCancel, itemType, itemHand,
itemRect);
                    HiliteControl(ControlHandle(itemHand), 1);
                                {make button appear to have been pressed}
                    Delay(kVisualDelay, myIgnore);
                    HiliteControl(ControlHandle(itemHand), 0);
                    MyModalFilter := TRUE;
                    myItem := iCancel;
                END;
        END;
    diskEvt:
        BEGIN
            DoDiskEvent(myEvent);
            MyModalFilter := TRUE;              {show we've handled the event}
        END;
    OTHERWISE
        ;
    END; {CASE}
END;
```

User Interface Code

```
{DoAboutBox: handle About... selections}
   PROCEDURE DoAboutBox (myWindow: WindowPtr);
      VAR
         myWindow:    WindowPtr;
         myDialog:    DialogPtr;
         myItem:      Integer;
   BEGIN
      myWindow := FrontWindow;
      IF myWindow <> NIL THEN
         DoActivate(myWindow, 1 - activeFlag);

      myDialog := GetNewDialog(rAboutDial, NIL, WindowPtr(-1));
      IF myDialog <> NIL THEN
         BEGIN
            SetPort(myDialog);
            DoDefaultButton(myDialog);

            REPEAT
               ModalDialog(@MyModalFilter, myItem);
            UNTIL myItem = iOK;

            DisposeDialog(myDialog);
            SetPort(myWindow);
         END;
   END;

{DoMenuAdjust: adjust menus by enabling and disabling items}
   PROCEDURE DoMenuAdjust;
      VAR
         myWindow:    WindowPtr;
         myMenu:      MenuHandle;
         count:       Integer;
   BEGIN
      myWindow := FrontWindow;

      IF myWindow = NIL THEN
         DisableMenuItem(GetMenuHandle(mFile), iClose)
      ELSE
         EnableMenuItem(GetMenuHandle(mFile), iClose);

      myMenu := GetMenuHandle(mVennD);
      IF IsAppWindow(myWindow) THEN
```

User Interface Code

```
        FOR count := 1 TO kNumTools DO
            EnableMenuItem(myMenu, count)
        ELSE
            FOR count := 1 TO kNumTools DO
                DisableMenuItem(myMenu, count);

        IF IsDAccWindow(myWindow) THEN
            EnableMenuItem(GetMenuHandle(mEdit), 0)
        ELSE
            DisableMenuItem(GetMenuHandle(mEdit), 0);
        DrawMenuBar;
    END;


{DoMenuCommand: interpret and act on menu selections}
    PROCEDURE DoMenuCommand (menuAndItem: LongInt);
        VAR
            myMenuNum:  Integer;
            myItemNum:  Integer;
            myResult:   Integer;
            myDAName:   Str255;
            myWindow:   WindowPtr;
    BEGIN
        myMenuNum := HiWord(menuAndItem);
        myItemNum := LoWord(menuAndItem);
        GetPort(myWindow);

        CASE myMenuNum OF
            mApple:
                CASE myItemNum OF
                    iAbout:
                        BEGIN
                            DoAboutBox;
                        END;
                    OTHERWISE
                        BEGIN
                            GetMenuItemText(GetMenuHandle(mApple), myItemNum,
                                            myDAName);
                            myResult := OpenDeskAcc(myDAName);
                        END;
                END;
            mFile:
                BEGIN
                    CASE myItemNum OF
```

User Interface Code

```
                    iNew:
                        myWindow := DoCreateWindow;
                    iClose:
                        DoCloseWindow(FrontWindow);
                    iQuit:
                        DoQuit;
                    OTHERWISE
                        ;
                END;
            END;
        mEdit:
            BEGIN
                IF NOT SystemEdit(myItemNum - 1) THEN
                    ;
            END;
        mVennD:
            BEGIN
                myWindow := FrontWindow;
                CASE myItemNum OF
                    iCheckVenn:
                        DoVennCheck(myWindow);
                    iDoVenn:
                        DoVennAnswer(myWindow);
                    iClearVenn:
                        DoVennClear(myWindow);
                    iNextTask:
                        DoVennNext(myWindow);
                    iCheckArg:
                        DoVennAssess(myWindow);
                    iGetVennPrefs:
                        DoModelessDialog(rVennDPrefsDial, gPrefsDialog);
                    OTHERWISE
                        ;
                END;
            END;

        OTHERWISE
            ;
    END;
    HiliteMenu(0);
END; {DoMenuCommand}


{DoContentClick: handle a mouse click in the content area of a window}
```

```
PROCEDURE DoContentClick (myWindow: WindowPtr; myEvent: EventRecord);
    VAR
        myRect:      Rect;                          {temporary rectangle}
        count:       Integer;
    BEGIN
    IF NOT IsAppWindow(myWindow) THEN
        exit(DoContentClick);              {make sure it's a document window}

    SetPort(myWindow);                         {set port to our window}
    GlobalToLocal(myEvent.where);

{See if the click is in the tools area.}
    SetRect(myRect, 0, 0, kToolWd * kNumTools, kToolHt);
    IF PtInRect(myEvent.where, myRect) THEN
        BEGIN                         {if so, determine which tool was clicked}
            FOR count := 1 TO kNumTools DO
                BEGIN
                    SetRect(myRect, (count - 1) * kToolWd, 0,
                                count * kToolWd, kToolHt);
                    IF PtInRect(myEvent.where, myRect) THEN
                        Leave;       {we found the right tool, so stop looking}
                END;
            IF DoTrackRect(myWindow, myRect) THEN
                DoMenuCommand(BitShift(mVennD, 16) +
                        ((kNumTools + 1) - count));{handle tools selections}
            exit(DoContentClick);
        END;

{See if the click is in the status area.}
    SetRect(myRect, kToolWd * kNumTools, 0,
                myWindow^.portRect.right, kToolHt);
    IF PtInRect(myEvent.where, myRect) THEN
        BEGIN
            exit(DoContentClick);
        END;

{The click must be in somewhere in the rest of the window.}
    DoVennClick(myWindow, myEvent.where);
    END;


{DoMouseDown: process mouseDown events}
    PROCEDURE DoMouseDown (myEvent: EventRecord);
        VAR
```

User Interface Code

```
        myPart:      Integer;
        myWindow:    WindowPtr;
    BEGIN
        myPart := FindWindow(myEvent.where, myWindow);
        CASE myPart OF
            inMenuBar:
                BEGIN
                    DoMenuAdjust;
                    DoMenuCommand(MenuSelect(myEvent.where));
                END;
            InSysWindow:
                SystemClick(myEvent, myWindow);
            inDrag:
                DoDrag(myWindow, myEvent.where);
            inGoAway:
                DoGoAwayBox(myWindow, myEvent.where);
            inContent:
                BEGIN
                    IF myWindow <> FrontWindow THEN
                        SelectWindow(myWindow)
                    ELSE
                        DoContentClick(myWindow, myEvent);
                END;
            OTHERWISE
                ;
        END;
    END;


{DoKeyDown: respond to keyDown events}
    PROCEDURE DoKeyDown (myEvent: EventRecord);
        VAR
            myKey:       char;
    BEGIN
        myKey := chr(BAnd(myEvent.message, charCodeMask));
        IF (BAnd(myEvent.modifiers, CmdKey) <> 0) THEN
            BEGIN
                DoMenuAdjust;
                DoMenuCommand(MenuKey(myKey));
            END;
    END;


{DoIdle: handle null events}
{currently we use this for auto-processing in Venn diagram windows}
```

```
     PROCEDURE DoIdle (myEvent: EventRecord);
        VAR
           myWindow:    WindowPtr;
           myHandle:    MyDocRecHnd;
     BEGIN
        myWindow := FrontWindow;
        IF IsAppWindow(myWindow) THEN
           IF gAutoAdjust THEN
              BEGIN
                 myHandle := MyDocRecHnd(GetWRefCon(myWindow));
                 IF myHandle^^.needsAdjusting THEN
                    DoVennIdle(myWindow);
              END;
     END; {DoIdle}


{DoOSEvent: handle OS events}
     PROCEDURE DoOSEvent (myEvent: EventRecord);
        VAR
           myWindow:    WindowPtr;
     BEGIN
        CASE BSR(myEvent.message, 24) OF
           mouseMovedMessage:
              BEGIN
                 DoIdle(myEvent);        {right now, do nothing}
              END;
           suspendResumeMessage:
              BEGIN
                 myWindow := FrontWindow;
                 IF (BAnd(myEvent.message, resumeFlag) <> 0) THEN
                    DoActivate(myWindow, activeFlag)        {activate window}
                 ELSE
                    DoActivate(myWindow, 1 - activeFlag);   {deactivate window}
              END;
           OTHERWISE
              ;
        END;
     END;


{DoMainEventLoop: the main event loop}
     PROCEDURE DoMainEventLoop;
        VAR
           myEvent:    EventRecord;
           gotEvent:   Boolean;                        {is returned event for me?}
```

User Interface Code

```
    BEGIN
       REPEAT
           gotEvent := WaitNextEvent(everyEvent, myEvent, 15, NIL);
           IF NOT DoHandleDialogEvent(myEvent) THEN
               IF gotEvent THEN
                   BEGIN
                       CASE myEvent.what OF
                           mouseDown:
                               DoMouseDown(myEvent);
                           keyDown, autoKey:
                               DoKeyDown(myEvent);
                           updateEvt:
                               DoUpdate(WindowPtr(myEvent.message));
                           diskEvt:
                               DoDiskEvent(myEvent);
                           activateEvt:
                               DoActivate(WindowPtr(myEvent.message),
                                       myEvent.modifiers);
                           osEvt:
                               DoOSEvent(myEvent);
                           keyUp, mouseUp:
                               ;
                           nullEvent:
                               DoIdle(myEvent);
                           OTHERWISE
                               ;
                       END; {CASE}
                   END
               ELSE
                   DoIdle(myEvent);
       UNTIL gDone;                    {loop until user quits}
    END;


BEGIN
   DoInitManagers;                     {initialize Toolbox managers}
   DoSetupMenus;                       {initialize menus}

   gDone := FALSE;                     {initialize global variables}
   gNumDocWindows := 0;                {initialize count of open doc windows}
   gPrefsDialog := NIL;                {initialize ptr to Preferences dialog}

   gAppsResourceFile := CurResFile;    {get refnum of the app's resource file}
   gPreferencesFile := -1;             {initialize res ID of preferences file}
```

```
    DoReadPrefs;                        {read the user's preference settings}


    DoVennInit;
    DoMainEventLoop;                    {and then loop forever...}
END.
```

Glossary

A5 world   An area of memory in an application's partition that contains the QuickDraw global variables, the application global variables, the application parameters, and the jump table—all of which are accessed through the A5 register.

action procedure   A procedure that performs an action in response to the user holding the mouse button down while the cursor is in a control.

activate event   An event indicating that a window is becoming active or inactive. Each activate event specifies the window to be changed and the direction of the change (that is, whether it's becoming active or becoming inactive).

active application   The application currently interacting with the user. Its icon appears on the right side of the menu bar. See also **current process, foreground process.**

active control   A control in which the Control Manager responds to a user's mouse actions by providing visual feedback.

active window   The frontmost window on the desktop, the one in which the user is currently working. The active window is designated by racing stripes in the title bar, active controls, and highlighted selections.

address   A number that specifies the location of a byte in memory.

alert   An alert sound, an alert box, or both. Alerts warn the user of an unusual or potentially undesirable situation occurring within an application. See also **alert box.**

alert box   A window that an application displays on the screen to warn the user or to report an error to the user. An alert box typically consists of text describing the situation and buttons that require the user to acknowledge or rectify the problem. An alert box may or may not be accompanied by an alert sound.

alert resource   A resource (of type `'ALRT'`) that specifies alert sounds, a display rectangle, and an item list for an alert box.

alert sound   An audible signal from the Macintosh speaker that warns the user of an unusual or potentially undesirable situation occurring within an application. An alert sound may or may not be accompanied by an alert box.

Alias Manager   The part of the Operating System that helps you to locate specified files, directories, or volumes at a later time. The Alias Manager creates and resolves alias records.

alias record   A data structure created by the Alias Manager to identify a file, directory, or volume.

allocate   To assign an area of memory for use.

Apple event   A high-level event whose structure and interpretation are determined by the Apple Event Interprocess Messaging Protocol.

Apple Event Manager   The part of the Macintosh system software that allows applications to send and respond to Apple events.

Apple Menu Items folder   A directory located in the System Folder for storing desk accessories, applications, folders, and aliases that the user wants to display in and access from the Apple menu.

application global variables   A set of variables stored in the application's A5 world that are global to the application.

application heap   An area of memory in the application heap zone in which memory is dynamically allocated and released on demand. The heap contains the application's `'CODE'` segment 1, data structures, resource map, and other code segments as needed.

application parameters Thirty-two bytes of memory in the application partition that are reserved for system use. The first long word is the address of the first QuickDraw global variable.

application partition A partition of memory reserved for use by an application. The application partition consists of free space, the application heap, the application's stack, and the application's A5 world.

auto-key event An event indicating that a key is still down after a certain amount of time has elapsed.

background-only application An application that does not have a user interface.

background process A process that isn't currently interacting with the user. Compare **foreground process.**

bitmap A set of bits that represents the positions and states of a corresponding set of items, such as pixels.

block See **memory block.**

button A control that appears on the screen as a rounded rectangle with a title centered inside. When the user clicks a button, the application performs the action described by the button's title. Button actions are usually performed instantaneously. Examples include completing operations defined by a dialog box and acknowledging an error message in an alert box.

checkbox A control that appears onscreen as a small square with an accompanying title. A checkbox displays one of two settings: on (indicated by an X inside the box) or off. When the user clicks a checkbox, the application reverses its setting. See also **radio button.**

close box The small white box on the left side of the title bar of an active window. Clicking it closes the window.

Command-key equivalent Refers specifically to a keyboard equivalent that the user invokes by holding down the Command key and pressing another key (other than a modifier key) at the same time.

Communications Toolbox A part of the Macintosh system software that you can use to provide your application with basic networking and communications services.

compact See **heap compaction.**

compatibility The ability of an application to execute properly in different operating environments.

content region The part of a window in which the contents of a document, the size box, and the window controls (including the scroll bars) are displayed.

context The information about a process maintained by the Process Manager. This information includes the current state of the process, the address and size of its partition, its type, its creator, a copy of its low-memory globals, information about its `'SIZE'` resource, and a process serial number.

context switch A major or minor switch.

control An onscreen object that the user can manipulate with the mouse. By manipulating a control, the user can take an immediate action or change a setting to modify a future action.

control definition function A function that defines the appearance and behavior of a control. A control definition function, for example, draws the control. See also **standard control definition functions.**

control definition ID A number passed to control-creation routines to indicate the type of control. It consists of the control definition function's resource ID and a variation code.

control list A series of entries pointing to the descriptions of the controls associated with the window.

Control Manager A collection of routines that applications use to create and manipulate controls, especially those in windows.

control record A data structure of type `ControlRecord`, which the Control Manager uses to store all the information it needs for its operations on a control.

cooperative multitasking environment   A multitasking environment in which applications explicitly cooperate to share the available system resources. See also **multitasking environment.**

current directory   The directory whose contents are listed in the dialog box displayed by the Standard File Package. See also **default directory.**

current menu list   A data structure that contains handles to the menu records of all menus in the current menu bar and the menu records of any submenus or pop-up menus that an application inserts into the list.

current process   The process that is currently executing and whose A5 world is valid; this process can be in the background or the foreground.

cursor   Any 256-bit image, defined by a 16-by-16-bit square. The mouse driver displays the current cursor and maps the movement of the mouse to relative locations on the screen as the user moves the mouse.

dangling pointer   A copy of a master pointer that no longer points to the correct memory address.

data fork   The part of a file that contains data accessed using the File Manager. The data usually corresponds to data entered by the user; the application creating a file can store and interpret the data in the data fork in whatever manner is appropriate.

default button   In an alert box or a dialog box, the button whose action is invoked when the user presses the Return key or the Enter key. The Dialog Manager automatically draws a bold outline around the default button in alert boxes; applications should draw a bold outline around the default button in dialog boxes. The default button should invoke the preferred action which, whenever possible, should be a "safe" action— that is, one that doesn't cause loss of data.

default directory   The directory used in File Manager routines whenever you don't explicitly specify some directory. See also **current directory.**

default volume   The volume that contains the default directory.

desk accessory   A "mini-application" that is available from the Apple menu regardless of which application you're using—for example, the Calculator, Note Pad, Alarm Clock, Puzzle, Scrapbook, Key Caps, and Chooser.

desktop   The working environment displayed on the Macintosh computer: the gray background area on the screen.

Device Manager   The part of the Macintosh Operating System that supports device I/O.

dialog box   A window that's used for some special or limited purpose, such as to solicit information from the user before the application carries out the user's command. See also **modal dialog box, modeless dialog box,** and **movable modal dialog box.**

Dialog Manager   The part of the Macintosh Toolbox that provides routines for creating and manipulating alerts and dialog boxes.

dialog record   A data structure of type `DialogRecord` that the Dialog Manager uses to create dialog boxes and alerts.

dialog resource   A resource (of type `'DLOG'`) that specifies the window type, display rectangle, and item list for a dialog box.

directory   A subdivision of a volume, available in the hierarchical file system. A directory can contain files and other directories (known as subdirectories).

disabled item   In an alert box or a dialog box, an item for which the Dialog Manager does not report user events. An example of a disabled item is static text, which typically does not respond to clicks.

disk   A physical medium capable of storing information.

disk initialization   The process of making a disk usable by the Macintosh Operating System.

Disk Initialization Manager   The part of the Macintosh Operating System that manages the process of initializing disks.

disk-inserted event   An event indicating that a disk has been inserted into a disk drive.

display rectangle   A rectangle that defines the size and location of an item in an alert box or a dialog box. The display rectangle is specified in an item list and uses coordinates local to the alert box or a dialog box.

disposed handle   A handle whose associated relocatable block has been disposed of.

divider   A gray line used in menus to separate groups of menu items.

document   (1) A file that a user can create and edit. A document is usually associated with a single application, which the user expects to be able to open by double-clicking the document's icon in the Finder. (2) Any collection of information that is displayed in a document window.

document record   An application-defined data structure that contains information about the window, any controls in the window (such as scroll bars), and the file (if any) whose contents are displayed in the window.

document window   A window in which the user enters text, draws graphics, or otherwise enters or manipulates data.

double indirection   The means by which the Memory Manager or an application accesses the data associated with a handle variable.

drag region   The area occupied by a window's title bar, except for the close box and zoom box. The user can move a window on the desktop by dragging the drag region.

edition   The data written to an edition container by a publisher. A publisher writes data to an edition whenever a user saves a document that contains a publisher, and subscribers in other documents may read the data from the edition whenever it is updated.

Edition Manager   The part of the Macintosh system software that allows applications to automate copy and paste operations between applications, so that data can be shared dynamically.

empty handle   A handle whose master pointer has the value NIL (possibly indicating that the underlying relocatable block has been purged).

enabled item   In an alert box or a dialog box, an item for which the Dialog Manager reports user events. For example, the Dialog Manager reports clicks in an enabled OK button.

event   The means by which the Event Manager communicates information about user actions, changes in the processing status of the application, and other occurrences that require a response from the application.

event-driven programming   A way of structuring an application so that it is guided by events reporting a user's actions and other occurrences in the computer.

event filter function   An application-defined routine that supplements the Dialog Manager's ability to handle events—for example, an event filter function can test for disk-inserted events and can allow background applications to receive update events.

event loop   A section of code that repetitively retrieves events from the Event Manager and dispatches to the appropriate event-handler.

Event Manager   The collection of routines that an application can use to receive information about actions performed by the user, to receive notice of changes in the processing status of the application, and to communicate with other applications.

event priority   The order in which an event of a particular type is returned to an application.

event record   A data structure of type EventRecord that your application uses when retrieving information about an event. The Event Manager returns, in an event record, information about what type of event occurred (a mouse click or keypress, for example) and additional information associated with the event.

extension   See **system extension.**

Extensions folder   A directory located in the System Folder for storing system extension files such as printer and network drivers and files of types 'INIT', 'scri', and 'appe'.

file   A named, ordered sequence of bytes stored on a Macintosh volume, divided into a data fork and a resource fork.

file fork   One of the two parts of a file. See also **data fork** and **resource fork.**

File Manager   The part of the Macintosh Operating System that manages the organization, reading, and writing of data located on physical data storage devices such as disk drives.

file system   A method of organizing files and directories on a volume.

Finder   An application that works with the system software to keep track of files and manage the user's desktop display.

Finder Interface   A set of routines, data structures, and resources that you can use to coordinate your application with the Finder.

folder   A directory. See **directory.**

Fonts folder   A directory located in the System Folder for storing fonts.

foreground process   The process currently interacting with the user; it appears to the user as the active application. The foreground process displays its menu bar, and its windows are in front of the windows of other applications. Compare **background process.**

fork   See **file fork.**

fragmentation   See **heap fragmentation.**

frame   The part of a window drawn automatically by the Window Manager, namely, the title bar, including the close box and zoom box, and the window's outline.

free block   A memory block containing space available for allocation.

global coordinate system   The coordinate system that represents all potential QuickDraw drawing space. The origin of the global coordinate system—that is, the point (0,0)—is at the upper-left corner of the main screen. Compare **local coordinate system.**

global variables   See **application global variables, system global variables,** and **QuickDraw global variables.**

glue routine   A routine, usually written in assembly-language, that allows a high-level language to call a low-level routine. Also, any short special-purpose assembly-language routine.

graphics port   A complete, individual drawing environment with an independent coordinate system. Each window is drawn in a graphics port.

handle   A variable containing the address of a master pointer, used to access a relocatable block. See also **pointer.**

heap   An area of memory in which space is dynamically allocated and released on demand, using the Memory Manager. See also **application heap.**

heap compaction   The process of moving allocated blocks within a heap to collect the free space into a single block.

heap fragmentation   The state of a heap when the available free space is scattered throughout the heap in numerous unused blocks.

help balloon   A rounded-rectangle window that contains explanatory information for the user. With tips pointing at the objects they annotate, help balloons look like bubbles used for dialog in comic strips. Help balloons are turned on by the user from the Help menu; when Balloon Help assistance is on, a help balloon appears whenever the user moves the cursor over an area that is associated with it.

hierarchical menu   A menu to which a submenu is attached.

high-level event   An event sent from one application to another requesting transfer of information or performance of some action.

high-level event queue   A separate queue that the Event Manager maintains to store high-level events transmitted to an application. The Event Manager maintains a high-level event queue for each open application capable of receiving high-level events.

icon   An image that represents an object, a concept, or a message.

inactive control   A control that has no meaning or effect in the current context—for example, the scroll bars in an empty window. The Control Manager dims inactive controls or otherwise visually indicates their inactive state.

inactive window   A window in which the user is not working.

interapplication communications (IAC) architecture   A standard and extensible mechanism for communicating among Macintosh applications.

item list   A resource (of type `'DITL'`) that specifies the items—such as buttons and static text—to display in an alert box or a dialog box.

item number   An integer that identifies an item in either a menu or dialog box. Menu items are assigned item numbers starting with 1 for the first menu item in the menu, 2 for the second menu item in the menu, and so on, up to the number of the last menu item in the menu. Dialog items are assigned numbers that correspond to the item's position in its item list. For example, the first item listed in a dialog item list is item number 1.

jump table   An area of memory in an application's A5 world that contains one entry for every externally referenced routine in every code segment of the application. The jump table is the means by which the loading and unloading of segments is implemented.

keyboard equivalent   A keyboard combination of one or more modifier keys and another key that invokes a corresponding menu command when pressed by the user. See also **Command-key equivalent.**

key-down event   An event indicating that the user pressed a key on the keyboard.

key-up event   An event indicating that the user released a key on the keyboard.

local coordinate system   The coordinate system defined by the port rectangle of a graphics port. When the window manager creates a window, it places the origin of the local coordinate system at the upper-left corner of the window's port rectangle. Compare **global coordinate system.**

localization   The process of adapting an application to a specific language, culture, and region.

lock   To temporarily prevent a relocatable block from being moved during heap compaction.

low-level events   The type of event returned by the Event Manager to report very low level hardware and software occurrences. Low-level events report actions by the user, changes in windows on the screen, and that the Event Manager has no other events to report. Compare **high-level events, operating-system events.**

low-memory system global variables   See **system global variables.**

Macintosh Operating System   The part of Macintosh system software that manages basic low-level operations such as file reading and writing, memory allocation and deallocation, process execution, and interrupt handling.

Macintosh script management system   The Script Manager, script-aware parts of other text managers, the WorldScript extensions, and one or more script systems.

Macintosh system software   A collection of routines that you can use to simplify your development of Macintosh applications. See also **Macintosh Toolbox** and **Macintosh Operating System.**

Macintosh Toolbox   The part of the Macintosh system software that allows you to implement the standard Macintosh user interface in your application.

Macintosh User Interface Toolbox   See **Macintosh Toolbox.**

major switch   A change of the foreground process. The Process Manager switches the context of the foreground process with the context of a background process (including the A5 worlds and low-memory globals) and brings the background process to the front, sending the previous foreground process to the background. See also **context, minor switch.**

manager   A part of the Macintosh system software.

master pointer   A pointer to a relocatable block, maintained by the Memory Manager and updated whenever the block is moved, purged, or reallocated. All handles to a relocatable block refer to it by double indirection through the master pointer.

master pointer block   A nonrelocatable block of memory that contains master pointers. A master pointer block in your application heap contains 64 master pointers, and a master pointer block in the system heap contains 32 master pointers.

memory block   An area of contiguous memory within a heap.

Memory Manager   The part of the Operating System that dynamically allocates and releases memory space in the heap.

menu   A user interface element you can use in your application to allow the user to view or choose an item from a list of choices and commands that your application provides. See also **hierarchical menu, pull-down menu, pop-up menu,** and **submenu.**

menu bar   A white rectangle that is tall enough to display menu titles in the height of the system font and system font size, and with a black lower border that is one pixel tall. The menu bar extends across the top of the startup screen and contains the title of each available pull-down menu.

menu bar definition function   A function that draws the menu bar and performs most of the drawing activities related to the display of menus when the user moves the cursor between menus. This function, in conjunction with the menu definition procedure, defines the general appearance and behavior of menus.

menu bar resource   A resource (of type `'MBAR'`) that specifies the order and resource ID of each menu in a menu bar.

menu definition procedure   A procedure that performs all the drawing of menu items within a specific menu. This procedure, in conjunction with the menu bar definition function, defines the general appearance and behavior of menus.

menu ID   A number that you assign to a menu in your application. Each menu in your application must have a unique menu ID.

menu item   In a menu, a rectangle with text and other characteristics identifying a command that the user can choose.

menu list   A data structure that contains handles to the menu records of one or more menus (although a menu list can be empty). Compare **current menu list.**

Menu Manager   The collection of routines that an application can use to create, display, and manage its menus.

menu record   A data structure of type `MenuInfo` that the Menu Manager uses to maintain information about a menu.

menu resource   A resource (of type `'MENU'`) that specifies the menu title and the individual characteristics of items in a menu.

menu title   The word or icon in the menu bar or in a window that shows the location of a menu.

minimum partition size   The actual partition size limit below which an application cannot run.

minor switch   A change in the context of a process. The Process Manager switches the context of a process to give time to a background process without bringing the background process to the front. See also **context, major switch.**

modal dialog box   A dialog box that puts the user in the state or "mode" of being able to work only inside the dialog box. A modal dialog box resembles an alert box. The user cannot move a modal dialog box and can dismiss it only by clicking its buttons. See also **modeless dialog box** and **movable modal dialog box.**

modal dialog filter function   An application-defined function that filters events passed from the Event Manager to your application when one of its modal dialog boxes is being displayed.

modeless dialog box   A dialog box that looks like a document window without a size box or scroll bars. The user can move a modeless dialog box, make it inactive and active again, and close it like any document window. See also **modal dialog box** and **movable modal dialog box.**

modifier keys   The Shift, Option, Command, Control, and Caps Lock keys.

mouse-down event   An event indicating that the user pressed the mouse button.

mouse location   The location of the cursor at the time an event occurred.

mouse-moved event   An event indicating that the cursor is outside of a specified region.

mouse-up event   An event indicating that the user released the mouse button.

movable modal dialog box   A modal dialog box that has a title bar (with no close box) by which the user can drag the dialog box. See also **dialog box, modal dialog box,** and **modeless dialog box.**

multitasking environment   An environment in which several independent applications or other processes can be open at once. See also **cooperative multitasking environment.**

nonrelocatable block   A block whose location in the heap is fixed. This block can't be moved during heap compaction or other memory operations.

null event   An event indicating that no events of the requested types exist in the application's event stream.

open application   An application that is loaded into memory.

Operating System   See **Macintosh Operating System.**

operating-system event   An event returned by the Event Manager to communicate information about changes in the operating status of applications (suspend and resume events) and to report that the user has moved the mouse outside of an area specified by the application (mouse-moved events). Compare **low-level events, high-level events.**

Operating System Event Manager   The collection of low-level routines that manage the Operating System event queue.

Operating System event queue   A queue that the Operating System Event Manager creates and maintains. The Operating System Event Manager detects and reports low-level hardware-related events such as mouse clicks, keypresses, and disk insertions and places these events in the Operating System event queue.

package   A collection of system software routines that's stored as a resource and brought into memory only when needed. See also **manager.**

part code   An integer between 1 and 253 that stands for a particular part of a control. The `FindControl` and `TrackControl` functions return a part code to indicate the location of the cursor when the user presses the mouse button.

partition   A contiguous block of memory reserved for use by the Operating System or by an application. See also **application partition** and **system partition.**

patch   To replace a piece of ROM code with other RAM-based code (by storing a new entry into the trap dispatch table). Also, a resource that contains the new code.

pixel   The smallest dot you can draw on the screen.

point   The intersection of a horizontal grid line and a vertical grid line in the coordinate plane. Defined by the `Point` data type.

pointer   A variable containing the address of a byte in memory. See also **handle.**

pop-up menu   A menu that appears elsewhere than the menu bar. The Control Manager provides a control definition function for applications to use when implementing pop-up menus.

PPC Toolbox   See **Program-to-Program Communications (PPC) Toolbox.**

preferences file   A file, usually located in the Preferences folder, that records a user's configuration settings for an application.

Preferences folder   A directory located in the System Folder for holding files that record users' configuration settings for applications on a particular Macintosh computer.

preferred partition size   The partition size at which an application can run most effectively. The Operating System attempts to secure this partition size upon launch of the application.

process   An open application, or, in some cases, an open desk accessory. (Only desk accessories that are not opened in the context of another application are considered processes.)

Process Manager   The part of the Macintosh Operating System that provides a cooperative multitasking environment by controlling access to shared resources and managing the scheduling, execution, and termination of applications.

process serial number   A number assigned by the Process Manager to identify a particular instance of an application during a single boot of the local machine.

Program-to-Program Communications (PPC) Toolbox   The part of the Macintosh system software that allows applications to exchange blocks of data with each other by reading and writing low-level message blocks.

pull-down menu   A menu that is identified by a menu title (a word or an icon) in the menu bar.

purge   To remove a relocatable block from the heap, leaving its master pointer allocated but set to NIL.

purgeable block   A relocatable block that can be purged from the heap.

QuickDraw   The part of the Macintosh Toolbox that performs all graphics operations on the Macintosh screen.

QuickDraw global variables   A set of variables stored in the application's A5 world that contain information used by QuickDraw.

QuickTime   A collection of managers and other system software components that allow your application to control time-based data.

radio button   A control that appears on screen as a small circle. A radio button displays one of two settings: on (indicated by a black dot inside the circle) or off. A radio button is always a part of a group of related radio buttons in which only one button can be on at a time. When the user clicks an unmarked radio button, the application turns that button on and turns the other buttons in its group off.

RAM   See **random-access memory.**

RAM disk   A portion of the available RAM reserved for use as a temporary storage device. A user can configure a RAM disk or disable it altogether using controls in the Memory control panel.

random-access memory (RAM)   Memory whose contents can be changed. The RAM in a Macintosh computer contains exception vectors, buffers used by hardware devices, the system and application heaps, the stack, and other information used by applications.

read-only memory (ROM)   Memory whose contents are permanent. The ROM in a Macintosh computer contains routines for the Toolbox and the Operating System, and the various system traps.

reallocate   To allocate new space in the heap for a purged block and to update the block's master pointer to point to its new location.

rectangle   The area picked by intersecting the grid lines of any two points in the coordinate plane.

release   (1) To free an allocated area of memory, making it available for reuse. (2) To allow a previously held range of pages to be movable in physical memory.

relocatable block   A block that can be moved within the heap during compaction.

resource   Any data stored according to a defined structure in a resource fork of a file; the data in a resource is interpreted according to its resource type.

resource file   The resource fork of a file.

resource fork   The part of a file that contains the files' resources. A resource fork consists of a resource map and resources.

resource ID   A number that identifies a specific resource of a given resource type.

resource map   In a resource file, data that is read into memory when the file is opened and that, given a resource specification, leads to the corresponding resource data.

resource name   A string that, together with the resource type, identifies a resource in a resource file. A resource may or may not have a name.

resource specification   A resource type and either a resource ID or a resource name.

resource type   A sequence of four characters that uniquely identifies a specific type of resource.

resume event   An event indicating that an application has been switched back into the foreground and can resume interacting with the user. See also **suspend event.**

return receipt   A high-level event that indicates whether the other application accepted the high-level event sent to it by your application.

ROM   See **read-only memory.**

script   A writing system for a human language.

Script Manager   The part of the Macintosh system software that manages script systems.

script system   A collection of software facilities that provides for the representation of a specific writing system. It consists of keyboard resources, a set of international resources, one or more fonts, and possibly a script system extension.

segment   One of several logical divisions of the code of an application. Not all segments need to be in memory at the same time.

Segment Manager   The part of the Macintosh Operating System that loads and unloads your application's code segments into and out of memory.

signature   A resource whose type is defined by a four-character sequence that uniquely identifies an application to the Finder. A signature is located in an application's resource fork.

size box   A box in the lower-right corner of windows that can be resized. Dragging the size box resizes the window.

size region   The area occupied by a window's size box. See **size box.**

size resource   A resource (of type 'SIZE') that specifies the operating characteristics, minimum partition size, and preferred partition size of an application.

stack   An area of memory in the application partition that is used to store temporary variables.

stack frame   The area of the stack used by a routine for its parameters, return address, local variables, and temporary storage.

Standard File Package   The part of system software that allows you to present the standard user interface when a file is to be saved or opened.

stationery pad   A document that a user creates to serve as a template for other documents. The Finder tags a document as a stationery pad by setting the isStationery bit in the Finder flags field of the file's file information record. An application that is asked to open a stationery pad should copy the template's contents into a new document and open the document in an untitled window.

submenu   A menu that is attached to another menu.

suspend event   An event indicating that the execution of your application is about to be suspended as the result of either a major or minor switch. The application is suspended at the application's next call to WaitNextEvent or EventAvail. See also **resume event.**

switch   See **major switch** and **minor switch.**

system extension   A file of type 'INIT' that contains executable code. System extensions are loaded into memory at system startup time.

System file   A file, located in the System Folder, that contains the basic system software plus some system resources, such as sound and keyboard resources. The System file behaves like a folder in this regard: although it looks like a suitcase icon, double-clicking it opens a window that reveals movable resource files (such as sounds, keyboard layouts, and script system resource collections) stored in the System file.

System Folder   A directory containing the software that Macintosh computers use to start up. The System Folder includes a set of folders for storing related files, such as preferences files that an application might need when starting up.

system global variables   A collection of global variables stored in the system partition.

system heap   An area of memory in the system partition reserved for use by the Operating System.

system partition   A partition of memory reserved for use by the Operating System.

system resource   A resource in the system resource file.

terminate   To end the execution of a process. A process can terminate by crashing, by quitting, or by being killed by some other process.

Text Services Manager   The part of the system software that manages the interactions between applications that request text services and text service components that provide them.

Time Manager   The part of the Macintosh Operating System that lets you schedule the execution of a routine after a certain time has elapsed.

title bar   The bar at the top of a window that displays the window name, contains the close and zoom boxes, and indicates whether the window is active.

Toolbox Event Manager   See **Event Manager.**

transfer mode   A specification of which Boolean operation QuickDraw should perform when drawing or when transferring a bit image from one bitmap to another.

unlock   To allow a relocatable block to be moved during heap compaction.

unpurgeable block   A relocatable block that can't be purged from the heap.

update event   An event indicating that the contents of a window need updating.

update region   A region maintained by the Window Manager that includes the parts of a window's content region that need updating. The Event Manager generates update events as necessary, based on the contents of the update region, telling your application to update a window.

user items   Items in a dialog box that are managed largely by an application, not by the Dialog Manager. These items are designated by the constant `userItem`.

user state   The size and location that the user has established for a window.

Vertical Retrace Manager   The part of the Operating System that schedules and executes tasks during a vertical retrace interrupt.

visible region   The part of a window's graphics port that's actually visible on the screen—that is, the part that's not covered by other windows.

volume   A portion of a storage device that is formatted to contain files.

window   An area on the screen that displays information, including user documents as well as communications such as alert boxes and dialog boxes. The user can open or close a window; move it around on the desktop; and sometimes change its size, scroll through it, and edit its contents.

window definition function   A function that defines the general appearance and behavior of a window. The Window Manager calls the window definition function to draw the window's frame, determine what region of the window the cursor is in, draw the window's size box, draw the window's zoom box, move and resize the window, and calculate the window's structure and content regions.

window definition ID   An integer that specifies the resource ID of a window definition function in the upper 12 bits and an optional variation code in the lower 4 bits. When creating a new window, your application supplies a window definition ID either as a field in the `'WIND'` resource or as a parameter to the `NewWindow` or `NewCWindow` function.

window list   A list maintained by the Window Manager of all windows on the desktop. The frontmost window is first in the window list, and the remaining windows appear in the order in which they are layered on the desktop.

Window Manager   The part of the Macintosh Toolbox that provides routines for creating and manipulating windows.

Window Manager port A graphics port that represents the desktop area on the main monitor—that is, a rounded-corner rectangle that occupies all of the main monitor except for the area occupied by the title bar.

window record A data structure of type `WindowRecord` (or `CWindowRecord`) in which the Window Manager stores a window's characteristics, including the window's graphics port, title, visibility status, and control list.

window type A collection of characteristics—such as the shape of the window's frame and the features of its title bar—that describe a window.

zoom box A box in the right side of a window's title bar that the user can click to alternate between two different window sizes (the user state and the standard state).

Index

M

Macintosh Operating System 11–12
Macintosh script management system 13
Macintosh system software 3
Macintosh Toolbox 7–11
major switches 167
managers 6. *See also* system software
master pointer blocks 40
master pointers 40
`MaxApplZone` procedure
  and `ApplLimit` global variable 33
`'MBAR'` resource type 154
`'MDEF'` resource type 52
`MemError` function 177
memory
  allocating 35, 38, 40, 42
  locking 42–43
  organization of 29–38
  purging 43–44
Memory Manager 11
  and application heap 35–36
  data types 39–40
menu bar
  creating 74
  specifying 154
menu commands
  keyboard equivalents 119, 152, 157
menu item numbers 156
menu items 151
  disabling 162
  enabling 162
`MenuKey` function 160, 161
Menu Manager 10, 151–162
  introduced 6
menu numbers 156
`'MENU'` resource type 152–154
menus 151–162
  adjusting 161–162
  creating 74, 152–156
  defined 151
  disabling 162
  dividers in 152, 157
  enabling 162
  handling selections 156–159
  required 152
`MenuSelect` function 156, 161
menu titles 151
minimum partition size 168
minor switches 167
modal dialog boxes 133–134, 144–148
  creating 145–146
modal dialog filter functions 146–148
`ModalDialog` procedure 144, 146, 167
modeless dialog boxes 134–135, 137–144

  creating 137–138
  handling events in 141–144
moods, syllogistic 23
`MoreMasters` procedure 41
mouse-down events
  in menu bar 156
  in the menu bar 120
  in windows 119–123
mouse-up events 79–81
movable modal dialog boxes 144
`MoveTo` procedure 5
`MoveWindow` procedure 121
movies 17
Movie Toolbox 17
MPW 57
MultiFinder 165
multitasking environment 165–167

N

`NewHandleClear` function 21, 118
`NewHandle` function 20, 42, 43
`NewPtr` function 40, 118
`NewRgn` function 96
`NewWindow` function 4–5, 42, 112
nonrelocatable blocks
  advantages of 42
  data type for 40
  defined 38
null events 72, 167
  handling 173–174

O

`OpenDeskAcc` function 159
`OpenRgn` procedure 96
operating environment
  checking features of 20, 178–181
operating-system events 72
`OSErr` data type 176
ovals 89

P

packages 8, 20
`PaintRect` procedure 89
part codes 119
partitions 29. *See also* application partitions; system partition

This Apple manual was written, edited, and composed on a desktop publishing system using Apple Macintosh computers and FrameMaker software. Proof pages were created on an Apple LaserWriter IINTX printer. Final page negatives were output directly from text files on an AGFA ProSet 9800 imagesetter. Line art was created using Adobe™ Illustrator. PostScript™, the page-description language for the LaserWriter, was developed by Adobe Systems Incorporated.

Text type is Palatino® and display type is Helvetica®. Bullets are ITC Zapf Dingbats®. Some elements, such as program listings, are set in Apple Courier.

The *Inside Macintosh: Overview* Team:

WRITER
Tim Monroe

DEVELOPMENTAL EDITOR
Antonio Padial

ILLUSTRATOR
Peggy Kunz

PRODUCTION EDITORS
Teresa Lujan, Josephine Manuele

PROJECT LEADER
Patricia Eastman

COVER DESIGNER
Barbara Smyth

The Entire *Inside Macintosh* Team
(1992 Snapshot):

PROJECT LEADER
Patricia Eastman

LEAD WRITERS
Dave Bice, Paul Black, Rob Dearborn, Sharon Everson, Tim Monroe

WRITERS
Dave Bice, Paul Black, Patria Brown, Julie Callahan, Sean Cotter, Rob Dearborn, Dee Eduardo, Doug Engfer, Sharon Everson, Ed Fernandez, Tony Francis, Gary Hillerson, Marq Laube, Sue Luttner, Judy Melanson, Tim Monroe, Diane Patterson, Rich Pettijohn, Laine Rapin

TECHNICAL CONSULTANT
Ray Chiang

LEAD EDITOR
Laurel Rezeau

DEVELOPMENTAL EDITORS
Sue Factor, Sanborn Hodgkins, Antonio Padial, Anne Szabla, George Truett

EDITORIAL CONSULTANT
Lorraine Aochi

ILLUSTRATORS
Ruth Anderson, Deborah Dennis, Sandee Karr, Peggy Kunz, Bruce Lee, Barbara Smyth

LEAD PRODUCTION EDITOR
Josephine Manuele

PRODUCTION EDITORS
Gerri Gray, Teresa Lujan, Rex Wolf

COVER DESIGNER
Barbara Smyth

PUBLISHING LIAISON
Martha Steffen

Inside Macintosh

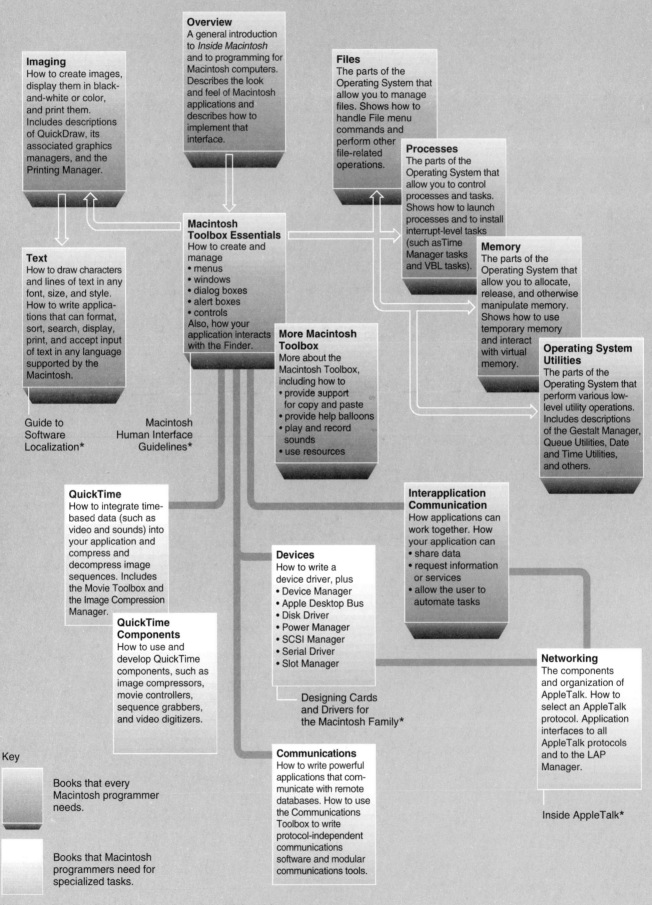

Imaging
How to create images, display them in black-and-white or color, and print them. Includes descriptions of QuickDraw, its associated graphics managers, and the Printing Manager.

Overview
A general introduction to *Inside Macintosh* and to programming for Macintosh computers. Describes the look and feel of Macintosh applications and describes how to implement that interface.

Files
The parts of the Operating System that allow you to manage files. Shows how to handle File menu commands and perform other file-related operations.

Processes
The parts of the Operating System that allow you to control processes and tasks. Shows how to launch processes and to install interrupt-level tasks (such as Time Manager tasks and VBL tasks).

Memory
The parts of the Operating System that allow you to allocate, release, and otherwise manipulate memory. Shows how to use temporary memory and interact with virtual memory.

Text
How to draw characters and lines of text in any font, size, and style. How to write applications that can format, sort, search, display, print, and accept input of text in any language supported by the Macintosh.

Macintosh Toolbox Essentials
How to create and manage
• menus
• windows
• dialog boxes
• alert boxes
• controls
Also, how your application interacts with the Finder.

More Macintosh Toolbox
More about the Macintosh Toolbox, including how to
• provide support for copy and paste
• provide help balloons
• play and record sounds
• use resources

Operating System Utilities
The parts of the Operating System that perform various low-level utility operations. Includes descriptions of the Gestalt Manager, Queue Utilities, Date and Time Utilities, and others.

Guide to Software Localization*

Macintosh Human Interface Guidelines*

QuickTime
How to integrate time-based data (such as video and sounds) into your application and compress and decompress image sequences. Includes the Movie Toolbox and the Image Compression Manager.

QuickTime Components
How to use and develop QuickTime components, such as image compressors, movie controllers, sequence grabbers, and video digitizers.

Devices
How to write a device driver, plus
• Device Manager
• Apple Desktop Bus
• Disk Driver
• Power Manager
• SCSI Manager
• Serial Driver
• Slot Manager

Interapplication Communication
How applications can work together. How your application can
• share data
• request information or services
• allow the user to automate tasks

Networking
The components and organization of AppleTalk. How to select an AppleTalk protocol. Application interfaces to all AppleTalk protocols and to the LAP Manager.

Designing Cards and Drivers for the Macintosh Family*

Communications
How to write powerful applications that communicate with remote databases. How to use the Communications Toolbox to write protocol-independent communications software and modular communications tools.

Inside AppleTalk*

Key

Books that every Macintosh programmer needs.

Books that Macintosh programmers need for specialized tasks.

*Not part of *Inside Macintosh*, but contains related information.

Please keep me informed about future volumes in
New Inside Macintosh.

Name   _____

Company   _____

Address   _____

             _____

City   _____

State   _____

Zip   _____

Please tear out card, put in an envelope, and mail to:
Chris Platt
Addison-Wesley Publishing Company
One Jacob Way
Reading, MA   01867

APDA
Your main source for Apple development products

Get easy access to *New Inside Macintosh* and over 300 other programming products through APDA, Apple's worldwide source for Apple and third-party development products. Ordering is easy. APDA offers convenient payment and shipping options.

Call today for your FREE APDA Tools Catalog

1-800-282-2732	U.S.
1-800-637-0029	Canada
(716) 871-6555	International

Site licensing is available for many of the development tools. For information, contact Apple Software Licensing at (408) 974-4667.

© 1992 Apple Computer, Inc. Apple, the Apple logo, APDA, and Macintosh are registered trademarks of Apple Computer, Inc.